McLevy Returns

Such as met 'Jamie' for the first time might have taken him for a well-to-do farmer from the Emerald Isle on a visit to Scotland intent on a 'deal'. He was of medium height, square-faced, and clean-shaven, and always wore a tall silk hat, from beneath the broad brim of which a pair of quick black eyes scrutinised the crowd as he sauntered along the streets accompanied by his faithful companion Mulholland.

Edinburgh Evening News, *1922*

Also published by Mercat Press:
McLevy: The Edinburgh Detective

McLevy Returns

Further Disclosures of the Edinburgh Detective

MERCAT PRESS
EDINBURGH
www.mercatpress.com

First published in 2002 by Mercat Press Ltd
10 Coates Crescent, Edinburgh EH3 7AL
www.mercatpress.com
Stories first published in 1861 in *Curiosities of Crime in Edinburgh* and *The Sliding Scale of Life*

ISBN 184183 0313

Set in Bodoni at Mercat Press
Printed and bound in Great Britain by
Bell & Bain Ltd., Glasgow

Contents

Preface *vii*

The Blood-Stained Moleskin 1

The Holy Land 9

The Jewel-Box 18

The Jostle 22

The Whisper 33

The Thieves Wedding 42

The Sea Captian 49

The Society-Box 57

The Miniature 65

The Conjuror 74

The Handcuffs 83

The Red Ribbons 91

The Orange Blossom 96

The Pewter Spoon 107

Long Looked-For, Come at Last 114

The Swan 122

The Half-Crowns 130

The Topcoats 142

The Belfast Key 153

The Padlock 163

The Boots 169

The Ingenuity of Thieves 173

The Urchin 183

The Pirates 189

Decision 196

Nievie, Nievie, Nick-Nack 200

The Hay-Seeds 208

The Ash-Backet 218

The Look-Out 225

Preface by the Editor

From *Curiosities of Crime in Edinburgh*, 1861

The cases of detection contained in this volume are only a part, and a very small part, of the experiences of Mr James M'Levy, taken from among no fewer than 2220 instances, where he almost uniformly got convictions. The strange adventures will speak for themselves, and will at once suggest the great difference between a species of literature which can be safely read, as being a true account of what happened, and another which, pretending to be true, is only fiction, with a few and sometimes no grains of truth at the bottom. In this latter kind must, I fear, be held to be included the greater part of those books which have been latterly given out as the experiences of detective officers, the authors being not only not of that class of men, but often entirely unacquainted with them or their ways, and drawing their materials—the more wonderful the more successful—from their own prolific brains. The name of Mr M'Levy is the guarantee of this book; and well it may be, for he is known throughout the kingdom, not only for his honesty and veracity, but for the possession of those many qualities which go to form a successful detective officer; nor, indeed, will it be too much to say, that while he is beyond question without a competitor, now or heretofore, in Scotland, he has very few, if any, in England. It is needless to enumerate these requirements, among which a native sagacity, ingenuity, decision, and courage, are indispensable, but I may remark, that he is well-known for having uniformly illustrated these by urbanity, moderation, and kindliness—qualities not always found in people of this class.

The advantages to which a book of this kind may be turned seem very evident; for, while all pandering to an appetite for details of crime has been carefully avoided, there is set before the reader such an array of examples where misdeeds have been brought to light as if it were by miracle, that no one can read them without being impressed by the conviction that in these times, when the dark paths of vice are so carefully watched, it is scarcely possible to be wicked without being in some way or another found out.

The cases given in this volume constitute, as I have said, a small portion of M'Levy's detections; but if this be, as I hope it may, considered a fault, it is one which it is the intention of the author to mend.

The Blood-Stained Moleskin

❖

MISS Balleny, a maiden lady with considerable means, and advanced in years, occupied a first flat, with front door, and an area flat beneath, in Buccleuch Place. From some peculiar choice, it would seem, and not from necessity, she kept no regular servant, employing a woman to come occasionally, and do any duties she could not herself perform; nor is it thought she had any extreme penuriousness in her nature, that led to this choice; rather, it would seem that she preferred being alone, having discovered perhaps that the Edinburgh servants are not remarkable for either fidelity or affection towards their employers. It is certain, at least, she was an inoffensive lady, and in many respects amiable and kindly in her feelings.

One night, in February 1845, she was preparing to retire to rest, it being near ten o'clock,—seriously disposed, she had been reading her Bible, and engaged in those thoughts that become one of her years. It has often been remarked, as a strange fact in the economy of nature, that the nearer to a catastrophe, the further the thoughts from it—a kind of security into which we are lulled by a false quietude, betokening a continuance of that peace which we could have wished to be unbroken, and which at least might be expected by those who desire to be in friendship with all men. She was startled in the midst of her lonely musings by a noise, as if some one was endeavouring to force an entry through one of the windows of the lower or area flat. Greatly fluttered, she groped her way to the lobby, which ran from the front area-door to the back, and before she got half-way along it, she encountered a man. Giving a suppressed choking scream, she retreated towards the kitchen, where, being followed by the man, he seized a heavy poker, and struck her a terrible blow on the head. This, with all its severity, had not it would seem deprived her of sense, for she had set forth such a yell of agony, that it was heard by some of the neighbours. I have heard it said that the intention to kill is rather confirmed and made furious by a thrilling cry—a species of resistance which, expressing horror, is felt by a murderer as an impeachment of his cruelty, besides rousing his fears of being detected; and it is thought that the cruel man was thus roused, for he laid on blow after blow, till the head of his victim bore cuts to the bone as the bloody traces of the terrible onslaught. A single minute or two sufficed for the work—the woman was bathed with blood, and the hand was again raised to put a certain end to life, when an alarm was raised by the neighbours. The poker was instantly dropped, and the murderer, flying along the dark passage, tried the door to the back; it was locked, and he escaped by the window just as the neighbours were at his heels. He got off, but not without being so far noticed, that they could speak to his general appearance and dress.

Immediately afterwards, doctors were called, the interest displayed by the sympathisers excluding for a time all efforts at tracing the man. So far as was thought, he had made a clean escape, for the indistinct notice got of him could not have amounted to identification, and the lady, almost at the point of death, could not be questioned, nor, as the attack took place when there was scarcely a glimmer of light, could it be expected she would be able to add much to the vague notice of those who saw him escape. I was at the house next day, but it was four or five days after before I could be permitted to question her; and even then, I found it possible to get only some marks which could not afford me much aid. I ascertained, however, partly from her own lips, in broken accents, and partly from the neighbours, just as much as satisfied me, that the man was a young fellow about eighteen or twenty, and that he wore a lightish moleskin jacket and trousers. Nothing could be more indefinite, as the dress is that worn by thousands of working men, and the age amounted to nothing.

Next day I was in the High Street, not knowing well how to turn, for where, in the wide expanse of the old town, filled with so many dens, and those often crammed with people of all kinds, was I to find the owner of *the* moleskin jacket and trousers? There were hundreds around me dressed in this common garb: he might as well be among these as in a house, for being certain he was not seen, he would not think it necessary to skulk; and then he had taken nothing with him by which the crime could be brought home to him. The allusions I have made to chance may tire readers, as well as lay my narratives open to suspicion; yet certain it is, that at that minute, when my eyes were busy surveying the crowded street, my attention was suddenly arrested by one I knew to be a thief, and who wore a moleskin jacket and trousers. I immediately walked after him, and it struck me that his dress looked like as if it had been washed and dried very recently. This made me curious; and as he walked on, I quickened my steps till I came nearer him, so as to have a better view of his jacket. I thought I could perceive blotches here and there, very like as if marks of blood had been ineffectually attempted to be washed out. I became at length so satisfied, that I stopped him.

"George," said I, for I knew him of old, "you have got your jacket newly washed; but, oh, man, it's not well done."

"What do you mean?" said he.

"Why," said I, "you have forgotten to rub out the stains of Miss Balleny's blood."

In an instant every trace of blood was absent from his cheek, however it stuck to his moleskin—yes, he was instantly pale, and struck dumb.

"Come," said I, "I wish to examine those marks better, and I would rather make the investigation in the office."

I accordingly took him there, in the midst of all the ordinary protestations and threatenings, and soon got my suspicions confirmed by the opinions of others. As soon as Miss Balleny was supposed to be able to stand the look of him, he was taken to her bedside. I shall never forget the look of that lady, as she brought her nervous eye to bear upon the man who was supposed to be he who did all that bloody work upon her. A shiver seemed to run over her whole body, as if the sight had brought back to her the terrible feelings of that lone and dark hour. It seemed that there had been some glimmer, either from the kitchen fire or from the street lamp through the window, I forget which, but there had been enough to enable her to distinguish his dress and general appearance; for, after gazing at him for a time, she said, "O God, that is the very man!" We afterwards got some of the neighbours to add something like identification, and we thought we had enough, with the blood-stains, to authorise a conviction.

The Crown officer having got all the evidence that was to be had, George Kerr was brought to trial before the High Court for the attempt to murder and the housebreaking. Miss Balleny was put into the box as the principal witness; but it became soon apparent that the poor lady had suffered too much to permit of the continuance of that recollection which had served on occasion of the prior meeting. Her mind was gone. At one time she was positive, at another only suspicious, at another doubtful, only to be more positive again, as the changing thought flickered through her brain. The other witnesses were decided enough as to the dress and generalities; and the washed blood-stains were as decidedly spoken to as marks of such a kind could be; but the fatality lay in Miss Balleny's incapacity; and the jury, after a discriminative charge, brought in a verdict of "not guilty."

All my efforts had thus gone for nothing; but my pride of detection was hurt, and I felt much inclination to stick by my man. I accordingly ascertained that he had gone by the boat to Stirling; and though he had thus left my bounds, he did not take with him my desire to look after his welfare. Nor was it long before my kind demon helped me in my solicitude, for a day or two afterwards the Stirling authorities sent us information that the shop of a Mr Meek had been broken into, on *that* very evening Kerr had left Edinburgh, by a young man answering to his description, and a sum of money, as well as a silver watch, had been abstracted as booty.

It was now my duty to watch again for my man, though I had small hope he would return so soon to town; nor did he. He had gone direct to Glasgow, with the view of getting the silver watch disposed of at a pawn-shop. There he was signally unfortunate, for the Stirling authorities had sent a description of the watch and the man to the Glasgow police, who had spread the intelligence among the pawnbrokers. Accordingly, when Kerr offered the article at a pawn-shop there, the man to whom it was presented declared immediately that it was stolen, and, sliding between Kerr and the door, endeavoured to detain him. The effort was vain. Kerr darted past him, and outran his pursuers.

Of all this we got timely knowledge, and now I had another chance. Always keeping the moth-instinct in view, I suspected that he would be back to his old haunts; and in this case I was made more than usually hopeful, in counting that the money taken at Stirling must have been spent, and the want of wings to fly further would send him crawling to his old nest. My former inquiries had enabled me to know that his mother lived in Macdowall Street. Thither I went, and somehow or other I felt a kind of certainty that I would find him. I knocked at the door with much confidence, and perhaps, on that account, with much humility and gentleness. Mrs Kerr herself answered, and I remember the conversation—

"Well, Mrs Kerr, have you any one living with you?" asked I.

"Nobody, sir."

"Quite sure?"

"Perfectly sure. I'm a lone woman, and after what has befallen my poor innocent son, I am very miserable."

"And so you may well be," said I, "for that was a terrible business; but have you no notion where George is?"

"No, no. I have never seen him since that day of the trial; and I fancy the poor fellow is so ashamed of having been suspected of murder that he'll never show his face in Scotland again."

"And have you no lodgers?" I inquired.

"Not a living soul, sir."

"Well," said I, "I'll just step in and see."

"You are very welcome," she answered, just in that involuntary way that has told me a hundred times that there is somebody in some place where there is nobody; and so we often need to act against the rule that a person cannot be in two places at the same time.

And passing her, I looked round the place she used as a kitchen. No concealing place there. I then opened the other room, and saw nobody; nor did I expect, as she had time enough before answering my knock to make any convenient arrangements.

"Here is a closet," said I.

"No, sir; just a cupboard for odds and ends."

"Locked," said I. "Do you usually lock up your cups and saucers?"

"What I use are in the kitchen," she replied, getting, as I saw, alarmed.

"And have you not got the key?"

"No, it is lost."

Ah! the old story, I thought.

"Well, if it is lost," said I, quietly, "it is the more necessary that search should be made for it. You go and get it *where* it was lost."

"How could it be lost if I knew where it is?" said she, thinking me serious, no doubt.

"Why, that is just a curious part of the case," said I; "and another is, that if you don't go and get it where it was lost, I will get an axe in the kitchen and break open the door."

"What? do you think my son is there?" said she, in affected wonder.

"Yes," said I. "I think his shame has gone off, and he has faced Scotland again. Get me the key, quick, or——" and I made for the kitchen.

"There," said she, as she drew it out of her pocket; "the Lord's will be done."

And there, upon opening the door, was that blood-thirsty man who had so ruthlessly smashed the head of the aged lady, who never did him a trace of injury, standing bolt upright in a narrow cupboard, which scarcely permitted him to move.

"Ah! once more, George," said I.

The fellow absolutely ground his teeth against each other till I heard the very rasping; a scowl sat on his low brow, so demoniac that if I had not been accustomed to such looks it might have made me recoil; and I believe if he had had Miss Balleny's poker, or any other poker, he would have tried his skill at laying open heads on my cranium. But for all these indications the cure is unshrinking firmness; and sure I am, if I had shown a trace of weakness, he would have fallen upon me on the instant like a tiger.

"There is no use for these looks with me," said I; "you know me of old; so take the cuffs kindly, or worse will befall you."

"But, sir," cried the mother, when she saw her son bound, "is this never to be ended? Has George not been tried and found innocent?"

"Yes," said I. "But we are informed that he robbed a shop in Stirling that very night after he was released; so you see the trial did not shame him quite so much as you thought."

"It's a d—d lie!" burst out the fellow; "I have never been out of Edinburgh."

"To that I can swear," said the parent; for, although she had said, "The Lord's will be done," the mother came back again to lie for her murderous boy. No, no; there is no appeasing of this yearning. I have seen it working in all forms. Even if she had seen those hashes in the head of the poor lady, and the body drenched in blood, drawn by the hand of her son, she could not have stayed that yearning. The moment's horror would have been succeeded by a tear for the victim and a flood for the murderer. So true what some one said to me once—the mother's heart is the sanctuary that shuts out all detectives. It even makes sinners of good people, just as if, being the very stuff the nerve is made of, it kicks heels-over-head all the virtues, which are only phantom things flickering about in the brain.

I confess here to a weakness. When I was taking my man up to the office, I thought all the world was looking at me. Why so? Since ever that day I saw the mangled head of that poor lady, the vision had haunted me like a ghost, and, having failed in getting the murderer convicted, the spectre followed me more and more, as if insisting I should bring him still to justice; so when I walked him up, I thought, It is done now—I have got him, and, though he won't be hanged, he will be better than hanged, for he must get on the chain and the horrible clogs, and pull his legs after him in Norfolk Island, under a scorching sun, and then he will not be obliged to *draw* the bloody head after him, for it will follow of its own accord, and every gash will make gobs at him.

So we think, and yet I have my doubts whether a man who *could* bring a heavy poker down with all his strength on the head of an unoffending female—I take the one peculiar case—is capable of relentance. The softness is not in him. I do not say that God is not able to bring it, but I do say that where such a change comes it must be a miracle.

We next sent intelligence to Stirling that the now famous George Kerr was safe in our hands. Meantime we knew that the Glasgow police had sent on the watch there, so that the watch and the watch-stealer would meet opportunely, where Mr Meek could speak both to the one and the other. It soon got known to the Crown agent who it was that had broken into Mr Meek's shop, and I do not doubt that this knowledge helped to quicken the Stirling fiscal's wits in making a clearer case of the robbery than the Edinburgh official had been able to do. The trial was fixed for the next Circuit. Every effort was made, witnesses called from Glasgow, and all those ferreted out in Stirling that could say a single word to help so good a cause as bringing so cruel a man to justice. If it had been some years earlier, he might have been tried for his life as a housebreaker; but as it was, it turned out as well as could be expected. He was sentenced to ten years' transportation.

No case ever gave me more satisfaction than this. The people of Edinburgh had been disappointed by the issue of the former trial, and when it was known that he had been sentenced to transportation for a robbery committed on the day of his liberation, the satisfaction was great, and all the greater that the robbery made sure of the real heartless, incurable character of the villain. Indeed, it is not too much to say that the act was worse than murder, for the lady was so desperately maimed that her recovery, with ruined intellect, was rather an additional evil to that first inflicted.

The Holy Land

❖

THIS large building, so christened by Scottish humour,—a little grim in its profanity,—still presents its dark front to Leith Wynd, on the same line with the Happy Land. At the time of which I speak, it was occupied chiefly by great masses of profligate women, some in rags, some in silks, mixed up in grotesque confusion. However well I know all its dark apartments and holes, it is beyond my power to describe it in such a way as to be followed with satisfaction by my readers. The middle stair led, and leads still, to a number of flats—each of these divided into dwellings, some of only one room, and some of two or three, and the size generally indicating the proportion of inmates, for they were literally crammed with human beings. They were almost all appropriated to the same purpose,—prostitution, with its accompaniment, intoxication. Among them were what might be called establishments, got up in a very simple way, and with no more capital than served to purchase a few old beds, chairs, and fir tables. One worn-out unfortunate, who chanced to outlive the limited term without becoming a cinder-wife, would contrive to get these articles, often through the medium of some man with a few pounds to spare, and who would have a share in the earnings, and thus "set up." Presently the rooms, seldom exceeding three, were filled with the young cast-aways with which Edinburgh was filled, and who were always on the outlook for shelter, taking along with them their stock-in-trade, often enough only the flimsy rags on their bodies. Sometimes there was no mistress, the affair being a joint partnership among three or four of these young women—clubbing for the few articles of furniture, and each earning her own livelihood, and spending what she earned in her own way—the usual routine being bread and butter, eggs, tea, and whisky.

Neither of these kinds of places of business, where the proprietor or partners lived and got drunk on the premises, was without the indispensable bully, or "fancy man"—that very worst example of degraded human nature,—always a thief outside, and a sorner on poor female wretches within—acting at one time the cruel hawk, preying upon small game, and at another the "dirty Andrew," living on the droppings of gulls as they fly over him. On entering these places, I have found him lounging among the women, and, as if ashamed, slinking away into some dark hole, scowling and looking back with his swollen eyes. He knows his degradation well enough, but the shame is changed into revenge against every one who can yet hold up his head, a man among men; and, strange enough, he and his kind are the wretches upon whom these women, often pretty young creatures, throw away their affections,—or rather, I would say, from my experience, that there is scarcely an unfortunate to be found anywhere, even in the genteel palaces of sin, where they are seldom let out, who does not have her low secret "fancy," all the while the gay youths who go about her think they are the objects of her affections. Wherever, in short, these creatures are, there are the indispensable carrion-crows.

Not that they keep these hangers-on always for robbery, for often enough I have found concerted cases among two or three or four women, all leagued for the systematic plunder of the simpletons who are enchanted into their dens. On the second flat of the Holy Land, I had occasion to be acquainted with a nest of female conspirators of this kind, who executed their business without the assistance of a bully. Their names were Jean Mullins, Elizabeth Thomson, and Eliza Graham; and their plan owed its principal feature to the condition that they should so work their treble-bagged net that when the fish was secure they should be all in at the hauling. But how was this to be managed? It required some cleverness both of mind and body. Their rooms looked to the street, and when one took in her "cully" she made a signal by hanging a white cloth out at the window, so that the other two might come in and assist. If one could act best alone, the two others might retire to the other room; but when it was necessary to dose the victim with drink, it was advantageous that they should all three be at the work. That they had force, and adroitness to use it in self-defence, is evident enough; for they knew that there are men who, under the rage of being so deceived and robbed, can be very dangerous; but they laid their account with taking advantage of their united strength in attack, when, perhaps, the individual, though intoxicated, was wary and resistive.

No one who saw these girls could have doubted their formidableness, not from their strength alone, for they were only lithe and active. Their extreme youth was a recommendation to those who were likely to fall in with their wishes; and the good looks of at least two of them—Thomson and Graham—might promise well for the filling of the net. One night in December 1847,—a very cold one, with snow on the ground,—Mullins got into her toils a gentleman of the name of H—ll, from Manchester; and the good soul sighed ardently for his translation to the Holy Land, not that she hinted she had any intention of taking him to a place the name of which would, to a Scotchman, have given rise to suspicions, and even to an Englishman might have suggested some contrast. No, she wanted him only to her lodging, which was all her own, not a "house" where a bully might murder a cully, but a quiet kind of retreat, with nobody near but a good old woman, so discreet as to wink at ways of pleasantness which she herself had enjoyed. Mr H—ll was tempted, and went along with the siren.

And to that holy of holies she led him. Thomson and Graham, the moment they heard her coming in, retired to the farther room, leaving a fine glowing fire to welcome the stranger. How kind in the good old lady to have that fire in that cold night, to thaw their cold limbs, and be so propitious to love! After remaining for some time, Jean was satisfied that Mr H—ll would not drink. He was a *temperate* man, and resisted all liquors which tended to steal away the reason, and therefore she must act upon her own hook. That she did pretty effectually, if we might judge from his starting up in a terrible consternation and bawling out—

"You wretch, you have taken from me a £50 Bank of England note."

"You're a liar," cried Mullins; "you have lost it somewhere else."

"I deny it," rejoined the temperate gentleman. "I made sure by feeling for it at the foot of the stair before I came up to this door."

"Then you must have lost it on the stair," said she. "We were passed by two women, one of whom you pulled by the gown."

"Yes, but I could swear it wasn't she," he cried again.

"And what care I for your oath? See, here's a witness," she cried, as Eliza Graham opened the door, coming out of the inner room.

"Eliza," asked Mullins, "did you come up the outer stair a little ago, and go into your room by the lobby?"

"Yes," was the confident answer.

"And wasn't you at the foot of the stair when we came in?"

"Yes," with equal confidence.

"And didn't you see that thief, Bess Collins, who lives above us, come down the stair after we went up?"

"Yes," repeated the vixen, "and what's a great deal more, she told me she had got a haul of a £50 note out of Mullins' cully."

And so tickled was Jean with the sharpness of Graham, that she burst out into a derisive laugh, in which not only Eliza joined, but also Elizabeth, who had also rushed in to help the game.

The man stood thunderstruck, nor was he for a time able to speak.

"Come, then," said Mullins, thinking he was satisfied, "give me a dram for ill-using me, and we'll make up."

"Yes," said Eliza, "and I'll help you to catch Collins. Won't I be such a stunning witness against the thief!"

"Yes, and serve her right," broke in Elizabeth; "for it's she and the like of her who brings all us decent girls into bad character."

But H—ll was sharp enough—and the form of the house might have led an observant man to it; he rushed to get into the inner room to see what he suspected, that there was no opening from it to the lobby whereby Eliza Graham could have got in. But no sooner did he make the effort than the whole three laid hold of him.

"What to do there?" asked Elizabeth. "It is my private room; and why would you wish to go into the sleeping-place of a respectable female?"

"Not like a gentleman," said Eliza.

"Not a Scotchman, at least," said Mullins.

And so they really shamed him out of his purpose; but Mr H—ll was not yet done. He bethought himself of the police, and ran back to the window of the room where he was, with the intention of pulling up the sash and bawling out.

"If you do, you villain, we'll tumble you out to send you after Collins," cried Mullins.

And H—ll got terrified at the young furies, who stood pulling and dragging him, with wild looks and flaming eyes, as if they would have torn him to pieces.

If H—ll had been a powerful man, he would at least have ended the personal struggle, but though not strong, he had still the small amount of courage necessary to enable him to make a stand against three young and even slender females; so he began to lay about him in the hope of terrifying them, but they had been called upon before for a device to pacify an unruly victim.

"If you arn't quiet," said Mullins, "I have only to give three knocks on the door, and one will appear who will pacify you, so that you'll require no more peace in this world."

"A bully?" cried H—ll.

"Perhaps," answered Jean; "and must not poor unprotected girls be defended against liars who say we rob when we don't?"

Mr H—ll had scarcely courage to meet a man of that stamp, and then he had no doubt that such a scoundrel was not far off. He was, in short, nearly at his wit's end, and became quiet through a kind of despair.

"Just better walk out living, than be carried out dead," said Mullins.

"And go after Collins," added Elizabeth with a laugh.

What could the poor Englishman do amidst so much adroitness, boldness, and threatened cruelty? They had entirely mastered him, and there seemed only one chance for him. He was quite satisfied as to the manner of the transference of his note, and he knew the Edinburgh police was under good management; so he had presence of mind enough to appear to give in to the Collins theory. He would now repay them in their own Scotch money.

"And where will I find this woman Collins?" said he.

"Oh, everybody knows Collins," said Mullins, scarcely able now to restrain her satisfaction at getting quit of the police, their greatest terror; "she walks Princes' Street, from the Register Office to the foot of Hanover Street."

"And how is she dressed?" asked he again, but only as a device.

"Bonnet and green ribbons."

"And what like is she?"

"Ugly—turned-up nose, mouth like a post-office, and eyes like a cat."

Whereat the two laughed heartily.

"You can't miss her," said Mullins, again. "And if you're good, I'll tell you a secret," added Eliza Graham.

"I will be good and quiet," said poor H—ll, so wise behind the hand.

"She has the £50 note in her muff; just go up to her, snatch the muff, and bolt to your inn, and you'll find it."

"Very well," said H—ll, taking his hat, and running out; hearing, as he went—

"And you *won't* give us a dram for what we have told you? scurvy beggar!"

No sooner had he got down-stairs, than he hastened to the Police-office, where he reported the robbery of £50, by Jean Mullins, and gave the description of the three women and the house. I took charge of the business, as being familiar with the Holy Land, as well as every one, mostly, of its inmates. After a conversation, in which Mr H—ll, still excited, wished to enlarge on all these particulars, and which I saw the necessity of cutting short, I went and apprehended the girls, searched the house without success, and found only some silver on their persons.

No more could be done that night. The note had been conveyed to a resetter, and tracing is always a delicate affair. In this instance, I was not without my idea. There was a person of the name of Thomas Brown, who kept an old metal shop on the ground storey of the Happy Land, and I had strong reasons for believing that he acted as resetter to the thieves of the various flats. About ten next morning I was on the alert, but as the article I was in search of was so small and delicate an affair that it might have been put into a walnut, I saw I could have no chance of getting it if my shadow were cast in at that man's door. I knew, moreover, he would change it at a bank, and it was even profitable to give him time to get that effected. At ten, I ascertained—though not by calling—that he had gone out, and immediately set off to try if I could bring him within the verge of my eye. By going to the banks, any advantage thereby derived would be counterbalanced by my chance of falling in with Brown. I had a weary hunt that day. I could find him nowhere, and was about to give up that scent for my fortune at the various banks, when, at length, crossing the top of Leith Walk, I saw my metal merchant, accompanied by another person, coming direct up from Leith. A thought now struck me that, as it was not then uncommon for thieves to get their English notes changed at Leith, Brown and the other man had been down at the Bank of Scotland branch there, getting their object effected. I resolved, therefore, on letting Brown in the meantime go unnoticed, and take my chance of my "idea." I hurried, accordingly, to Leith, and found, upon inquiry, that the note had been changed at the bank there only a few minutes before. I regretted that the number of the note was unknown to Mr H—ll, and therefore to me, but I got such a description of Brown's friend that I had no doubt of the man. I got the note from the agent on receipt, and hurried to Edinburgh.

I went and apprehended Brown, and afterwards got hold of his friend, whose name is not in my book. Never was a man more delighted than Mr H—ll when he learnt the fate of the note; but the business was not yet finished. There could be no doubt of the travels of the small bit of paper, or the hands through which it had gone; but there was a difficulty. The bank-agent could identify Brown's friend; but, he being unwilling, who was to identify a note with a number not condescended on, because not known? Then, unless we could identify it as stolen, the bank would reclaim it. Nay, we could not get at either the robbers or resetters. Nor would it have been any better though I had got the fifty Scotch notes on Brown or in his house, because, whatever the presumption might have been, the legal proof that they were the change of this £50 note would have been wanting.

I had only one remedy. I went to Brown's friend.

"Now," said I, "you're in for Botany Bay."

"You must prove me guilty," said he, doggedly, for no doubt he had a share in the spoil.

"Why," replied I, "it is an easy matter that. The bank-agent at Leith will swear to you as having changed the note at his office."

"Well, and what then?" not much moved as yet.

"What then? It will be demanded of you where you got the note."

"No man is bound to tell where he gets his money," he replied, doggedly.

"No, certainly, if he does not feel the force."

"What do you mean?" said he.

"Simply this," replied I, "that as every honest man is ready to admit where his money comes from, your refusal will be taken as a confession, and you will be held responsible for the robbery."

"Are you sure of that?"

"Sure; and what a fool you are! Suppose you got it from Brown, and say so, you are free. You are a mile off from the women, and no one will blame you for being made a dupe of Brown, but rather pity you. Besides, you are doing your duty to your country."

This last speech did the job—the man broke down.

"Well," he said, "I did get the note from Brown to change, and I changed it, getting a pound to myself."

"And you'll swear this?"

"Yes," replied he, stoutly.

"All right," said I. "You will be liberated after the trial, with no scath."

So this strange case terminated. All the three denizens of the Holy Land, along with the dealer in *hard* goods, were tried before the High Court. One of the girls—I think Eliza Graham—was let off, on what special grounds I don't remember. Mullins and Thomson as the robbers, and Brown as resetter, were all sentenced to seven years.

I have always considered this case as one of the narrowest that ever went through my hands. It had a good effect. The Holy Land did not become more holy,—that was impossible,—but it became, for a time at least, more circumspect. A great many of the "Virgins of Jerusalem," in their white robes of innocence, were at the trial, and they would take home to the Holy Land the fate of their sisters.

The Jewel-Box

SOMETIMES we detectives have moments of despondency. As the world is made, thieves, robbers, and murderers will persevere,—it is their nature; and the more they achieve, the more they would. They are artists inspired by their art. On the other side, we must progress as well. We are the checks to nature when she gets rampant, and a little out-o'-sides; and we are vexed when she gets ahead of us. The charges on the side of our books against honesty had been—I am speaking of August 1845—getting heavier and heavier; and Mr Haining was nervous, because I was not bringing a *per contra.* Yet I was as keen in the nose, eye, and ear as ever; and never allowed a glimpse, sniff, or whisper to go without its proper attention and response. The artists were buzzing about me like blue-bottles, attacking fresh and stale, and yet their wings were unsinged. No wonder I was a little out of humour that day. I was walking down the High Street, with never a hope of a transportation to transport me, or a suspension to hang up my disappointment. My flies, to use my old metaphor, were either unsuited to the sky or the water, of they were known, though they were changed from the red-hackle of my anger to the palmer of my humility. On my way, I happened to fix my eye on Mrs Bushe, (before, Miss Noel,) hurrying up the High Street. Ah! there is an actress, as I am an actor; yet how different our deserts! She transports, so do I. She charms by singing, I by swinging. No great difference in what learned people call the literal way, yet how wide asunder in reality! Her friends applaud her, and throw money at her; mine curse me, and would starve me. Nor was I altogether pleased with old Mother Providence, for I had a notion that I did as much good in my way as she.

Will any man, more knowing than I, account for such thoughts, brought up by a passing vision? I had seen Mrs Bushe before, and never thought of such things; and why should I now, merely because the lady looked a little more excited than she was when singing "Nid noddin'," or "Auld Robin Gray?" I fear I would get no answer; nor do I wish any, for I've been long satisfied that there are things in the world—even my own leadings and wonderful chances, as they are called—which your very wise gentry could make no more of than my poor self.

Still sauntering, with my aide-de-camp behind me, I could scarcely get quit of my regrets at these young gamesters on every side of me, who made such a difference between me, by allowing me no influence over them, and her, whom they went with their stolen shillings to hear every night in the "gods" yonder, while I was among blue devils. I had got to the Bridge, had crossed, and was for down to the Canongate, where the stream, always turbid, with a shadow from the high sides, gives hope to the moral angler; and just as I passed the mouth of Halkerston's Wynd, the next to the Bridge on the left hand going down, I saw a clot of my celebrities standing a good way within it. No doubt they had arrived there by the stair behind the Theatre,—at least that was my thought,—and by and by they would emerge at the top. A glance satisfied me they were examining something. I beckoned my assistant—

"Down, and take a man with you, by the stairs by Adam Black's old shop,—get to the foot of the close, and there keep sentry. There's a nest in the middle of the close, and let none escape your way."

The man was off, and next I hailed two of the High Street perambulators—

"You stand here, each on a side; and if you see any young celebrities come running up the close, grip 'em, and hold fast till I come."

"All right, sir."

Giving time for my scout by the stairs, I walked down the close. The students of the piece of art which so claimed their attention were still there; and so studious were they, with all their heads huddled together,—so like Mr Faed's scholars over the schoolmaster's watch, busy taking down the works, all the while the dominie, with birch in hand, was looking in at the school door,—that they did not see my face until it was presented over the shoulder of him who held the object—no other than a splendid jewel-box, filled with gold chains, bracelets, necklaces, brooches, rings, and other *bijouterie*, which made even my eyes reel. Down went the lid with a click of the steel spring, and off flew the students in rays from all this glory. I seized, of course, him who held the treasure,—an old friend, who had given me as much pain by his prudence as he did others by his imprudence. As for the others, the bags of the net were ready, each with its *cul-de-sac*; and the harder they ran, the greater the bang against the woven hemp. Two went up and two down, and the fifth was mine, jewel-box and all.

When I got to the top of the close, I found each policeman with his charge; and, looking down, I saw my assistant and his companion coming up, equally engaged with their couple. A few minutes brought us together, as lovingly as the different feelings of the parties would permit. So we all marched on, with a gathering crowd about us, to the office.

But here comes the mystery. We had scarcely passed the Bridge, when whom do I see coming down in front of us?—the same lady, Mrs Bushe, whom I had met as I came down. I looked at her again, but was now in no humour for dreary comparisons. Nor did she look less intensely at me. How is this, thought I; is there any sympathy between this artist and me? And still she looked, with her eye fixed upon my jewel-box. Nor was this all, for she made her way through the crowd, and approaching me, said—

"Oh, you've got it? How clever!"

"What?" said I, as I went along, for I couldn't stop.

"The box."

"Yes; I have got a box."

"My box."

"Your box, madam? I do not know; but if you will have the kindness to follow up, I will speak to you at the office."

She fell back, and no doubt kept close to us. We are landed.

Having delivered my men, Captain Haining came up to me, joined by this time by the lady.

"God bless me, M'Levy," said the Captain, "you got no notice, did you? I sent a man after you, but he came back and said he couldn't find you."

"I got no notice, but I've got the box, and a very valuable one it is."

"Why, you must have met Mrs Bushe as she came up to give information of the robbery of her jewel-box."

"I did meet the lady, but she did not speak to me."

"No," said she, laughing with delight at the sight of her jewels all safe. "I didn't know Mr M'Levy, though I've heard his name, otherwise I would have claimed his services. But, good heavens! it seems like magic. Where got you it?"

"I have not only got your jewels, madam, but my jewels—ay, five of them—and very bright ones, too; true diamonds,—sharp, cutting, and extremely fine set-offs to detectives like me."

"But are they all there?—let us see," she said, anxiously, even nervously.

And opening the box, she scanned over the contents all so carefully, as if they had been darlings, as no doubt they were.

"Not a ring amissing!" she cried, exultingly; "wonderful interposition of Providence! for they are worth more than a hundred pounds, and many of them I am to wear this very night on the stage. You must take a ticket, Mr M'Levy, from me, for I would like you to be in the pit to-night, just to hear with what spirit I shall sing—

Oh, bright and rare
Are the jewels I wear.

And, laughing again, she thanked me, and went away, with Captain Haining's promise that the box would be sent after her, when an inventory was made, that she might sign.

But somehow the laugh of the lady was not joined in by those who admired jewels as much as she, and not the less that they were not their own. Nor am I sure that they ever overcame the sad disappointment, not even after the Sheriff congratulated them upon the jury's verdict of guilty, upon which followed the distribution among them of the months,—three getting six; one nine; and another twelve. After which they might still study those envied trinkets from the gods, as they did before those from the devils.

The Jostle

❖

SOME time towards the end of the year 1857, I happened to be coming round from Windmill Street to Chapel Street,—musing, of course, as usual; for it must be recollected that we are great students, though having vastly little to do with books,—except sometimes a directory or railway guide. I had got up to Chapel Street a small way, when suddenly a man, bouncing out of a shop occupied by one Flynn, came with a sudden broadside on my left shoulder. No doubt it was an accident; the man was in a hurry, and one don't mind these things much; but in my case there is this peculiarity, that having always been rather soft in my communication of force, I don't like to be impinged upon rudely, so I looked sharply round to see my bouncing gentleman, and just met his face as he turned round for an instant to see what effect his jostle had produced. I didn't know the fellow, but neither did I like his look, which was between the jimmy genteel and the healthy mechanical,—brushed down, and yet frowsy; hat shiny, yet with a *clour* or two, as if it had met with accidents on the road; buttons on his coat too new to match the threadbare streaks here and there; not yet out at elbows, but coming. Yet all this was little or nothing. There are plenty of such kind of people, who do not qualify themselves for my attention,—a kind of ne'er-do-weels for themselves and ne'er-do-ills for others,—more unfortunate than criminals,—bogles to their friends, and canny towards others. Yet I was struck by this man, principally in consequence of his style of face. Even if I had had no genius in that way, I could not have forgotten it. The principal feature was not like any nose I had ever encountered. It was a straight, sharp line till towards the end, where it bulged out to such an extent at both sides that it looked like a club, and seemed to bespeak pulling as some thing suited to it and deserved by it.

But if this organ was a temptation, there was something above it, in a pair of eyebrows, as well as the squinting lights that shone through them, which seemed to threaten vengeance to the hand that should be so tempted,—just as if that said expression above declared that it had the special care of what so temptingly lay below. Moreover, a scowl at me, who was really the aggrieved party, riveted the impression of features which stood in no need at all of any such auxiliary to make them stick to any mind—far less mine, so ominously retentive of peculiar faces.

I need not say that that face accompanied me, as that of one who was formed of a kind of clay suited to my handling. I could not account for the circumstance that such a person had been resident in Edinburgh for a time, without having thrown out signals to me that he was well worth my acquaintanceship; and the circumstance was the more extraordinary, that the house he came from when he jostled me—to get me, as it would seem, to look at him—was a resort of cardsharpers, perfectly well known to me. Be all that as it may, it is certain at least that the image of that face occupied my mind so exclusively—not only that day and night, but several others—that I fear some other profiles were deprived of that attention from me they deserved; but I was not accountable for this: if God has thought proper to paint "thief", "robber", or "murderer" on certain brows, it isn't for nothing; nay, it is for something—that the like of me should read the marks, and try to save the good and virtuous from the workings of the spirit which these terrible words are intended to indicate. But if it was certain that I was haunted by that nose so club-like, and those eyes which, being drawn out of the straight course, had got into a twist, from which they could not be untwisted by the eternal regularities of the good and the true,—so calculated as these are to simplify and strengthen vision,—so also was it certain that I entertained no doubt he would fall into my hands, but when, wherefore or how, was of course a mystery. Nay, I was even so presumptuous as to take the jostle, and the consequent shock to my nervous system—not very susceptible that—as a presage of my being to be called upon to protect the rights of society against a man so clearly *Cainified* to my hand.

Other affairs carried my attentions away in various other directions, but the complexity of these avocations was just no more than a pretty wide meshed net over the surface of a picture, and which scarcely interrupts the view of the piece; and among these calls upon me, a case in Aberdeen, far enough away from Chapel Street, was peculiar and exacting. I am speaking to a period only a few years ago—1857—and the time of the year October. A Mr Lundie, pawnbroker in Glasgow, with a branch doing extensive business in Aberdeen, got his premises in the latter town broken into one night. The affair was not only bold and desperate, but the number of gold and silver watches and valuable jewels of many kinds, was such that the whole of old Aberdeen was on fire. Groups of people stood at the door of the pawn-shop discoursing of the ingenuity of the housebreakers, others were examining the traces of the successful manœuvre, not only during the next day, but for several days; and, perhaps, there had not been so successful and extensive a depredation in that comparatively quiet town for many years.

Meanwhile the police had their nerves strung up to the mark. The town and suburbs were scoured; and at length two seemly gentlemen, who were so very ill at speaking the Doric of that district, that pure cockneyism shone through, and declared them to all intents and purposes foreigners, were taken up. What were these southern artists doing so far north? what attraction was there in Aberdeen brose over the roast beef of Old England? in the northern equinoctials over the southern? Vain questions, for there was no satisfactory answer; but then what right had the Aberdeen police to seize on these curious travellers, merely because a curious case of burglary had taken place in a town not over-pure in other respects—see the Register of Births—besides honesty. Why, no right at all, except that which belongs to a vague suspicion roused by bits of incongruities in dress, appearance, habits, and so forth, not very easily accounted for. So these English gentlemen having broken into the strong box of these suspicions, and, like conjurors, shown to the astonished police that there was actually nothing under the hat where the pigeon was, got off,—the police acting a little upon the dodge as well as from necessity; for the dismissal, it was thought would send the adepts to where the valuable booty was planked, with which they would go no doubt south, and be thereby nabbed perhaps by no less a personage than myself.

This trick among us sometimes works very well; and in this case it did not work ill. Information was sent to us in Edinburgh, that the gentlemen would likely pay our Modern Athens a visit, and after a time return to Aberdeen to unplank the plank. We not only got the names,—Thomas Williams and William Thomson,—but also a very graphic account of their persons. Now you will say that my stories have got joints added to them by my fancy; for what were the chances against me of one of these men being my jostler of the club organ? Not so formidable as you imagine. The secret with me has always been to be about the right place at the right time. What took me up by Chapel Street, but just that I knew that Flynn's house was to me an interesting one? and then thieves are wonderfully narrowed in their haunts. If my jack of clubs was to be anywhere, he would be among the cardsharpers at Flynn's, and a cardsharper does not consider it beneath him to shuffle gold watches in place of bits of pasteboard, if he can play the game with nothing in his pocket for stakes. It don't signify: the account from Aberdeen was a pen-and-ink sun-picture of my jack of clubs, so well drawn that I recognised him in a moment; nay, for aught I know, he was at that moment when he jostled the wayfarer M'Levy, and scowled back upon him, on his way to the pawnshop in Aberdeen, where Thomson was before him, making espials and arrangements, in their prudent way.

It was natural that I should wish, by way of revenge, to smile upon that face which had scowled upon me; but, although I considered it very probable that the Aberdeen police were right in supposing that the gentlemen had come to Edinburgh to wait until the plank was ripe for lifting, and do a little by-play at Flynn's in the meantime, it was not for me to show my face there, to flutter the wings that were to carry them to my dovecot with the straws in their bills. No; I behoved merely to set a watch, which I did without any effect; and then came another communication from Aberdeen,—and how the police there got the information I never learned,—that on Friday the 2d of October the burglars had started from Edinburgh for the north, with the intention to remove the booty. So my club had proved a trump over my ace of hearts, and my next object was to watch them when they came south, which they would very soon do. Though, strangely enough, the northern gentlemen of the second sight had come to know what seemed to me almost impossible to be known, they were ignorant of that which seemed likely they would know, that the enemy had again taken a direction towards my beat.

Thieves and robbers *observe* Sunday;—the blessed day drives them into their dens, where

"Sabbath shines no Sabbath-day to *thieves*;"—

that is, as a holy day on which God is to be worshipped, and sins repented of, but as an unholy day so far as their desecration can go. The very sternness of soul which makes them the breakers of God's law is aggravated and irritated by the sound of the Sabbath bell and the crowded tread of worshippers; for how otherwise can we account for that day being chosen for their hellish jubilees—ay, for the very advantage they take of houses left empty that the house of God may be full? What then?—the advantage they think, in their madness, they derive from the observation of the day of peace and rest, we turn round, till the head of the scorpion bites its tail in the midst of the fire of retribution. Yes, we must observe their observation; and so on the next Sunday I expected something which might turn the tables upon them. No more watching of Mr Flynn's door, where I had been jostled, and where it was now my turn to jostle, but not scowl. I took with me, in the evening, four assistants,—for I knew that meet whom I might they would not, on the Lord's day, be solitary beings, immured in separate rooms, communing with their spirits in retirement, but congregated in clusters, triumphing over their wickedness, under the sympathetic power of the *esprit de corps*. Arriving at Flynn's, I told my men to stand back and be ready for a rush,—perhaps a fight; for my "club" would not turn out a sapling among willows, bleating as the zephyrs blew. I knocked, and the door was opened by Flynn himself, but immediately shut again,—upon my baton interposed close by the lintel. I pushed in, and three of my men followed, with scarcely any noise, the fourth being for the outer escapes.

"Now," said I, as I wheeled and took hold of the key and turned it gently in the smooth lock, "let hush be the word. If you, Flynn, raise a syllable higher than a loud breath, you are *up* on the instant."

The man was mute—he could not help himself; and even the wife found a rein to her tongue, somewhere about the back nerves, which are amenable to fear. They remained in the front shop along with the men, who stood guard at the door. I knew the form of the house, and my knowledge of that guided my movements. There was a kind of kitchen adjoining the shop; the communicating door was shut—a good-enough omen. Beyond that there was a room, usually the scene of holiday cardsharping, and off that a dark closet, where I promised myself some light, neither from window, gas, nor candle. I have got light through the points of my fingers before now. So making no noise, I approached the door to the kitchen, opened it upon the instant, and there saw two men busy at a Sunday dinner which would not have shamed the feast church-goers fairly think they are entitled to on the day of rest, after two good sermons—things which I have heard said are appetising, though for what reason I know not. Yes; there was, in his proper person, my master of clubs,—even he who at the door of that shop had been so unpolite as to jostle me, a simple lounger in the streets, and not even so much as looking at him,—and Thomson too; in short, the two English thieves who had taken an affection to the Aberdeen watches and jewels.

"Don't disturb yourselves, gentlemen," I said. "Eat away; that's a good roast joint, so well loved in England, and it may be a good long time before you see another."

The sound of the knives and forks ceased on the instant. They started to run.

"Be seated," said I; "there are three valets at the door, ready to wait upon you. So go on with your dinner, for after your run from the north you must be hungry."

I saw Williams's eyes fixed on me with that twist so like the beak of the crossbill, when applying its nippers to a chesnut. I could not tell whether he saw in me the man whom he had encountered so rudely before at Flynn's door; perhaps he did; and if so, could it be supposed that he possessed a mind from God so strangely formed that it could not by any means work out a rough problem of natural religion, which is often accomplished by blind fear? I can't tell; these things are a foot or ten thousand miles beyond the cast of my plumb; but I can at least say, that as I looked at him, and remembered the extraordinary circumstance of our meeting, I was impressed by a feeling which, if I had not been on my watch, would have turned the black of my eye up under the lid to seek light in darkness.

"Just remain," I said again; "I will be with you instantly, and if you cry, your flunkies at the door will attend to you. There can be no bolting, you know, in spite of bolts. I have taken care of that. So steady."

Irony is one's only weapon where mildness is mocked and sternness resisted. Williams's scowl got darker, but not more dangerous, as his hand grasped the knife which he held in his hand; but I knew it would be only the knife that would suffer.

"There is the hot joint," said I, as I watched him; "that's the mark for the knife."

And leaving them in that fix,—with the roast before them, which they could not eat, however hungry, and the valets behind them, whom they could not call, except to give them hotter plates than suited fingers fonder of cold gold,—I opened the door leading to the back-room, and there found nine cardsharpers, seated round a table, so busy trying to cut each other as well as the cards, that they had not heard any part of the melodrama in the kitchen or front shop. So much the better; yet, as the window was being looked after outside, I had not much to fear. By several of these I was known.

"All busy on the Lord's-day," I saluted this graceless crew of the darkest and most determined vagabonds on the face of the earth.

And the growl was terrible,—just as if a kennel had seen Reynard's nose smelling a bit of their dead horse within the ring. I knew the growl would, like the wind, be contented in this case with its own sound; yet I may remark, that thimblers and cardsharpers are a class of men far more dangerous to the *person* than are the shoplifters and pickers,—the latter have at least a little of that boldness of character which is not so often found associated with cruelty as you find the dark cunning of the former.

Now, not a single word or sound but that rumbling growl. Nor was it for me to dally with such men by rubbing irony against the sharp file of their wrath. I had another object in view just then. They were safe, and so far I was satisfied. The door leading to the dark closet I have mentioned was a little ajar. I had no light, and did not wish to call for one at that juncture. I had found my way in very dark places before; and, as I have hinted with some weak egotism, my fingers are pointed with phosphorus like lucifer matches. I groped my way,—the more easy that I had groped there before, but not to any good purpose; nor indeed, to say the truth, was I very hopeful even now, considering, as I did, that these men were, as the slang goes, so *up*, that I could not come down upon them in that easy way,—I mean I could scarcely suppose that that closet would be selected as a planking hole. At the same time, I was aware that the jaunting members of the fraternity (for that the entire inmates in both rooms formed one corps I had no doubt) had newly returned home for a late dinner, and a hungry man likes to satisfy his appetite before he takes out the soiled shirts to be given to wash. So I groped my way, feeling about and about. There were carpet bags hung on pegs round and round. I grasped them hard, not for soft goods, and I know the grip of a watch as well as any man. Nothing there in any of these bags to gratify my touch, yet all the while there was a flustering and whispering among the sharpers, inspiring enough to have given me hope. Was I to be discomfited, and, after all my somewhat confident irony, to be laughed at by these scoundrels in the way they can so well do, giving me a chorus to my song of triumph, like a satirical note at the bottom of a page making a mockery of the text? It was like it; and no one can tell what it is for a detective to be "done" by his children careering on the top of a "fault" in his scent.

I stood for a moment in the middle of the closet, considering what I should do, whether to carry the hopeless bags out to the light, or get a candle in, when just as I had resolved on the latter alternative, and had brought my right leg round to turn my body to the door, my foot encountered a bag lying on the floor pretty close to the wall,—and oh, that touch of the toe, so much more fortunate than my fingerpoints! Nothing but a watch could have resisted so neatly that touch; nay, I could have sworn I had broken a glass, for there followed the impulse just such a pretty tinkle as one might expect from a musical glass—musical to me in my downcast hopes—touched in rather a rough way. My hand was on the object in an instant. I took it up, gripped it, and gripped it again, as doctors do for a knot that should not be among the soft parts; and there I could feel, one after another, thirty or forty of these round resistances, all as well marked in their rotundity as little Altringhams, with *shaws* too, no doubt.

I had got what I wanted, and presently came out.

"Does this bag belong to any of you gentlemen?" I inquired.

No one spoke.

"Will nobody claim it?" I insisted, opening the intermediate door, and taking in the two of the roast-joint interlude within the verge of my appeal.

Why are mankind accused of selfishness, and a love especially for such fine things as watches and rings, when we find such an occurrence as I now witnessed can happen among those whose rapacity is said to be born of their very "mother wit"? Every one of these men denied after another that he had any connexion with or claim to this pawnbroker's shop in a bag; and with such evidence of self-denial as I thus often encounter, it may well be wondered at that I should not have long ere now given up my unfavourable opinion of mankind.

"Well," said I, "if the bag don't belong to you, I am certain that you belong to the bag; and, as the bag must go with me, and as I don't think that what belongs naturally or artificially to a thing ought to be cut off from it, you will all of you go with the bag to the Police-office."

Terrible commotion, threats, growlings, scuffling, denials, interjections, "disjunctive conjunctions."

"It won't do," said I; "get your hats."

And they soon came to their senses. When the time comes, no one can give in more handsomely than an outlaw, so as to become an inlaw, just until he can break out, again to break in, somewhere else than into a police-office or court of justice.

In the course of half-an-hour these eleven gentlemen, with Flynn and his wife, were safely at their "home". The bag was opened. Let me transfer from my book the numbers:—23 silver watches; 17 gold watches, many of them superb; 170 gold rings, several very rich and of great value; 50 gold chains, many of them massive and weighty. It is scarcely possible to imagine a detective's feelings on pulling out of a mysterious bag the very things he wants. Even the robber, when his fingers are all of a quiver in the rapid clutch of a diamond necklace, feels no greater delight than we do when we retract that watch from the same fingers now closed with a nervous grasp; or, what is nearly the same thing, draw it out of his bag. Ah, but not the same thing in other respects here. The jewellery was no doubt identified as that of the Aberdeen pawn-shop; and, though I assumed that these thirteen belonged to the bag in some way, unfortunately it was only an assumption. And, accordingly, the Aberdeen authorities felt this difficulty.

Nor did it tend to diminish it, that, when we landed at the railway station, we encountered an extraordinary scene. Somehow it had got wind there that the robbers were expected. I have remarked that the robbery had made a great sensation in the quiet town of old Aberdeen. Well, no sooner had we arrived with our charge, than we were met by a perfect scene of triumph. Old Aberdeen seemed to have poured forth all her children that night to witness those adroit fellows who had so deceived the sharp ones of "the Doric order" there. Never was such a scene. Why, it might have seemed that the town was so virtuous that a robbery was as great a wonder there as it would be, or would have been, in that strange country I have heard some speak of,—called Arcadia, I think,—where there are not, and never has been, any necessity for detectives at all. (I think I shall pass the last of my days there, if I knew where to find it.) The whole street, from the station to the Police-office, was crammed with people, all prepared to give us a great reception; and so surely it was, for a louder shout I never heard than that which rose and resounded as we passed along with our thirteen prisoners, neatly handcuffed. But, alas! even we have enemies other than our children. Our fathers, the judges and great officers, sometimes think us fast youths. Those "guv'nors" are so exacting and fastidious, they don't go into our humours. They asked proof of the possession of the said bag of gold, and legally no one was responsible for it but Flynn and his wife, who, though the custodiers thereof, denied that they had any knowledge of it; and then they were no more amenable to justice than the innkeeper is who is found to have in some bed-room of his premises a golden waif or drift-cast, brought there by whom he knows not.

Those men, of whom I had taken so much care, were accordingly taken from us, and let off, to plunder the lieges, and I was left with the sole consolation of having recovered some £300 or £400—all for a pawnbroker, who ought to have taken better care of his pawns. A conviction of my "club" would have repaid him for the jostle he gave me. I am in his debt to this hour, though I have no doubt he could not be got anywhere now in this hemisphere to give me a proper discharge. This case is, therefore, more a confession on my part than a detection. I don't like it much,—it goes against the hair, and brings sparks of anger, not altogether consistent with my incombustible nature. The club nose, however, remains; and who knows what may happen before I go to Arcadia?

The Whisper

❖

I HAVE often thought of the different kinds of outlaw characters which have fallen in my way. If you take the general term "thief," then you can arrange them into sneakers, fighters, bolters, and pleaders. I need not go into a description, where the traits are so evident; but if I were asked to say which of the kinds is the most troublesome, I would fix upon the first. You can overcome a fighter, watch a bolter at the window, replead a pleader, but a sneak, gifted with cunning, who lies, crawls, lurks, winds, and doubles, requires all your wits. To match them all demands many powers both of body and mind, but, beyond all, courage, both moral and physical; and it is not to be wondered at, nor attributed to me as self-praise, if I say that in my experience I have not found many men who combine the gifts. One man has one, another another, and they are useful each in his department, where the character of the criminal is known. That, however, cannot be ascertained till the gentleman has been tested, and the whole tribe flit about so much that they become *new* in the various towns.

David Howie, originally belonging to North Leith, was famous about 1836, chiefly for his escapes by *bolting*; not that he escaped always, for we had him several times through our hands, but that he had as yet been successful beyond our wishes, and had a great objection to the other side of the water. We repeatedly were within arm's-length of him, but his recklessness in leaps from windows, his speed, and confidence in these qualities, enabled him to baulk us oftener than any man I have known. Still he stuck to Edinburgh; a strange fatality that in thieves and housebreakers,—their remaining in a town where they not only know that they are known to the officers, but where they have been again and again convicted. However this may be explained,—and I won't attempt it,—it is clear enough that as the knowledge of them increases, they become gradually defiant. They become settled in a trade which they think (and, as our society is formed, they are not far wrong) it is absolutely necessary they should follow; the necessity being, of course, a consequence of their own acts; which necessity again renders it necessary that society should have nothing to do with them.

Howie, unlike many of them, tried other places,—that is, "went to the grouse,"—and we thought we were quit of him; but intelligence reached us from Stirling, in the same year, 1836, that he had cleared out a watchmaker's shop there, got the stolen property sent to London, and escaped the fingers of the officers by leaping from a high window, in his old Edinburgh style. A considerable period elapsed. It was known afterwards that he went to London, and got the large quantity of watches and jewelry disposed of. Knowing, as I did, that he must now have been what they call "flush," I expected him to his old haunts. I had experience as well as theory to justify this expectation. A "flush" thief has the same yearning to get back to his native place that a rich Indian has, after he is sure he can overtop his old school-fellows. Nor are they without an object; often a great desire to figure among the girls, whose affections are competed for, and earned just as the gentleman has it in his power to gratify them with money. Perhaps, were I permitted to look out of my profession a little, I might say they are not unlike their neighbours in this respect, though I would not take it upon me to say that *every* man has a side-look to the sex in his efforts to make cash to gratify them when wives.

At least, in Beau Howie's case, I was just as sure that he would have a "fancy" with him, or get one here on his return, as I was satisfied he would turn up in the old dens. Nor was I wrong. "The Bolter" was in due time seen, dressed in the first fashion, so that he would not have shamed "plush" at the club-house in Princes Street if he had gone to ask whether His Grace or My Lord was in town; but our David was, in one respect, even more sensible than another of that name,—insomuch, at least, as he did not demean himself so as to earn the ridicule of his "fancy." Nowhere, indeed, can we see the wonderful effect of dress and money working with more effect than in the attraction a "swell" exercises over the lower class of unfortunate females. He is a very god among them; but David had made his choice of a help-meet and a worshipper in a woman—Ann M'Laren—whom we all knew as "The Hooker," from her art in transferring,—a dark gipsy-looking wench, with eyes that could see to the bottom of a pocket a foot deep, and fingers that could search it for other things than a psalm-book; and withal, so far as genius and a pretty face went, quite worthy of so clever a fellow as "The Bolter," and so accomplished a gentleman.

The moment I heard he had taken up with this woman, I considered him secure, for women make a dangerous "trail" to men of this stamp,—not that they betray willingly, which they seldom do, but their activity, and gossiping about their "fancies," and the endless ramifications of their small ways, soon get to our ears. I had only to trace the female to find the male bird; but soon found that she was, as they call it in their slang, alive or awake. One day, I got my eye upon her in the High Street. She had no time for doubling that day, and was bolder, or perhaps off her guard, for no creature can be for ever a watcher,—the mind must have a rest; perhaps, too, she was hungry. At any rate, I traced her to a stair in the Grassmarket; but I must wait long enough to be certain it was not merely a house of call. Indeed, from my knowledge of the stair,—and what stair was I not compelled to know?—I was pretty well made up to the conclusion that there she and David passed their sweet lives of innocence and ease. By inquiries, I was able to fix upon the room they occupied. There were several windows connected with the lodging, and these required to be looked to. It was a part of the many wonders told of "The Bolter," that, knowing his genius for leaping, he took his lodging accordingly; not on the ground-floor, because he might expect an ordinary watch at the window,—nor very high, for then he might break his neck,—but something between, not beyond his hope of getting to the ground, but greatly beyond the notion of a policeman that he would attempt it. I must have him at any chance for the Stirling affair, and required not to be scrupulous. Otherwise I must give up, and wait for a new charge. A little refining on the danger of his not being identified by the Stirling witnesses,—and, after all, he was only suspected,—or of not finding any of the watches,—which I could hardly expect,—would have ruined my enterprise. "The Bolter" was too important a personage to let slip, from my fears of myself being liable to the charge of taking up a man innocent, at least, of any *unpunished* crime.

I selected the hour of midnight, the most auspicious for many reasons,—though, no doubt, often cruel, for while a man is most easily taken in bed, so it is proportionally hard to drag him from the twining, soft arms of love to the encircling grip of unkindly iron; but, then, what right had he to call me and my men from our homes and beds to look after him? I had several officers prepared for an encounter. There were all the windows to guard, because he might leave one room and fly to another. To make sure work, I posted a man at every window, ready to receive David in his bolt, reserving for myself the high privilege of paying my respects to him personally.

All was ready,—a dark and still night, no light at the back of the lodging where the men stood concealed, and scarcely a sound anywhere, except the echo of some tread of a late passenger going along the Grassmarket. I ascended the stair with no more noise in my step than a velvet-footed cat would make in nearing a rat-hole. Got to the landing-place,—listened at the door,—no noise. Gone to bed, thinks I, happy in each other's bosoms. Hard fate of mine, to be obliged to part such hearts! but then a comfort it was to part those whom God had not joined,—and then, peradventure, join them again in a honeymoon trip over the sea. It was no fault of mine that their lives had not been lovely. Knocked very gently,—no answer. Again,—no answer, but a whispering. "It is, Davie," I heard Ann say; "get up." Anon came a rumbling noise, the meaning of which I understood,—they were barricading the door. Then with my knowledge of the man, it was for me now to be obstreperous, yea, as noisy as I could. In a *battue* you profit by making as great a kick-up as possible, to get the animals in the safe place. I would either catch him or drive him out of the window into the kindly embrace of my nurses outside. These crazy doors are no impediments; I placed my back to the pannels, my foot to the opposite side of the narrow passage, and drove it in with a crash, for the table and chairs behind flew off, adding their confused noise to that of the splintered door. At that instant the window drew up, and all I could see of "The Bolter" was the tail of his shirt as he disappeared from a height of fifteen or twenty feet. Thinking I had not seen the flight, Ann ran to the window, drew it down, and met me, prepared; and I, knowing he was safe, was as much at my ease.

"Where is Howie gone?" said I.

"You are on the wrong scent," said she; "he doesn't live here."

"And whose clothes are these?"

"These! why, they belong to my husband, who has gone out. If you will wait"—(no doubt to give David time to get off)—"I will tell you all about it. My man's name is—"

"I am not curious, Ann," said I, "about your *husband*; I only want to search the house. This I accordingly did, smiling as I saw "The Hooker" so keen to hook *time* by even helping me in my search where she knew nothing was to be found. Yes, there was absolutely nothing. The watchmaker's stock had melted away into the usual fluidity in London,—a result a little alarming to me, if I had been by nature capable of being alarmed, which I am not; for though "The Bolter" was sufficiently habit and repute to justify his being at that moment snug in my nurses' arms, I had yet no charge against him, except the old suspicion of the Stirling affair,—a suspicion merely,—and I stood exposed to the risk of being defeated by a verdict of "not guilty,"—always, in such cases as this, as disagreeable to me as agreeable to the panel.

The longer Ann could get me to wait the more light-hearted she got,—waxing merry as the hope rose upon her that she had "done me" by detaining me from a pursuit of her master, lover, and copartner. I was in no hurry to undeceive her, and, moreover, I had no available charge against her. I knew her subtlety too well to try to get anything out of her. So quietly bidding her good-night, and hoping her husband would soon be in to comfort her for my intrusion, and the smashed door and broken tables and chairs, all of which she passed over without a charge for breakage, I left her. On reaching the foot of the close, I found the shirted David in the embrace of his tender nurses, having been caught in the arms of one of them just as he threw himself from the window. We proceeded to deposit him in his crib, sending back afterwards for his clothes.

Next morning I had a conference with the Captain. Information was sent off to Stirling, but he feared we would be defeated, in consequence of nothing being found in the house. I was a little uneasy, and was meditating as to whether I could make sure work by getting some other charge against him. And now occurred one of those extraordinary coincidences which have made my life a romance to myself. I happened to be standing in such a position down stairs—thinking of what I was to do—as rendered it quite possible for me to hear a prisoner speaking to any one outside in the close; and just at that moment I thought I heard the very low and cautious sounds of two persons conversing. I could gather scarcely anything, but I was satisfied a woman outside was talking to one within the bars. I have already alluded to my sense of hearing, from which I have derived so much advantage. Yet withal I could catch but little. I detected the words, "Run and make away with the boots," spoken in a kind of loud hissing whisper. Next instant I saw Ann standing in the close.

Losing no time, I proceeded to the Grassmarket; got into the room easily enough, for the broken door was not yet mended; got hold of *the boots*; and met Ann at the close-foot, as she was hurrying, with flushed face, and the keen light of anxiety glancing from her gipsy eyes, to execute the commission.

"I have got them," said I; "and will save you the trouble of carrying them up to your husband, who did not return to you last night."

If the glance which followed had been steel—and it had all the light of steel—I would have detected no more in this world.

On getting to the office, and searching the books, I ascertained that a pair of boots had the day before been taken from the house of Mr Craig, in Church Lane, leading to Stockbridge. To Mr Craig I went. They were the very boots; and that gentleman described to me how they were taken. They happened to be standing on a table opposite the window, and were abstracted by some one who quietly drew up the sash, and deliberately *let it down again.* With my information thus obtained, I looked in upon Howie.

"I have brought the boots, David, which you asked Ann to go down to the Grassmarket for. What purpose do you intend to turn them to here?"

"What!" he cried, "has the b–tch betrayed me, after having spent all my money upon her?"

"No," replied I; "I knew you were anxious about them, and got before her."

"How, in the devil's name, could you know unless you had got her over?"

"That's my business."

"You're the old man," he said coolly enough, for he had no notion that I could discover their owner; "always in compact with the devil, but you'll not hang me yet."

"I don't want. But were did you get these boots?"

"Try to find out," he growled. "They're paid for anyway; no one could stop me at the *shop door.*"

"*Window*, David, lad."

He knew he was caught, and became as dumb as the boots themselves,—satisfied, I believe, that I was in compact with the devil.

He was thereafter taken to Stirling, that the fiscal might try to connect him with the clearing out of the watchmaker's shop. Meanwhile,—so soon do these "fancies" forget their loves,—Ann got another partner; and here, though not much inclined to notice matters out of my own peculiar line, I cannot help remarking how strangely these outlawed beings carry their ties of love and friendship. They are like the knots of ribbons on women's persons,—very nicely bound themselves, but binding nothing else; and, taken off at night, are pinned on next morning to some other dress. Habit enables them, both men and women, to mix old griefs—for they have griefs—with new joys, and these they have, of a crude kind, too. However true the "fancy" is to her swell, she always contemplates the probable shortness of her obligation, and is quite ready for a new bond when some very ungallant Sheriff or Justiciary Lord severs the existing one. I have known cases where one of these Arab-like creatures has sat in the court and sobbed at the fate of her darling mate, and when he was sentenced to death or banishment, hopping away with a new swell from the court, pass perhaps a month or two with him, then to sob for his fate; and so on. There is something affecting about many of them, which would melt very stony hearts. Often interesting, kindly creatures, with bosoms that would have been fountains of love and kindness to husbands and children, if they had been better starred,—and they had no voice in the casting of the form of their fates,—they throw away their devotedness on heartless soundrels, who make tools of them, and mistresses of them, only to leave them on an instant's notice. But then the very changes reconcile them to a fate they can't escape; and thus there is nothing but unhearty laughter and very hearty tears—love's griefs and love's tears again, love's mirth and love's groans for ever. But it does not last long, thanks to the fate that is so cruel to them. A few years is the average of their lives. You would be astonished were I to tell you how they have passed from my watchful eye. Three, or four, or five years, and a new set are on my city beat. They come and go like comets, blazing for a time with wild passions, and then away to make room for others. As for the real *artistes*, one has less sympathy. In place of being kept by men, they keep them—often prostituting themselves for them, robbing for them, suffering for them in a thousand ways, ay, even by imprisonment, and often cast away by the heartless scoundrels to die, or, what is worse, to rot without dying. In the case of our Ann, I traced her for a year or two, and then heard she had died of disease and want. She, no doubt, had had a foreboding of the fate of "The Bolter," nor was it false. He was sent to Stirling as I have said. The fiscal could not identify him as the robber, and he was sent back to us. The charge for the boots remained. It was urged against him as an old offender, and there being no doubt of his guilt, he got seven years. His fate hung upon a whisper; for if I had not overheard the direction to Ann, to make away with the article, I would not have thought of tracing *their* origin any more than that of the rest of his fashionable clothes—all of which we would have thought he had bought and paid for out of the proceeds of the watches and jewelry, very soon spent, as all the money of such persons is, let it be what it may. Nay, they can't keep it. It burns their hands till it is cast away, and then the hands itch again for the touch.

I believe Howie never knew that the breath of a whisper sent him "over the seas and far awa'."

The Thieves' Wedding

❖

I HAVE already alluded to the subject of the flinty-heartedness of the fraternity among whom I have so long laboured, and I may illustrate the same feature by another case, which is calculated as well to show a peculiarity somewhat better known—the elasticity of their enjoyments, if the rant and roar of their mirth can go by a name expressive of a heartfelt affection.

Is there any reason in the world why thieves should not marry one with another? or rather, were we to bear in mind the words of the priest, importing the necessity of faith and confidence in each other, might we not rather expect that these celebrations should occur oftener than they do? The nature of the connexion might, indeed, suggest an addition to the formula, to the effect that they should be made to promise not "to peach" on each other; and as for the words, "Whom God hath joined together let no man separate," these might be dispensed with, to save the judges and such as I from breaking a law of the Bible. The "duty", "obedience", and "affection" might remain as approved by experience. But however decorous these unions, (and pearls, you know, have to be called unions, as well they might,) it is certain that we see very few of them. When they occur, they are very genuine, in so much as the contracting parties *know each other*,—a peculiarity almost entirely confined to their case; but, as I have said, they occur very seldom. They seem to have a sort of instinct that they are liable to changes of *dwelling* as well as changes of *country*, and hence their notion that it is better for both males and females to join their fortunes and affections in that loose and easy way, which enables them to snap the silken bands when it is necessary to assume the iron fetters.

So much of prosy prelude to that gay scene which occurred in Bailie's Court, head of the Cowgate, in January 1855, when Richard Webb and Catharine Bryce were, amidst the strains of the Tam Lucas of the feast, made man and wife. That they knew each other was beyond doubt, for had not the gay Catharine been twice condemned for shop-lifting, and Richard carried the honours of as many convictions for the minor crime of theft? Yes, it would be well for our Beatrices and Birons if they knew beforehand tempers so well developed. When did you ever hear of thieves disgracing themselves by going to the divorce courts? They are contented with the justiciary, or even the sheriff. They despise, too, restorations of tocher; and as for the one turning witness against the other's frailties, you never hear of it.

This celebration, when I heard of it, appeared to me curious. I don't say ludicrous, because marriage is an august ceremony, originated in Paradise, and so very often ending there. And why should not M'Levy be among his children, to whose happiness he had devoted so many years of his life, of toil and danger? I know that you will say, Why should he not be there? And to be sure there he was. I got indeed no invitation, any more than I did when the handsome hawker was to have been joined, by a "closing thread" well birsed, to the disappointed snab. When people are insulted in this way, they get over it by calling it an oversight—yet they don't put the parties right by going as I did, and showing that degree of magnanimity which consists in heaping coals of fire on the head.

As Bailie's Court, in the Cowgate, does not often respond to the strains of a marriage fiddle, there behoved to be a crowd, and it behoved that crowd to be witty at the expense of the happy pair; for when were not the poor, who form such crowds, envious? When I arrived, I found them all in that kind of uproar—hurraing at every new comer—which characterises scenes of this nature; and my appearance quickened the humour into such bursts as "M'Levy is to join them with handcuffs," "Let up the priest," "Where is your white cravat," and the like—jokes which were really not happy, in so much as the nuptial knot had already been tied, and the sacred restraints of the guests were loosened to the extent of the freedom of dancing. On going up-stairs, I found that all my suspicions of affront at not being invited were mocked by an open door for all comers, whence issued just such sounds of fiddle, feet, and fun, as one might expect. On my entry, there awaited me an honour which I believe would not have been awarded to the Lord Justice-Clerk; for my very appearance stopt the merrymakers when in full spring, just as if they were overawed by the appearance of a winged messenger. And no wonder, for I saw there many for whom I had procured lodgings, supplied with food, and even sent on an excursion to the sunny climes of the south; but no man has a right to enforce more gratitude than what is due to him, and I was vexed at throwing a cloud over so happy a scene.

"Go on, my lads and lasses," said I. "You know you belong to me, but this night you shall have your liberty."

"Give him a dram," cried the bride.

And straightway, to be sure, I got my glass of whisky; but not content with that gift, they pulled me into the middle of a reel, where I am not sure if I did not actually dance,—nay, I won't answer for it that I was not whirled round by some very passable arms, not only for good colour, but for softness.

I remained only for a short time. I had gratified my curiosity, and I wished to save them from the embarrassment of a presence in many ways suggestive of associations. I had not been disappointed; but I am sure that when I appeared again to the crowd without having Webb or Catharine with me, or at least some of the guests, they were disappointed—so envious, I am sorry to say, is that common nature of ours, and so impatient of the joys of others. Another thing gave a kind of satisfaction. I saw no chance for this celebration being disgraced by pocket-picking—an occurrence so common in crowds—for here truly there were no pockets to pick, that is, no pockets with anything in them, beyond a quid of tobacco and a pipe, or at most a few pence. You will see how this fond hope was destined to be disappointed.

Having joined my assistant, who waited for me at the foot of the stair, we went along to the Cowgate on the look-out, and having finished our survey, we turned to retrace our steps by the scene of the marriage. It was a frosty night, I remember, with thick snow, heaps of which were thrown up on the sides of the cart-ruts. As we were thus proceeding, I heard coming up the rapid steps of a runner; and who should this be but Bill Orr, one of my own. He stumbled against a heap of snow, and fell at my feet.

"What's all the hurry, Bill?" said I, as he was getting up.

But Bill clearly did not like the question, far less did he like the anticipation of being laid hold of, for he was up in an instant and off, much quicker than a wind-driven snow flake.

"Where's the pursuer?" said I to my assistant; "Bill Orr is not the man to run at that rate to get out of the snow."

The pertinancy of the question was no more apparent to me, than to you, or any one who notices the common actions of mankind, which display a proportion in their vivacity corresponding to the degrees of impulse; nor did the notion leave me that something was wrong with my old friend, and I was accordingly on the outlook. On coming again to Bailie's Court I was attracted by some noises, not at all like the fun I had witnessed before in that quarter; and on going forward, ascertained, from the lamentations of an old poors'-house pensioner—a very old woman, who in spite of her age and poverty had been attracted in that cold night by the festivity of the marriage—that she had been robbed; yes, a poors'-house pensioner robbed of the sum of four pennies and one halfpenny. Ludicrous enough; ay, but pitiful enough, too, when you remember that that fourpence-halfpenny would keep, and was intended to keep, that very *poor* pauper a day out of the very few she would see on this side of the grave. Don't wonder, therefore, at a grief which was intense, if it did not amount to as strong an agony as those shrivelled nerves could bear without snapping. I had here my sympathies; and if anything could add to my disturbance, it was that in spite of my hopes this auspicious wedding was disgraced.

"Be easy, my good woman," said I; "I will get both your fourpence-halfpenny and the heartless rogue that took it."

"God bless you, Mr M'Levy; ye've saved mony a ane's property, and ye're sent here this night to save mine."

And had she no right to think fourpence-halfpenny entitled to be designated *property*? It was at least her all; and when all is lost, it is, I suspect, of little importance whether it be a thousand pounds or a penny. Nor was she less miserable than one would be at the loss of a fortune,—only the *tear* was not there, perhaps because an out-door pensioner does not get nourishment with sap enough in it to produce that peculiar evidence (which is said to be limited to our species) of human grief.

And now there was another contrast between what was going on upstairs and that which was enacted below. There, merriment was the produce of thieving; here, the offspring of the same parent was sorrow.

"Wait there, my good woman," said I, "till I bring you your property and the thief."

And upon the instant there arose a cry of, "Hurra for M'Levy," which I received with becoming modesty.

So away I went back the road I had come; nor did I diverge till I came to the house of Mrs M'Lachlan, who sold beer and whisky to be *consumed* and to *consume* on the premises, where, in a room, surrounded by some of his own tribe, who should have been at the marriage, I discovered Bill Orr, with his own stoup before him, in all the confidence of security, and in all the joy of his fourpence-halfpenny.

"What was your hurry, Bill, when you fell?" said I. "You haven't told me that yet."

"Perhaps to get to this jug of ale in a cold night," replied the rogue.

"No," said I; "you wanted away from the poor old pensioner whom you robbed of fourpence-halfpenny."

Bill was choked with the truth.

"Mrs M'Lachlan," continued I, "has Bill paid for his stoup?"

"Ay, I never trust till the ale's drunk," replied she; "for sometimes it taks awa' the memory, and they get confused, and say they paid afore."

"A penny the stoup?"

"Ay."

"And therefore I expect there's threepence-halfpenny in your pocket, Bill. Turn it out." But he wouldn't, and I was obliged to extract it.

"And now, Mrs M'Lachlan," said I, "though stolen money cannot be reclaimed, when I tell you that our friend Bill here stole it from the pocket of an old woman-pensioner, you'll not refuse to repay it."

"No, though it were a shilling," replied she, as she put down the penny.

"Now there is one I shall make happy," said I, as I put the money in my pocket, and taking Bill by the coat I carried him off, without even permitting him to finish his pot, the remaining contents of which would be a half-penny to Mrs M'Lachlan for her penny.

So pulling Bill along—I might safely have allowed him to walk between me and my assistant, but I felt some yearning to hold him tight—I took my "pearl of Orr's Island" to Bailie's Court, where there waited for me my poor pensioner, as well as the crowd, who no doubt wanted to see whether I would fulfil my promise. The moment they saw Bill in my hands they raised three cheers, more grateful to me than the *éclat* of having recovered a thousand pounds. There stood the woman, and before her Bill, the personification of lusty youth preying on shrivelled old age; but Bill was as unmoved as a stone, and I thought of making him feel a little, if that were possible. I knew I had no right to give up the money, but I was inclined to make an exception, were it for nothing else than to save the credit of the thieves' wedding.

"Now," said I, "Bill, you will give this money to the woman, to whom it belongs."

And the rogue, finding it useless to disobey, took the money and handed it to the woman, in the midst of another shout. I never received so many blessings from a sufferer all my life as I did from this poor pensioner; and the feelings of the crowd, depraved as many of them no doubt were, showed that there was something at the bottom of the most callous spirits that responds to justice. But I was not satisfied, for I made him declare to his victim that he was sorry he had robbed her,—an admission due to the fear he entertained of being torn by the angry people. Nor was even this all, for I sent up to the wedding-party for a dram to the sufferer, whereby I still maintained the *honour* of the marriage, and had the satisfaction to see the old woman's eye lighted up as bright as that of the bride.

And having gone through all these manœuvres, which afforded me no little satisfaction, and perhaps more to the crowd, I again took hold of Bill, and dragged him as roughly to the Office as was compatible with my obligation not to punish a man before sentence.

Sometime after, Bill was tried by the High Court. He was an old offender, and this had its weight with the judge; but it was easily to be seen that the peculiar circumstances of the case had more than their usual weight. The judge became quite eloquent, and no doubt he had a good subject to handle, but a very impenetrable object to impress. Bill was as unmoved as ever; I am not sure if he did not laugh,—another example of what I have so often stated, that the hardihood of these creatures is not modified by punishment, nay, even transportation. Yet I have no doubt that if this young fellow's heart had been handled softly when it was capable of being mollified, he might have been of some use to his kind, if not a credit to himself. We have sometimes reason to doubt the effect of training even among the children of respectable people, but I suspect such a result arises from their being otherwise spoiled. The parents let out at the one end the web woven by the schoolmaster at the other, and thus education loses the character of its efficacy. With the "Raggediers" in an industrial school, no such spoiling would be permitted. The good tendency would be all in one way; and the devil would not, through the parents, be permitted to pull in the opposite direction. What though Bill Orr got a *year* for every *penny*, and one to boot for the odd halfpenny! He would be the same Bill Orr at the end as he was that night of the thieves' wedding.

So much for another phase of the "sliding scale," exhibiting, as it does, the facility with which the thief can *descend* even to the *zero* of criminality, as exemplified in this pitiful robbery,—the very minimum point, I may say, in the whole scale of theftuous depravity.

The Sea Captain

❖

I DOUBT whether the good philanthropical people are even yet quite up to all the advantages of ragged schools. The salvation of society from a host of harpies is not the main chance; neither is it that the poor wretches are sold into the slavery of vice and misery before they know right from wrong. There's something more. I have a suspicion that society loses often what might become its sharpest and most intelligent members in these half-starved youngsters, whose first putting out of the hand is the beginning of a battle with the world. I'm not to try to account for the fact, but I am pretty well satisfied, from all I have seen, that the children of these poor half-starved people are something more apt than the sons of your gentlemen. You who are learned may try your hand at the paradox, and make as much of it as you do of the other riddles of human life. Here is a plea for the John Poundses and Dr Guthries, of which they could make something. Every ragged urchin they lay hold of to make him learn from books has been at a school of another kind, where he has got his energies sharpened on a different whetstone from that found within a school, and then the school does its duty in directing these energies.

Just fancy what some of our card-sharpers would have been if their cleverness had been directed towards honest and lawful undertakings. I have known some of these gentlemen so adroit at the great problem of ways and means that they might have shone as Chancellors of the Exchequer. It is not their fault that we find them out. Their great drawback is, that they begin to be cunning and adroit before they know the world. All this close cunning defeats itself. The young rogues put me often in mind of moles. They work in dark holes, but they are always coming near the surface, where they hitch up friable hillocks to let air in, and so are caught. Nay, they sometimes hitch themselves out into the mid-day sun of justice. I have at this moment two or three of these misdirected geniuses in my eye whom I have traced from early childhood—ay, that period when the Raggedier officers should have laid hold of them.

In April 1854, an honest joiner in Banff of the name of Donald M'Beath, had taken it into his head that he would do well to go to England, where his talents would be appreciated. In short, Donald had working within him the instinct of that little insect so familiar to the Highlanders, the tendency of which is to go south—probably because it knows in some inscrutable way that Englishmen have thick blood. Then he had friends in Newcastle who had gone before him, and found out that the yellow blood corpuscles of the social body flowed there more plentifully than in Banff. Were I to be more fanciful, I would say that Donald M'Beath had the second sight—for money. He loved it so well that he had stomach for "ta hail Pank of England", and would "maype return in ta grand coach and ta grey horses." Nor had this love been as yet without fruits, for he had by Highland penury saved no less a sum than seven pounds, all stowed away in a seal-skin spleuchan, besides seven more which he had laid out on a capital silver watch—convinced that no Highland shentleman bearing a royal name, as he did, could pass muster in England without this commodity.

The Highlanders were never at any time in the habit of getting lighter or leaner by moving from one place to another, if they were not generally a good deal heavier at the end of their journey than at the beginning. So true to the genius of his race, he laid his plans so that, in progressing south, he would lay contributions on his "friends" all the way, in order that, if it "could pe possible," he might keep the seven pounds all entire—some extra shillings being provided for the voyage in the *Britannia* from Leith to Newcastle. How many Highland cousins suffered during this transport of the valuable person of the King's clansman till he got to Leith, I never had any means of knowing. We cannot be far wrong, however, in supposing that he shook them all heartily by the hand; and no pedigree of the M'Farlans from Parlan downwards, was ever courted with more industry than that of the M'Beaths, if it was possible to bring within the tree any collateral branch with M'Beath blood in his veins, meal in his girnal, and a bed fit for a Highlander. Then the shake of the hand, and the "Oigh, oigh" of true happiness, were the gratitude which is paid beforehand—the only kind that Donald knew anything of; or any other body I suspect—at least if I can judge from what I have received from so many to whom I have given lodgings, meat, and free passages.

Arrived at Leith, the first thing Donald did was to get out the little bit of snuff-coloured paper which contained the names of the cousins, and where, among the rest, was that of an old woman in the Kirkgate who was a descendant of the sister of Donald's grandmother, a M'Nab,—as unconscious of being related to the clan of the murderous king as any one could be, before such a flood of light was cast upon her history as Donald was well able to shed. He soon found her out; and though Janet M'Nab could make nothing of the pedigree, she could count feelings of humanity; and what was more, she had a supper and a bed to save an infraction upon the said seven pounds.

Next morning, after having partaken of a Highland breakfast from poor Janet, which could only be calculated by the professions of eternal friendship uttered by a Gael, Donald went forth to see the craft which in some cheap berth was to transport him to the land of gold; and, to be sure, it was not long till he saw the vessel lying alongside of the quay. No doubt she was to be honoured in her freight. It was not every day the *Britannia* carried a M'Beath with seven pounds in his pocket, a seven-pound watch in his fob, and a chest of tools, which was to cut his way to fortune. Then if it were just possible that the captain had ever been in Banff, or had in his veins a drop of Celtic blood—he would ascertain that by and by, he might even be a M'Beath or a M'Nab.

Much, however, as he expected from the clanship of the captain of the *Britannia*, who was not then to be seen, he had sense enough to know that that officer could not abate his passage-money. Nay, he knew that he must take out his ticket at the office on the shore, and thither he accordingly hied to make a bargain. Unfortunately these tickets are not liable to be affected by Highland prigging; but the loose shillings to which I have alluded allowed him still to retain untouched the seven pounds. Yea, that seven pounds seemed to have a charmed life, the charm being only to be broken by some such wonder as the march of some wood or forest from one part of the kingdom to the other, or by the man who should try to take it having been from the belly of a shark "untimely ript".

It wanted still some considerable time until the *Britannia* sailed, and Donald thought that he might as well get his chest of tools and bag of clothes put on board. He accordingly hied away to Mrs M'Nab's, and having returned his thanks for her kindness, if he did not promise her a part of his fortune "when it should be made," he got the packets on his broad shoulders, and proceeded to the vessel. He was more lucky this time. A seaman, very probably the captain, was busy walking the deck.

"Hallo, tare!" cried Donald to the seaman, "you'll pe ta captain?"

"Yes, all right," replied the other; "and you'll be a passenger for Newcastle; what have you got there?"

"My tool-chest and clothes," replied Donald; "fery valuable, cost seven pounds ten shillings."

"Heave them along the gunwale there," said the seaman, "they can be stowed away afterwards; but you're too soon, we won't heave off for an hour."

"Ower sune is easy mended," replied the Gael.

"And sometimes," in a jolly way, said the other, "we have time for a dram."

"Ay, and inclination maype too," cried Donald, quite happy.

"Come away, then, our lockers are shut, so we'll have it up the way, where I know they keep the real peat-reek, and I'll pay."

And Donald, leaving his luggage, but carrying with him a notion that the captain of the *Britannia* deserved to be one of her Majesty's Admirals of the Blue, followed his guide until they entered the house of the publican, whose name I do not at present recollect. Nor was this notion in any way modified even when they were seated at the same table with three very respectable-looking men, apparently engaged in the harmless pastime of playing at cards. Nay, the notion was evidently shared by the three strangers, who, although they had clearly never seen the captain of the *Britannia* before, offered him, with a generosity wonderful to Donald, a share of their liquor. On his side, the generosity was equalled by his insisting that they, whom he declared he had never seen before, should take a part of his. Never was there such generous unanimity among strangers; and even Donald was included in the newborn friendship. Then the harmless play went on. There were only three cards used, two diamonds and one clubs; and the game was so simple that the Gael understood it in a moment, for it consisted in a little shuffling, and if one drew the clubs, he was the winner of the stakes. The generous captain laid down a stake of a pound; one of the players laid down another; then the cards were shuffled in so obvious a manner that a child might have seen where the clubs lay; and so to be sure the captain saw what a child might have seen, drew the slip, and pocketed the two pounds. This was repeated, until the captain pocketed six pounds; and Donald seeing fortune beckoning on, tabled one of the seven with the charmed unity. None of these men had been cut out of the belly of a shark, and so Donald M'Beath's seven was made eight.

"Play on," whispered the captain, "while I go to look after your luggage."

And so to be sure the Highlander did. He staked pound after pound, gained once in thrice, got furious, and staked on and on till the seven was nil.

Then rose the Highlander's revenge; the watch was tabled against seven pounds, and went at a sweep.

"And now, py Cot, to croon a', ya *Pritannia* will be gone," he cried, as he rushed out in agony.

Frantic as he was, he could yet find his way to the part of the pier where he expected to see the vessel with the noble captain on board. The steamer was gone; and as he stood transfixed in despair, a man came up to him.

"Was it you who carried some luggage on board the *Britannia* about an hour ago?"

"Ay, just me."

"Well, then, I saw a man dressed in seaman's clothes carry it away. He seemed to make for Edinburgh, likely by the Easter Road."

"And whaur is ta Easter Road?" cried the Gael, as he turned round to run in some direction, though in what he knew not.

At length, after many inquiries, he got into the said road, and hurrying along at the top of his speed, he expected every moment to see the captain. He questioned every one he met, got no trace, and began to lose hope with breath; for, long ere this, he had seen the full scope of his folly, and suspected that the captain was one of the cardsharpers. Fairly worn out,—more the consequence of the excited play of his lungs and galloping blood than the effect of his chase,—he slackened his pace when he came to the Canongate. There he was—a ruined man, not a penny left, the hopes of a fortune blasted, even his tool-chest, with which he might have cut his way anywhere, gone,—a terrible condition, no doubt, not to be even conceived properly by those who have not experienced the shock of sudden and total ruin. No sight had any interest for him, no face any beauty or ugliness, except as it carried any feature like what he recollected of his cruel and heartless companions. Nor was he free from self-impeachment, blaming his love of money as well as the blindness of his credulity. While in this humour, and making his way by inquiry to the Police-office, he met right in the face, and seemed to spring up three inches as he detected the features of one of his spoilers. In an instant, his hand clutched, with the tension of a tiger's muscle, the gasping throat of the villain. The Highland blood was boiling, and you might have seen the red glare of his eye, as if all his revenge for what he considered to be the ruin of a life had been concentrated in that one terrible glance. The sharper, strong, and with all the recklessness of a tribe of the most desperate kind, was only as a sapling in his grasp.

"My money and my watch, you tam villain!"

Words which, accompanied by the contortion of Gaelic gesticulation, only brought about him a crowd, among whom two constables made their appearance. The sharper was transferred to their hands, glad enough to be relieved of his more furious antagonist, and all the three made for the Office.

It was at this part of the strange drama I came into play. The moment I saw the Highlander enter with his man, I suspected the nature of the complaint, for I knew he was from the country, and the sharper, David Wallace, was one of my most respected *protégés* in the card and thimblerigging line; but I required the information given me by the Highlander to make me understand all the dexterity of the trick which the pseudo-captain of the *Britannia* had practised. The club, I knew, consisted of four, David Wallace, Richard Kyles, John Dewar, and John Sweeny. It was regularly organised, each man having attached to him his gillet of a helpmate, ready to secrete or carry the watches and other property won by their lords at this most unequal game. I have always considered those daylight sharpers, who, without instruments other than three cards or three thimbles and a pea, contrive to levy extensive contributions on society, as men worthy to have been drawn into the ranks of honest citizens, where their talents could not have failed to elevate them into wealth. Even the manipulation of these simple instruments is more wonderful than the tricks of a conjurer. Fix your eyes as you may, be suspicious even to certainty that the player is cheating you, I will defy you to detect the moment when, by the light if not elegant touch of the finger, your pea has been slipped from the right thimble to the wrong, or the right card to the wrong—yea, to the end, you could swear that no deception has been or could be practised upon you; and even when your watch is forfeited you could hardly think but that your misfortune lay on some defect in your power of penetration. And so it does. You are cheated—nay, *fairly cheated.* You can't expect from such men that they should undertake not to deceive you. If they had no art, you would ruin them in five minutes, for all you would have to do (and you insist on the unfair privilege) is to watch the thimble under which your fortune lies and snatch it. There is, therefore, no pity due to the victims of these men's deceptions, and this we can say with a thorough condemnation of the men themselves.

As soon as I understood the transaction, it was my duty to detect the right thimble, and I had no fear of deception. I sent Wallace, under charge of a constable, to the Leith Office, and told M'Beath that I would have the three others there in the course of a couple of hours. I had no doubt that Dewar, the cleverest of them, had personated the captain, and that he had rejoined his associates to share the booty. I knew their haunt, a public-house in Bristo Street, and, taking Riley with me, I went direct to the place. My luck was nothing less than wonderful. Just as I entered I met my three men coming out of a room, and holding out my arms—

"Stop, gentlemen," said I; "I have got something to say to you."

But I didn't need to say it. They understood me as well as I did them.

"Captain Dewar of the *Britannia*," said I, looking to Dewar.

"At your service," replied the rogue, with a spice of humour, at which, in the very midst of their choking wrath, they could not help leering.

Well, the old process. "Search," said I; "I want seven pounds and a watch."

And calling in my assistant, I began my search. No resistance. They were too well up to their calling.

I found the watch on Wallace. No more. The pounds had been given to the fancies.

I kept my word by having them all three at Leith within a couple of hours, safely lodged in prison. They were afterwards tried by the Leith magistrates, aided by an assessor, and sentenced to sixty days each, with sixty more if they did not give up the money and luggage. The sentence seemed judicious, and in one sense it was; but the worthy bailies did not consider that they were offering a premium on the seductive and depredating energies of the trulls, who (long after the seven pounds was spent) in order to get their birds out of the cage, set about their arts and redeemed them from bondage.

The Society-Box

❖

THE way by which the ranks of thieves and robbers are recruited is by the *old* teaching the *young* the figure system. Yes, there is a proselytism of evil as well as of good. Society is always straining after the making of parties, and while churches are working for members, the old thieves are busy enlisting the young. The advantage, I fear, is with the latter, for there's something more catching in the example of taking another man's property than that of praying for grace. Of course I am here looking to the young, and I make this statement without caring much how your beetle-browed critic may take it.

I have known a good many of those dominies of the devil's lore, not a few of them with streaks of grey on their heads, who, having themselves been taught at the same desk, have taken up the trade as a kind of natural calling, and raised their pupils according to the old morality, "The sweet morsel of another person's property is pleasant to roll under the tongue;" and perhaps the more pleasant, too, that the tongue that *sucks* is the tongue that *lies*. There was Hugh Thomson, about the cleverest thief in my day, that rogue brought up as many youngsters in the faith as would have filled a conventicle; and what a glorious grip that was I got of him, just as he was trying to reap the fruits of his lesson, through the ingenuity of one of his scholars, William Lang! I would not have exchanged it for the touch of a bride's hand, with the marriage ring upon her finger.

In 1841, there was a Mr Brown who kept a spirit shop in the Low Calton, nearly opposite Trinity College Church. One of those modern unions called "Yearly Societies" was kept in his house, the members paying their contributions on the Monday evenings, which contributions, the produce of toil and sweat of poor, hard-working men, were deposited in the society box, and secured under lock and key. One Monday evening I was passing down the Calton on my way to Leith Wynd homeward, to get myself refreshed with a cup of tea. In the mouth of an entry, on the other side of the street called the North Back of the Canongate, I observed Hugh and his scholar Lang, engaged, no doubt, in the mutual offices of teaching and learning. I thought I might learn something too, and stepping into the recess of Trinity Church gate, I watched their movements. Shortly, Lang came out—he had become a man by this time, recollect—and having mixed with the workmen, who were going into Brown's shop to make their weekly payments, he went in among the rest.

At first, I confess, I could not understand this. The thief could make nothing of the workmen, even if unknown to them as a thief, which in all likelihood he was, and the idea of his trying the pocket line among fustian jackets never entered my head. But that there was some play to go on, where Thomson was patronising, I could have no doubt whatever. After a time, during which I took care that Thomson should not see me, Lang came out, and, having joined Thomson, the two went off together, with something that sounded in my ears as a laugh, and the meaning of which was made clear to me by a happy thought that occurred to me on the instant like a flash. I now wanted to see Brown by himself, but as the workmen were still going in and coming out, I was obliged to wait a considerable time. Selecting at length a moment when the coast was tolerably clear, I entered the shop. There, in the back room, was the sacred box, devoted to benevolence, and from which some widow and orphans might, before the year expired, receive something that would make *her* tear less scorching and *their* cry less shrill—some broken bones, too, broken through the labour and toil of the poor man for the rich one, might have less pain through the charm of that box. Thoughts these pretty enough to some minds, but to such as Thomson quaint, if not funny.

"Mr Brown," said I, as I entered, "will you be kind enough to show me your list of members?"

"Surely, Mr M'Levy." And he placed the book in my hands.

Running down the names I came to "William Lang, joiner," though all his *junctions* were between his hand and the property of another.

"I have seen enough," said I; "and now, Mr Brown, you will take especial care to carry your box up-stairs with you to-night to your dwelling-house."

And without giving him time to ask for explanations, which I did not feel much disposed to give, I left him. I knew that Brown shut up late on the pay-nights, and therefore having plenty of time that evening, even in the event of an emergency, I went home to get my tea. After which, and having cogitated a little under its reviving influence, I took another turn down Leith Wynd. I wanted to examine the iron gate leading to the church. On looking at it, I found that the lock was off, and consequently free ingress was afforded to any one wishing to enter. I went to a blacksmith's and got a chain and padlock, the use of which will be apparent, when I mention, that if I adopted the recess within the gate as a look-out, from which I could see Brown's shop, it was as likely to be so used by those we wanted to observe, as by ourselves, the observers.

Having made these preliminary arrangements, I proceeded to the Office, where I secured the services of one or two of the most active constables, besides my assistant, for I knew that having Thomson to cope with, we had something to encounter far more formidable than any other thief or robber within the sound of St Giles's. I was in all this, I admit, fired with the ambition of getting a man who had become as bold as Macbeth under the witches' prophecy. Having waited till about eleven o'clock, the hour when Brown generally closed, I repaired, accompanied by my men, to our place of retreat. We entered cautiously, and shutting the old gate with as little noise as possible, I secured the two halves with the chain and padlock, with which I had provided myself—a proceeding which, as it afterwards appeared, was necessary to the success of our enterprise, but the object of which my men could not at the time very clearly understand. Yet what more likely than that

Thomson and his gang should wish to reconnoitre us, as we wished to reconnoitre them. We were soon enclosed, and ready for observation. We saw the light put out in Brown's shop, and heard the locking of the doors both in front and at the back, or rather in the side of the entry which led up to the premises above which the spirit-dealer resided. But more than this, we saw the cautious cashier with the sacred box under his arm, as he stept up the entry—a sight which I enjoyed with a secret chuckle of satisfaction, for it was no mean pride to be up with a man such as Hugh Thomson.

It might be about twelve o'clock before we saw any symptoms of sport. Suddenly, three men, coming apparently from different directions, met, and whispering a few words parted, to act for caution-scouts to each other. Each took a round, casting wary glances to the right and left, and desultory as their movements were, I could recognise Hugh, Lang, and another, David L——, also an old pupil of Thomson's. It seemed to be Thomson's special care to look into the Trinity Church recess, and as we saw him coming forward, we retreated behind the pillars of the gate. He appeared to be taken aback as he observed the gate secured, and taking hold of a railing, he shook it; so that it was evident to me that the place we occupied had been fixed on for retreat, if not for observation. I had thus again the advantage of my old friend, and the moment he receded we resumed our posts. In a few minutes, the different scouts seemed to agree in the opinion that all was safe, and went direct to the work I had anticipated, the moment I saw Lang enter with the members of the society. The front door was not their object; it was the back, or more properly the side one in the entry, which, from the passage being right opposite to us, I could see along, though very indistinctly, scarcely more than to enable me to trace their dark figures against the light thrown in at the farthest opening. None but a keen trapper or snarer can appreciate the pleasure a detective of the true instinctive order feels when engaged in the capture of game so wild, shy, and cunning. Their very cunning is what whets our appetites, and I absolutely burned to embrace the dauntless leader of the gang.

Now we saw one separate from the rest, come up the entry, and begin to act the "goose-guard", dodging backwards and forwards, throwing up his head, and looking from one side to another. Inside the entry, meanwhile, some obstruction seemed to take place, even adroit as Thomson was; but presently we were surprised as a vivid flash of exploded gun-powder illuminated the passage. Though unprepared for this, I understood it at once. Thomson had a way of his own with *sullen* locks—placing a small parcel of powder into the key-hole, and pushing it home, so as to reach the wards, he exploded it with a match. The only thing I wondered at was the scarcely audible report—perhaps to be accounted for by the moderate charge, and the resistance of the guards which he intended to loosen. So long as they were in the entry, we could not move, even to undo the padlock and get the gate open and ready. Our moment was that of their entrance; and watching thus, with breathless anxiety, we saw that the door had been opened, by the disappearance of the shadows from the entry. Out we sallied. The "goose-guard", L——, is made secure in an instant. Two constables, placed one on each side of the front door. I and my assistant enter the close and get to the side door. Lo! it is locked. The gentlemen had wanted time, not only to rifle the box, but to enjoy themselves with ample potations from the whisky barrel; and no doubt their libations would have been rather costly to Mr Brown, as every minute besides would have been devoted to the abstraction of as many portables as they could carry away.

Finding the door barred, (for I think the lock must have been rendered useless,) we began to force it—a circumstance that really added to my satisfaction, as every wrench and thump must have gone home to the hearts of the intruders, now fairly caught in a novel man-trap. Nay, with the constables at the outer door, I didn't care what noise we made, provided we were not annoyed by curious neighbours; and then, to make the play more exciting, we heard them as busy with the front door trying to get *out*, as we were with the back one endeavouring to get *in*. Forced at length, and a rush in in the dark, the noise making the thieves desperate, so that their energies to force the front door might rather be termed fury. They succeeded, just as we were at their back; and in consequence of the door being in two halves, and one starting open while the constables' eyes were fixed on the other, Lang bolted, at the moment that Thomson was embraced by a powerful constable. Another constable was off immediately in pursuit of Lang; and such was my weakness, that when I saw Thomson struggling ineffectually in the grasp of the officer, one whom I had so often sighed for in secret, and eyed in openness, that I took him from the man with that kind of feeling that no person ought to have the honour of holding him but myself.

By this time Mr Brown was down among us in great consternation.

"Ah!" said he, "I see the reason now of your having told me to carry the society-box up-stairs."

"I fear that would have been nothing to your loss," replied I, "if we hadn't been as sharp as we have been. All's right."

Mr Brown's fears were appeased, and we then marched our gentlemen up to the Office, in which procession, so honoured by the presence of Hugh Thomson, I enjoyed one of my triumphs. Lang was sought for during weeks, but could not be found; and here I have to recount one of my wonders. One dark evening when I was acting the night-hawk out near the Gibbet Toll, I had gone considerably beyond that mark, and was returning. Dalkeith is a kind of harbour of refuge for the Edinburgh thieves when the city becomes too hot for them, and I had some hopes of an adventure on this road, otherwise I would not have been there at that hour, for it was late. The road to Portobello is also a hopeful place at times; but on that night I had some reasons, known only to myself, (and it was not often surmised where I was at any time,) for preferring the southern opening. Well, sauntering along I met a young fellow, but it was so dark that, at the distance of two or three yards, you could scarcely recognise anybody. I had a question ready, however, that suited all comers.

"Am I right for the city?" said I.

"Right in," was the reply.

And seeing the man wanted to be off, I darted a look at the side of his face. It was Lang's; and I suspected he had recognised *me* before I did *him*, for he was off in an instant on the way to Dalkeith, and I must take to my heels in pursuit, or lose him. I immediately gave chase, and a noble one it was, though the night was as dark as pitch, and every step was through liquid mud.

Lang was a good runner, and had, I fancy, confidence that he would escape, and that which he had to escape from might very well grease the heels of even a lazy fellow. He ran for freedom, that dear treasure of even a thief's soul; and I ran to deprive him of it, a feeling as dear to a detective. The race became hot and hotter, and I could see only the dark outline of the flying desperado, and I heard the sound of his rapid steps as the voice of hope. By the side of the road one or two people stood, and seemed to wonder at the chase, but no one ventured to interfere. We had run a mile and a half with no abatement of the speed of either, so that we were about equal, and if this continued we might run to Dalkeith; but this issue was rendered improbable by the fact, quite well known to me, that a *pursued criminal*, with a clever officer after him, may almost always be caught by loss of breath. The impulse under which he flies is far more trying to the nerves than that which impels the officer to follow, and hence it is that criminals are so often what is called "run down". The same remark is applicable to a chase of animals. Fear eats up the energies, the lungs play violently, and exhaustion is the consequence. And so it was here. I gained as time sped, and at length I heard the grateful sound of the blowing lungs. He felt his weakness, and the old bravado getting up, he stopt all of a sudden, and waited for me.

"Why, man," said I, "you have just to walk back again; so what's the use?"

"No use," he replied, doggedly; "only if you hadn't caught me I would have been well on to Dalkeith."

Plunging my hands into his coat-pocket, I pulled out a bundle of picklocks.

"Not cured yet?" said I.

"No," replied he, "and never will. You have spoiled a good job at Dalkeith with your d——d dodging."

"Are you a member of a Dalkeith society, too, Lang?" I retorted, good-naturedly.

"Something better," said he; "I might have had £10 in my pocket before morning, if you hadn't come between me and my game."

We began our walk homewards. I didn't require to take hold of him. We had measured our powers, and he knew he had no more chance in flight than in personal conflict, and he walked quietly enough. I would put my handcuffs to use, however, at the Gibbet Toll, to provide against the dangers of alleys favourable to a bolt. I remember I tried him on the soft parts, in regard to the society-box, reminding him that he was robbing the widow and the fatherless.

"Humph! what have I to do with the widow and the fatherless? I am an orphan myself, and there is a difference besides, for your widow and fatherless have friends, because they have characters, and I don't know but they are better cared for than I, who have neither the one nor the other. I am bound to a trade, as that trade is bound to me, and I must live or die by it. So there's no use for your blarney about widows and orphans. All you have to do is to take me up, and get me condemned and imprisoned, and I will be the same man when I come out."

No doubt he would; and why should I have doubted, who scarcely, in all my experience, could hold out my finger and say, "There's a man whom I have mended, and he is grateful to me for having been hard with him?" No wonder I am weary of my efforts at penal reformation.

I believe the nine months' imprisonment awarded to these three desperate fellows only steeled them to dare the committal of crimes deserving transportation for as many years. How true it is, that the current of vice and criminality proceeds, both in its ebb and flow, on a "sliding scale".

The Miniature

❖

It is not often that I have had to deal with irregular criminals, by which I mean those that are not moulded and hardened in infancy and early youth, but who, from some inherent weakness of nature have, by the force of example, or the spur of unlawful gratifications, been precipitated—sometimes against the silent admonitions of their better genius—into a breach of the laws. I have said already that those whom Mr Moxey used to call "abnormals" are comparatively few, and it is not difficult to see how it should happen that their cases are the most painful exhibitions of misery that can be witnessed in this—to most, I fear—very miserable world. In the normals the heart is all in one way. Seldom is there any conscience stirring to produce the terrors of retribution; nay, the conscience is often completely reversed, so that the struggle of pain or anxiety, if it exists, is between the impulse of selfishness and the check imposed by the restraining laws. If a regular thief is sorry for anything, it is for being detected before he has enjoyed the fruit of his ingenuity or violence. There are only two powers in opposition—self, and the world. God is not feared, simply because He is never thought of; religion has no sanction, because it is not known. In the irregulars again, their heart is divided between God and the devil. Yes, that's my blunt way of putting it. And we may naturally look for some misery, I think, where the poor sensitive mind of the human creature is made the theatre of a contest between such powers.

In September 1850, Mr M——o, solicitor in Regent Terrace, had his bank account in the National Bank operated upon by a forged cheque to the extent of £195. So far as I remember, the forgery was not discovered at the time: nor did the startling intelligence come to him singly—at least it did not remain long single, for there was a crop of minor fabrications that started up like lesser evils round a great one. The forger, whoever he might be, had begun in a small way, as these abnormals generally do—boggling at the first step, then another as the terror waned and the confidence increased, then another and another, till primed for the great leap at length taken. The small cheque-books often kept by gentlemen in the names of their children with the Savings Bank, for the purpose of inducing habits of care and economy, were forged to the effect of abstracting such accumulations of the little daughters as £3 10s., and thereby—small sums and small sufferers—and then came the great feat on the great victim. How true a history of the progress of vice—the sliding scale of crime; fear leading passion to prey upon the weak and helpless, and passion throwing off fear, to rush headlong upon the strong!

At first there was a great obscurity as to the depredator. It was with a recoil that Mr M——o thought of his clerks, until suspicion began to be raised by the fact of the absence from the office of one of them, of the name of William L—— O——, who (as usual) seemed to be the very last on whom the mind of a confiding master could fix as the author of an act so treacherous, heartless, and cruel. The determination was at length come to, that he should be secured, and the charge of doing so was committed to me. I got my description, and how true it is that almost every case of the kind presents marks of personal aspect the very reverse of those we would expect; nay, I would say that, with the exception of a *side look*, expressive of fear, there is nothing about the face of a criminal that would imply either one thing or another as to the existence of tendencies towards even the *greater* crimes. Hence the common expressions, "Who would have supposed it?" "He was so unlike it," and so forth; all perfectly true. I have seen a devil with the meek face of an infant not less often than I have witnessed the softness and smoothness of infancy overlying nerves of steel leading to powder-pouches of fury and revenge. So be it; but I would not give a very long or very decided squint for all your fanciful expressions of this devilry or t'other; and so in this case. I had enough of marks;

but I soon learned that I was now, or later, sure of my man, for I ascertained that, like most other novices, he had taken to drink, to keep up his nerve and down his shame—a resource which throws a sought-for personage into my hands the quickest of any. He had changed his lodgings, and for a time I could only find traces of his passage through taverns, as he flew, sometimes trembling with drink and horror, from one to another, seeking from a fiend, whose gift is delirium, that peace which can only be got from one who behind a rough providence hides a smiling face. His friends, who knew nothing of the charge against him, told me that he had gone with the quickness of a shot into this wild life, and that they considered him mad. I knew otherwise. I deemed that his disease was not remorse, though all such fits are placed to the account of that mysterious power; he was simply under the despair of terror, and as the impulse of fear is the quickest of all passions to take the wind out of a man, I had no doubt I would overtake him between the fiend's temple and the suicide's death-bed.

Nor was my expectation long delayed. The search among the lodgings was difficult; he must have changed in lucid intervals, for he cleared away so effectually all behind him, that no one could tell me where he now lived. But at length I discovered his retreat. Placing a couple of constables at the foot of the stair for fear of a window-drop, I ascended to his room, at the door of which I placed my assistant. It was not a case for premonition by knocking, so I opened the door, which was merely on the lock-catch, and behold my sporter of the little Savings-Bank portions! He was sitting at a table, with a glass and bottle before him; but I could mark from the state of the bottle that his potations at this time had only commenced; nor was I blind to the conviction that the drinkfever was still careering through his veins; the old signs so familiar to me—the trembling hands—the flush—the tumid swellings at the top of the cheeks—the hare-brained eye, with its lightnings of fear.

I doubt if he knew who I was, but he needed no personal knowledge of me to quicken an apprehension that responded, no doubt, to every movement, even to that of a mouse. The first look of me bound him to the easy-chair,—not made for terror-ridden criminals these rests,—to which he fixed himself by hands grasping the soft cushioned arms; his mouth gaped quite open, so that I could even see his parched tongue, as it quivered like a touched jelly-fish, and his eye shot like a fox's when the hounds rush on him with their yell. I am not exaggerating—I doubt if any one man can in such a case; at least all language appears to fall far short in depicting the real state of a man in this young offender's position. Even the best describers in such cases are only botchers. We see only physical conditions,—mere palpable signs given in the flesh; nor know aught of the spirit, with its agonising recollections of home,—father, sisters, brothers,—hopes once entertained of a successful future to shed happiness upon them,—all blasted and destroyed, and the only contrast a jail and ignominy.

Yet amidst all this I had a calm part to play.

"You are Mr William L—— O——?"

"Yes."

"You were clerk to Mr M——o, of the Regent Terrace?"

As I uttered the words, I saw in an instant a change come over him, of a kind I have often noticed in people merely nervous from temperament and not drink. He clasped the arms of the chair more firmly, his trembling ceased as if in an instant, and his eye became steady. Yes, the energy of the instinct of self-preservation shot up through the drinkfever, confirmed his nerves, and prepared him for an onset. I have seen fear run into firmness like the congelations of a liquid metal; but such appearances, which I have learned to understand, never in any case shook my suspicions.

"Yes," replied he; "and what then?"

"Not much," said I, "in so far as I am interested, but something in so far as Mr M——o and his young daughters are concerned."

"I have left his employment, and do not intend to go back," was the answer, framed to avoid the main chance.

"I am not going to take you back to *your* office, but rather to take you up to *ours*, with a view to get some explanation of certain forgeries on the National and Savings Banks, perpetrated by some one."

"Then *get* that some one," said he, waxing firmer.

"I am just going to take him," replied I, a little nettled, and taking out my handcuffs.

The sight of these produced another effect, which may be said to be inconsistent with human nature. For my part, I don't know what human nature is, except just so far as I see it, and I never saw much consistency in it. The attempt to be firm, against the nervousness produced by his week's drunkenness, seemed to give way, as if suddenly let loose by the opening of some unseen aperture, and the effort to say something strong was changed into a kind of hysterical laugh—something like the cackle of a goose, and dying away into loud breathings. This was the mere going down of the barometer; it got up again on the courage side.

"I deny all knowledge of these forgeries," he cried.

"Well," said I, "it will only put us to a little trouble in proving it. In the meantime, accept the handcuffs."

To this I got no reply. He seemed to be struggling for stronger words of defiance, but they would not come at his bidding, and I heard nothing but a jabber, which expressed nothing but determination. I called in my assistant, and while he lay back in the chair we put on the cuffs—observing, as I have done before, the clenched hand, with the perspiration in the act of oozing out between the rigid fingers. Can any man imagine the fearful agony that could effect this, or the state of that conscience-riven and bursting heart?

Having raised him up, a little bit of romance introduced itself into this very prosaic affair, and, as it did not come out at the trial, was never known. He was standing by the side of a bureau, and suddenly he snatched with his left hand a *miniature* (that indispensable appurtenance of the romance-wrights), and placed it in his breast.

"What is that?" said I.

"The portrait of my mother," he said, and the tear stood in his eye.

"Let me see it," said I, taking hold of it; and examining it, I found that he had told me what was false. It was the portrait of a young woman, not above twenty years of age, with long black ringlets—exceedingly beautiful, of course—they all are in the velvet-coated case; but as I am no despiser of a good face, I may admit she was really a fair creature,—ay, even as regards beauty, such a one as a man with more *love* than *duty* would even forge for.

"Why," said I, "this is the portrait of a young lady. Why did you tell me a lie?"

He paused for a moment. His heart got big, all his hardness had gone, and with a choking voice he said,

"I don't want it to be known that she was connected with me, or ever saw me. So for God's sake give it me back."

I saw the impolicy of complying with this request, and put the miniature in my waistcoat pocket.

"No," said I, "you deny the forgery, and this face may lead me to a witness!"

"Never!" he cried, "she is too innocent to know aught of evil."

"Be it so," said I; "I will make no improper use of it, and whatever may happen, I promise to return it to you."

With this he seemed satisfied,—and we took him up to the Office, where he was locked up in a cell, with but little light, and where, I fear, in the dark hours he would see, in the magic lantern of a criminal's fancy, many more familiar faces than that of the mysterious original of the portrait. A mother's, at all events, would not fail to be illuminated there.

Somewhat troublesome as the apprehension of this unfortunate young man had been, it was far more easy than to procure the proper evidence to support an indictment. It turned out, to the annoyance of the authorities, who had no doubt of his guilt, that the imitation of the handwriting of Mr M——o was so skilfully executed, that the cheat was almost too much for the engravers. Forgery is, in this respect, a peculiar kind of crime. You may prove that the forger drew the money; but what then, if he was the person that ought to have drawn it for his master? Then, of whatever respectability the proprietor of the forged name, he is only a witness on his own behalf. Suppose the imitation *inimitable*, where are you? Yet it is to be confessed that so fine a case seldom happens, so that what I have said about the devil's limp is true here. It seems to be almost beyond the power of a human being to write the name of another in all respects so like that it cannot be detected, even although he has been in the practice of doing so several times a-day for years. But what is still more wonderful, as I've been told—for I am now speaking much from hearsay—it is even more difficult to imitate a rude and illiterate hand than a learned one; just as if Providence cared more for the poor, who cannot so well guard and protect themselves against such attempts.

The indictment was, however, prepared and served, and as the case was now more in the hands of the engravers, I had little to do with it; but I could not get quit of my portrait. There it was, still in my waistcoat pocket, just as if I had been some love-smitten swain, doing the romantic, notwithstanding my advanced years; so, thought I sometimes, if I had dropt down dead, or hung myself on a tree, or thrown myself over the Dean Bridge, as wiser men have done before me, what a story might have been founded on this miniature, and how appropriate for a woodcut stuck in front of my works! Doubtless some italic letters would have been in request by the printer:—"This great man hanged himself for love. The object of his affections was never known, and must remain a mysterious secret till that time when all things shall be revealed."

But even such thoughts as these had passed away. One night I went home late. I lighted my gas and sat down by the fire, in one of those reveries which have always taken possession of me when alone; very unlike other people's reveries, I suspect—for while these are occupied about catching money, or sweethearts, or fame, and sometimes the faces of departed friends, mine never had any other object than the catching of men. From a dream of this kind, and far removed from the case of the young man O——, I heard my door open, and, looking up, saw before me the figure of a fine tall young woman, muffled up in a cloak, and with a veil drawn closely under her chin, and held there by a gloved hand. Even I was amazed; for though I have had strange visitors, there was a something about this one that I am not much in the habit of seeing, at least within the walls of my humble dwelling—something of style and breeding so much above my Bess M'Diarmids and my Jean Brashes, that I was put off my calculations as to character.

"Are you Mr M'Levy?" said she, in a clear silvery voice.

"Ay, ma'am, at your service."

"It was you, I think, who apprehended the unfortunate young man, Mr L—— O——?"

"Yes."

"When you took him away from his lodgings, did you see about him the miniature of a young female?"

"Yes," replied I; and here my practical character began to show signs of activity. I suspected my mysterious visitor had under her veil the fair face from which that miniature had been painted, and my detective instincts carried my hand to my waist pocket.

"Now, my young lady," said I, "we have a peculiar curiosity about concealed things. If you will show me your face, I will tell you whether this miniature I hold in my hand is the one you are inquiring after."

"That I dare not do," replied she, with a tremble.

"Then I cannot show you the picture," said I.

"Would money move you?" said she.

"Not unless gold could cut or dissolve steel," replied I.

"Ah, then, I am miserable indeed!" she said. "I would not for the whole world that my friends, who are of rank, should know that the miniature of their relative had been found in the possession of a forger."

"I see no occasion for that coming out," said I; "the picture is of no use at the trial, and I can prevent every chance of such a circumstance obtaining publicity."

"Oh, Heaven bless you for the words!" she cried. "Can I trust you?"

"Yes," said I; but becoming again official, and not relishing the idea of being *done* by a female, I could not help adding, "But if you can have faith in my promise as regards the *picture*, why do you doubt me as respects the *original*?"

"I cannot—I dare not," she ejaculated, as she held the veil more firmly. "Adieu! I trust to your pity for one who truly deserves compassion."

And my mysterious visitor departed. I never heard or saw more of her; but I have since frequently thought of that lovely face, as portrayed no doubt truthfully in the miniature, and formed numerous conjectures:—the disappointed hopes, it might be, of early affection,—the bleeding heart, brooding in secret over the shame of such a connexion,—or, stranger still, the misplaced sympathy of a woman's love clinging with mistaken tenacity to the unworthy object, notwithstanding the disgraceful crime of which he had been convicted,—these and many others have often passed across my mind as the mysterious visit occurred to me. Nor is it possible to contemplate this affair without wondering at the fatality of the youth, with beauty if not rank in his power, and yet preying on the portions of children.

I have only to add, in conclusion, that the unfortunate young man was found guilty, and sentenced to fourteen years' transportation,—a life of misery entailed, and everything worth living for obscured and forfeited, by the unprincipled and criminal desire of display and prodigality. What a lesson for those holding confidential positions against listening for a moment to the insidious wiles of the tempter!

The Conjuror

❖

THE more I consider my eventful life, the more I am satisfied that there are coincidences that cannot be explained on the common calculations of Chance, because, though I have attributed many of my lucky hits to her, whom I call my patroness, yet I am quite sure her ladyship, though by no means a Lady Bountiful, is very much a Lady Grateful, who insists on something being done by her favourites to deserve her attention—perhaps a little flattery, though I am not much in that way.

About 1840, a very young boy, in Bo'ness, was sent by his masters,—shipowners, I think, there,—with £200 to place in the bank to their credit. As he went along, he was met by a man, holding a good character, and following the profession of a schoolmaster. Seized, it must have been, by the very demon of ambition, or perhaps sick of unbreeching and birching,—which seemed to do no good in the world, as the people were all as bad notwithstanding as he felt himself to be in his heart, in spite of all the birching he himself had got,—he fell upon the boy, who, he had suspected, was the bearer of money, and by sheer force took the whole sum from him. How, in so small a place, and at noon-day, he could have escaped, is a mystery I never heard cleared up, but true it is he did escape from the town, notwithstanding of the hullaballoo that got up in the neighbourhood. If he had taken to any of the country-leading roads, especially that to Edinburgh, he would have been seized; and I have always held the probability to be, that he sought refuge in some of the low, disreputable houses, where the inmates have a strong sympathy for custodiers of cash, so long as it lasts, thereafter kicking them out; and "serve 'em well."

We got, of course, information; but, after some weeks, I concluded that the man had either never come to Edinburgh, or had quickly left it. His crime was there, however, where it made a considerable noise from its peculiarity; for though dominies have often vices, it is seldom they betake themselves to the highway. When I know a man is not under the changeful wing of an alibi, he must be got of course—that's certain. That's a rule with me; but never having considered myself omniscient, the moment I am satisfied a man is not on my beat I can be easy. But then my beat was certainly a pretty wide one, and the difficulty was to find out one negative among so many positives as some two hundred thousand; and somehow I am a hard hoper, so that my conclusion was rather a forced matter in this case.

About a week or ten days after the affair, I was one night taking a turn along Bristo Street, a little in the knight-errant way, looking out for some pretty Lady Virtue, in defence of whom, under the brutalities of her ungallant sons, I might break, not a spear, but a head. On the pavement there stood two young girls, speaking, with their bonnets nid-nodding against each other, and looking with eyes so scandalously full of scandal of some very captivating kind, that I was induced to stop.

Thereupon one, shooting out her face so as to be very near my ear, said, "Whisht!"

"What now, my lasses?"

"Fine night."

"Where do you belong to, now? Edinburgh lasses—eh?"

"No, Bo'ness," said one of them.

"Bo'ness! Oh, you must have heard of the school-master who robbed the boy?"

"Ay, and just speakin' o' him," said the second.

"Do you know him?" asked I, just with the proper carelessness.

"Brawly; he has whipt me before now, and I wadna care though he was hanged in his ain lang tawse, for his cruelty to me mony a day."

"Well, perhaps I may help you to repay him," said I; "one good turn deserves another."

"Why? there's no one near."

"Nae saying; he's in that public-house there," pointing with her finger.

"Stop there till I come," said I, and instantly, walked in.

I got into a room where there was a man, threw my eye over him, and there to be sure was Mr——. I took no time to scan; you only raise suspicion. A glance gave me the "nose somewhat turned up;" the "demure face," as if so tired of whipping urchins; "gray eye," far ben, so indicative of foxiness; "big upper lip," of sensuality; "no whiskers," where whiskers should *have been*; and, beyond all, the look of great reverence, as if he had been bred to psalm-singing.

"Fairish night," said I.

"Middling," was the gruff reply of my schoolmaster.

"Bring me a bottle of ginger beer," I cried, suddenly, to the man of the house.

If any one will guess why I called for a drink I despised on a coldish night, when perhaps I needed something to warm me under the freezing look of his reverence, I'll give him my baton. Just guess now, and fail. It was not, I assure you upon my honour, that I might treat the girl whom he had whipped. Be so good as keep that in mind, because you might call me a fool for proposing a puzzle which was no puzzle.

My beer came in, and, going to the door, I brought in the whipped Jenny.

"Take a little beer, lass," said I, cheerfully.

But she couldn't, for her eyes were fixed on the dominie,—in the recollection probably of the tawse,—and her whole body shook.

"No fear," said I; "no tawse here, lass."

But still she stared and he stared, and they would have kept staring until all the froth on the beer had passed into thin air, if I had not put an end to it.

"You know the man?" said I to the girl.

"Ay—that's him," replied she, still staring at him, as if the old charm of the tawse tingled somewhere about her body.

"Who?" rejoined I.

"Mr——, the schoolmaster o' Bo'ness."

"Well, give me your name and address," said I, getting out my pencil, and proceeding to make the important entry in that terrible red-book of mine. "Now, my bonny lass," continued I, "your name is *given up* to the dominie, who'll *decry* you; but never mind. You may go now, but 'still remember me.'"

And she went, still all of a tremble, and forgetting her beer entirely.

"Well, I have the pleasure of having before me Mr——, late schoolmaster at Bo'ness?"

"It's false, sir."

"At any rate a supposition's no crime, and just let us suppose it."

"I'm not to suppose any such thing."

"Don't want you—it isn't necessary. It is only necessary that I should, and, what is more, *I do.* And I also suppose you have something in your pocket which would be very interesting to me."

"I am a respectable man——"

"I'm not disputing it."

"And I see no authority you have to inquire what I carry with me."

"Well, you may put me down as impertinent. I am sorry for it, but I am often obliged to be uncivil—can't really help it. Turn out."

"'Twill do you no good," said he, sulkily, and fumbling in his breeches-pocket.

"There's all the money I have,"—putting some silver upon the table,—"if you're a robber, take it."

"I don't happen to belong to that fraternity, I am a robber-catcher."

I had got the *whip*-hand of the reverend dominie. He shook violently, and knit his brows to make amends.

"You are pale, my good sir," said I, "and my beer's done, but I see you have got some in your coat-pocket,"—pointing to the top of a bottle sticking out, and which I had seen when I called for my own, through sympathy or fun; for we sometimes, when prosperous in our calling, get merry at the expense of vice. And why not? Are we not men? Have we not eyes, noses, hearts to feel, and lungs to laugh, and all the rest?

"What mean you?" he said, looking at me as if those far-ben eyes had come an inch out of their dark holes.

"Just to give you a drop of your favourite beverage," said I, pulling out a bottle from his right pocket. "Ah! and here is one for me as well," taking another from the left; "and here's a third for Madam Justice," taking the remaining one from his breast-pocket.

"I get beer at this house," said he, "and bring back the bottles to get more."

Here I was certainly a little taken aback. The explanation was really plausible, and I thought for a moment my drollery had been folly—that however brisk the beer I had called for, my joke had been stale.

"And now you see," said he, profiting by my disadvantage, "what you have made of your impudence."

But then, I think I have said that Vice is liable to infirmities. When she gets merry she gambols, like the moth, and rushes into the candle; or crows like the cock, who, getting on the heap-top, and then into the claws of the eagle, would never, but for the cocky-leerie-la of his jubilation, have been seen by his big friend. Yes, my reverence here committed a mistake;—probably though he had not, I would have been up with him. And then, with all the coolness in the world, he actually took up one of the bottles, and was putting it into his pocket.

"What! didn't you say you had brought these empty bottles?—for that they are empty," I continued, as I lifted one, "there can be no doubt; and why put them back into your pocket again to trouble you by taking them out a second time?"

"That's my business," said he.

"And this is mine," said I, taking up a poker in one hand and a bottle in the other, and knocking the head and upper part clean off, when there appeared a nicely rolled up bundle of notes, about £50.

The sound of the broken bottle brought in the landlord.

"Just in time," said I, taking the man by the coat, and drawing him forward.

"You see this?—it may be necessary you testify to it. This bottle, which I have taken from this gentleman, is more wonderful than that one I have read of in 'The Devil on Two Sticks,' for it contains this bundle of notes. Let us try our luck again," I continued, as I broke the second, and then the third, each revealing a similar bundle of notes, amounting in all to £180.

"Do you put pound-notes in your ginger-beer bottles when you cork them up for sale?"

The man laughed, even in the midst of his bewilderment. "The deevil o' the like o' this ever I saw!" he said; "what is the meaning of it? Ah, I see, you're a conjuror."

"Just so."

"I wish you would conjure some of my bottles that way. Faith, an' I'd soon be a rich man."

"I only do it to my friends," I replied, as I took a look of Master Reverence; "but no more of this joking; you have seen what you have seen, and can speak to my conjuring when you are called upon by an officer from the Sheriff."

The man began to see a little better.

"I understand," said he.

"Well, you may go."

"And now, sir," addressing my prisoner, "you will please go with me to the Police-office; I will take care of your bottles."

"What to do there?" he said, scarcely now able to speak with fear.

"To answer to the charge of robbing the boy —— in Borrowstounness, a week ago."

I now began to gather up my broken bottles; and as I proceeded, I heard him sighing and breathing laboriously; words came too, as if he had forgotten I was there. The spirit was working within; the conscience up in war, tearing him; he threw himself back on the chair, with his legs out, and as he hauled these shuffling along the floor, he still muttered—I could scarcely make it out, yet I was satisfied of these strange words, which I have never forgotten, and never will forget—

"Good God! this very girl I punished severely without a fault, because I had a grudge against her father!"

So, so, I thought; and what hand led me here so that I should come upon this girl, and what power stopped me, what power opened my mouth? Silence! I am only a humble instrument for discovering the secret ways of man's wickedness. Yes, I have often been impressed with this feeling when people thought I was merely pleased with my own poor efforts. Maybe they did not know me, for these thoughts are not just suited for the Police-office; and then, I have been obliged to stand the look of great judges, who, while they complimented me, no doubt looked upon me as a poor machine, only moved by strings pulled by a love of being thought clever, while they, who act upon my detections, are so wise and so honourable. But every man to his trade—shoemaker, poet, judge, and last—excuse me—the ferreter out of evil. It is easy to "charge" on such labours as mine,—easy to pronounce the word guilty, as proved by them,—easy to hang, as a consequence of them; and yet no man has less reason to complain than I myself.

"I love a penitent," said I, as I turned round to the miserable man.

He did not relish the compliment; such people never do.

"Mind your own business; you have been insolent in your wit."

Ah, there's no pleasing them: if you are harsh, they say you are riding over them; if mild, you are gloating over your superiority; if humorous, you are cruel and ironical.

"Suppose then," said I, "I command you as a suspected—"

"Just suspected."

"As a suspected robber of a poor helpless boy, not much beyond your birch—"

"Peace, man; your words enter my soul."

"Who might have been suspected of having appropriated that money, and been ruined for ever, to—"

"Peace, peace!"

"Walk up to justice;—will that please you?"

"True, true!" he ejaculated; "what will please him who has displeased God, and therefore himself? Were you to speak as an angel, I would call you devil; and devil you are!"

"Well, you will admit that the boy's masters, when they get the contents of the bottles, will not have so bad an opinion of me; you know there's a reward."

"But none to me," he sobbed, as his head fell on his breast; "my reward will not be here."

"Not sure but it may begin here, and in a way which may lead you to rejoice that it does not end here. A little sharpness quickens a man's conscience, and when that begins to cry out, you know there's a voice that answers."

"Well, you are not so bad a fellow after all," he said; and, rising, "now I will go with you quietly, for I think God's mind is in me, and perhaps He may lead me through tribulation to exultation."

"But what put the bottles in your head?" said I, changing the subject, for really I felt curious, though I have seen all manner of hiding-places, even the tender arm-pits of women,—yes, their mouths speaking sweet, endearing words,—but a ginger-beer bottle was new to me.

"Because," replied he, "after my first run I got thirsty, and having, in a public-house, got a drink of ginger beer, and as the empty bottle stood before me, I thought it would be a good means of hiding. No doubt the devil put this in my head, because he knew there was a man in Edinburgh who understood the devil's ways, and would find me out. But what," he asked, after a pause, "made you call for ginger beer when you entered? The words went to my very heart."

"Because," said I, "the devil induced you to allow a neck to stick out. I suspected in an instant that the money was there."

"Strange, indeed!"

"And I was so amused with myself, that I called for a bottle, just as a playful way—for I do my business with good humour—of intimating to you that I knew your trick."

We had talked more than I am in the habit of doing generally. I took him, with the broken bottles and notes, up to the office.

"There," said I, to the Captain, "is the Bo'ness gentleman, and there is the money—all bar fifty pounds—and there are the bottles where the money was secreted."

These were enigmas; but when the Captain understood them, he did not know what to say, between a desire to laugh and some restraint he could not comprehend.

"Ah!" said he, at last, "M'Levy, we should have a pulpit here, where people might be taught by us, as preachers, that God has many ways of finding out the wicked."

The prisoner was sent on to Linlithgow, along with the notes and broken bottles, and afterwards sentenced to fourteen years. The Judge complimented me handsomely; not so the offerers of the reward, for they never gave me a penny. The £25 went to the girls. I did not begrudge the gift; and yet, somehow, though not fond of money, more than is necessary for my humble wants, I think I should have got a five-pound note to wet my throat with ginger beer when following up the devil.

The Handcuffs

❖

IN the year 1836, which was in Mr Stewart's time, information came to the office from the quiet town of Peebles,—so quiet, that Lord Cockburn says, in some of his books, "if you want to make a public proclamation anywhere so as not to be heard, go to Peebles, and it is buried for ever,"—that the house of a gentleman there had been robbed on a Wednesday night, and a number of articles, among which were a new greatcoat and a pair of Wellington boots, had been carried off. However deaf Peebles may be to a proclamation, it certainly—at least among the high authorities there—cannot be charged with insensibility to the breach of the laws, for a capital account it was which we got, embracing all the particulars, the articles carried off, and the description of a person, once a servant in the family, who was suspected of the breaking-in and the abstraction. There was only one want—not a hint of the direction the burglar had taken,—whether east, west, north, or south; only that he was off somewhere.

The affair was entrusted to me, but I wanted that indispensable condition of hope—the certainty, or at least probable suspicion, of his being in Edinburgh. However, I transferred the image of the fellow to my mind's eye by that inside photography I have a knack in. I never knew where the light comes from, but the image, if once there, does not need any "gall" of anger to fix it, rather only the honey of love. I had him set up in that inside-plate accordingly, as large and living as life:—six feet two—dark complexion—leg-of-mutton whiskers—drooping nose, as if too heavy for the forehead to sustain—small mouth under the same, sadly oppressed by the said nose, and as if afraid to open under so formidable an incumbrance—something of a squint, under a bush of eyebrow. As for clothes, uncertain, unless he exchanged in the morning, and put on the new greatcoat and boots, which, for the sake of completing the picture, I supposed he had done; and so I had my man's image safe in my mind's keeping. But where was the original? I have always had a yearning for those comparisons, however odious, between the mind-sun-picture and the real walking, breathing piece of humanity itself, however low and degraded; but the desire is fruitless without the one of the two sides of the comparison.

Two days passed without issue, and it was now Saturday night. I had had the image all right for twice twenty-four hours, but where was the lantern? Even that would show me the honest man in the dark,—more difficult then to be seen, though present, than at noonday, as in the old case; nor have we more of that class now than then, I suspect. I wanted my "idea," and it was not a case exactly of time; another day might as well pass without diminishing my chance of success. I would wait for my "idea," just as the poets do, I'm told—not considering themselves bound to work unless they're sure they have it, though some tell me that many try without it. Better they than I, for I never did any good without mine. It might come by chance. True, what have I not done, in my small way, by chance? Ay, but Chance never smiled on me unless I poked her (is she female?) some way; so that my "notion," after all, has been, in the getting of it, my own work, only perfected by a higher hand.

In this dubious, stupid kind of state I left the office, intending to go home; nor, before I came to Toddrick's Wynd, had I any intention to poke up my favourite goddess; but, just as I was passing by the entry, my right leg I found inclined to the south, and the one leg carried the other, and both my head, which, so drowsy was I, seemed to be quite guiltless of the change from my right line home to bed down that same close. Habit, I fear, had some part in this wilfulness of my lower members. A Mrs Taylor lived down the wynd, a famous keeper of a half-respectable kind of lodging-house—a species of pool whence I have drawn many a kipper, as well as full-roed fish, newly run, with no other bait than a sombre "March-dun," or sober "May-bee"—and with a lazy floating line, too, without a bit of harling or whipping. Yes, I had been so often there, that I might be said to have formed a habit of going, for that kind of comfort without which I do not think I could live in this world of man-and-woman wickedness.

Having opened the good woman's door,—I call her good, because, if her lodgers were often only half-respectable, she was wholly so, at least in my eyes,—I entered with my usual familiarity, and sat down with her by the fire. I have said I wanted comfort, and so I began my old way of asking for it.

"Any lodgers just now?"

"Ay, a man frae the country. He came early in the morning, and got his breakfast. He is to sleep a' night at ony rate."

"What like is he?" I inquired.

"A perfect Anak amang the Philistines! Ye're a guid buirdly man yersel'; but, my faith! ye're naething to him. The man, I fancy, is guid eneugh; but I wadna redd you meddle him—I mean if he were ane ye had ony care for—without at least twa assistants."

"Can you describe his face?" said I, really in the expectation of getting nothing.

"Indeed, no," replied the good woman, "for it's lang since I gave up spying into men's faces, whaur I never, in my best days, saw muckle to look at, but a nose amang a bush o' hair, and twa een aye glowerin' at us women folk; but, besides, my niece Jenny gave him his breakfast, and I've scarcely seen him;—but, Guid save us! here he is," she added, as she heard a heavy foot in the lobby.

And so, to be sure, the big lodger entered, very confidently, drew in a chair, and sat down. I threw my eye over him on the instant, not of course very inquiringly,—for, indeed, as I have already said, a glance generally does my purpose,—and there was the nose, so much too heavy-like for the forehead, and the mouth under the incumbrance of the nose, the leg-of-mutton whiskers, and the squint, all so perfect, that my mind-sun-image leapt within me, as if it would be out to its original, there to lose itself in flesh and blood. Enough for the justification of my modesty and simplicity, and taking-it-soft method—nay, I'm not sure if the man had observed whether I looked at him at all or not, and, as for the future of our companionship, I did not need. I had something else to do—I had caught my "idea," as well as its original; but then the one was a fancy, and the other a "Tartar."

The conversation was meanwhile leading to trades and occupations; how it began I cannot tell; but all of a sudden it came into my head to say to my man, "You'll be a hawker, no doubt?"

"Are *you* a hawker?" replied he, rather in a surly tone, as if offended.

"Yes," said I.

"I thought as much," growled he, "for we think everybody we meet should be like ourselves."

"And yet we don't find that always," I rejoined, softly. "But I could wish every man were as well to do as I am, for I have six men on the road, and a horse seldom off it."

"The horse will be for yourself?" said he.

"Yes; I could not get on without my Rory; for, you know, I have all those six fellows to look after."

"Why, don't they return at the end of their rounds?" inquired he, again.

"Yes, if they are able."

"And what's to disable them?"

"The fiend drink," said I, somewhat sorrowfully. "They get into wayside publics, and sometimes lie for days—all the while my goods are being stolen."

"And what do you do with them when you find them in this state?" said he. "Turn them off, I fancy, and get more sober men?"

"No: were I to do that, I would be changing every week, and with no chance of getting better ones; for if they don't drink, they cheat, and a drunken honest pedlar is better than a sober dishonest one."

"Why, then, you must just let them sleep off their drink," said he, "and trust to a sober run to make up for the drunken one?"

"No; I hasten to the spot, and having caught the fellow as he begins to look clear, I handcuff him, and bring him into town with the pack on his back. There I relieve him, and keep him without wages as a punishment, just as long as I think necessary; and when

I think he is determined to do better, I give him his pack again, and begin his pay."

"And is this strange punishment often necessary?" said he, as his curiosity became excited by my novel method.

"Why," replied I, "no longer ago than Wednesday morning, I was obliged to set off for Peebles, where one of my chaps was lying drunk—and I think I met you" (a chance thrust) "coming out of the town with a bundle, and that was just the very reason that made me suppose you were one of our order."

"Well," said he, thus taken suddenly, "I did leave Peebles on Wednesday morning with a bundle, but I am not a hawker."

"No offence; it is a good honest calling. Once upon a time a great part of the country trade of Scotland was done by hawking, and a pedlar was often worth thousands."

"May be," said my giant; "but if I were one of your men I would be very drunk indeed if you could handcuff me."

"Perhaps I wouldn't try one of your size and mettle," said I, "unless you were very drunk."

"And then what the use?" rejoined he. "Drunkenness is a very good handcuffing itself, though I never saw the instrument I have heard so much of, nor would I like to deserve it. But, man," he continued, after a pause, during which he perhaps thought he did deserve the application of the check, and maybe shook a little at the prospect of feeling it, "what are handcuffs—what like are they? Could a strong man not snap them, and then snap his fingers at the officer?"

"A very simple thing," said I, drawing out a good specimen, which I cherish as my stock-in-trade, maybe with no less affection than Simpson did his bit of hemp, though, in point of respectability, I don't want the two things to be compared. "Here is my wrist-curb for my disobedient pedlars."

I even put the thing into his hands.

"A very simple affair," said he, with a sneer; "but I am d—d if that would hold me, unless it be applied in some queer way."

"Well," said I, "I never saw one of my men break it or get loose."

"How *do* you apply it?" said he, looking curiously.

"Why, just this way."

And in, I hope, my usual kindly manner, I put his right hand into the kench.

"How is that to bind a man?" he again sneered.

"Not finished yet, my dear fellow. I bind the other end to my *left* hand thus, and there you are."

"Well, rather kittle, I admit," said he, looking not quite comfortable-like; "and I would just as soon be out of it."

"But you have not tried it yet," continued I. "Sometimes a man is unfortunate, and while we are yet innocent and free we might be nothing the worse for preparing for an eventual future, you know. Just suppose that I were not a hawker, but one of those very uncomfortable men called detective officers, and that I wanted to walk you up to the Cross. Let us see—come along, now; quietly, my good fellow—this way"—leading him out—"so, this way—so," till I got him to the outer door leading to the close. "So,—how quiet you are! You don't resist. Why don't you? So"—up the close a bit—"you said you could snap it, or get loose, and then snap your fingers, and yet don't you see?"

Even all this time my man thought it play, but whether it was that suspicion seized him, or he merely wanted to try the game, I cannot say, but he began in earnest to struggle; but it would not do. I held him firm by the right arm, and whenever he used the left, I quelled him easily by *my* right.

"Enough of it," said he, at last.

"Not just yet," said I, with an *impressive* softness. "I want to see if I can take you up as far as the Police-office."

"The Police-office!" he roared, with a tremendous growl. "The Police-office and be d—d! Why there?"

"To be searched and examined," I replied, still keeping my temper, "and perhaps committed for breaking open your old master's house at Peebles, on Wednesday night, and stealing, among other things, the greatcoat that's now on you, and, I believe, also the boots now on your feet."

I felt his right arm fall as if palsied. I could see by the lamp at the head of the close that he was as pale as pipeclay. There was not so much pith in this big man as would have sufficed to break a rosin-end of good hemp, nor did he speak a single word. All I heard was his labouring breath, as he heaved his strong ribs, so that he might give room for the play of his heart. I was now safe from an attempt at escape, for we had reached the top of the wynd, where the man in charge of the street immediately came up to my assistance. But somehow I got filled with the demon of pride. I had an ambition to walk him up alone, and though, no doubt, the appearance of the policeman might have contributed to the continuance of my now easy victory, yet I verily believed he was still incapable—such is often the effect of that striking down of the confidence and courage of a conscious criminal, by a calm announcement, coupled with a mere strap of leather—of offering any resistance.

And thus I took him to the room of the lieutenant, where Captain Stewart happened to be at the time; and here it was he first found voice.

"I am brought here by a hawker. I am not one of his pedlars, and no more drunk than he is himself," he cried, his mind suggesting some faint hope which, for a moment, blinded him to his fate.

"Why, M'Levy, you have caught our Peebles friend," said the captain, laughing, but wondering, too, at my new vocation of pedlar; "there's the height, the nose, and all the rest, as large as life. Where, in the name of all that's wonderful, did you find him?"

"Stranger still," said the lieutenant, "where's your assistant? You couldn't handcuff that giant alone?"

"He's handcuffed, anyhow," said I; "call some of the men, for I want to be relieved."

He was, in a few minutes, safer still—locked up for the night.

Don't, I beg of you, suppose that we are such ill-disposed and gloomy beings, who frequent this outer chamber or entrance to the dempster's hall, that we never have the luxury of a little quiet mirth. Bless you all, except, of course, those who will not come quietly up to see us, we are quite humane in our way—no hyæna's laugh or crocodile's tears amongst our fraternity. We can even enjoy such mishaps as the discomfiture of those who try to put mirth to flight in many a domestic heaven; and can even afford, without detriment to our hearts, to be merry over grief, when it is the grief which follows God's behest against the disturbers of man's rest. Then it is only making the balance even, for how glorious do our enemies, whom we yet treat as friends, get in their midnight triumphs of pilfering, robbing, and murdering their fellow-creatures, who not only never injured them, but often served them well, but, alas! not wisely. So I need no apology for that heartily-passed half-hour, during which I explained the capture of my man—one of my six pedlars; but withal, it was nothing but the confidence my superiors had in me that prevented them doubting, not only the means I employed in getting the wrist of this truly big thief into the strap, but my ability to bring so great a giant all so quietly from Toddrick's Wynd to the Cross of Edinburgh. I was at least comforted, even by Widow Taylor, at whose house I had sought consolation for my two days' disappointment, and went home to bed without a touch of compunction.

Next day, my pedlar, with his pack—collected from several brokers—along with him, was sent to Peebles, where the Sheriff and Jury gave him nine months, to confirm him in a resolution, no doubt formed when he pled guilty, that he would not, even at the bidding of a hawker, try on a pair of handcuffs again.

The Red Ribbons

❖

ONE day, also in Captain Stewart's time, a gentleman came to the head-office late in the afternoon. There were several detective officers present, ready for any emergency. He was much excited; more so, indeed, than was consistent with the principal cause of his application, but not more than might have been expected from the circumstances attending it. He stated, that in the morning of that same day he and his wife had left his house in Haddington Place (a flat) to go to the country, where they intended to sojourn for some time. Their children, and the care of their house, they left to the sympathy and trustworthiness of the servant, a young girl, in whom, for her gentleness, religious feelings, and general good conduct, they had the most unbounded confidence. For some reason which, I think, he did not state, he returned himself in the afternoon, and, to his horror, found the door locked, and no trace of the key. He knocked, but all that he heard was the weeping and wailing of his children, all very young, and one, indeed, only newly weaned. Even amidst this very eloquent evidence of something being wrong, he could not at the instant, nor for some time, suspect any foul play on the part of the gentle Helen, but after waiting longer, he heard one of the young creatures sobbing behind the door, and crying out that Nelly had gone out long ago, and that they had got nothing to eat. He was now satisfied that there was something very wrong, and, hurrying for a blacksmith, he got the lock picked, and, the door opened.

On getting inside he observed an extraordinary scene. The newly-weaned child had been laid in the cradle, where it had wept itself nearly blind—its eyes swelled, and its face all wet with its tears.

Another was lying on the ground, in a perfect agony of fear; a third was sitting looking wistfully out of the window, which it could not open, and where it had been knocking and crying to the passers-by for hours, without having been responded to; and two others were running backwards and forwards, not knowing for what object, but just in obedience to an impulse that would not permit of rest. But what was more strange, they had, from sheer hunger, got hold of a loaf of bread, no doubt to eat it ravenously; and yet there was the loaf untouched, as if the desire to eat had been overcome by their fear, so that, while the stomach craved, the muscles of the mouth disobeyed even this primary instinct. But he had not yet seen everything. On examining further, under the suspicions excited by the sobbing, weeping words of the poor young creatures, he found that the bureau where he kept his money had been broken up with a poker, and sixteen pounds extracted. He now understood everything too well, and having got a neighbour to attend to the children, and give them something to eat, he hurried up to the office. Captain Stewart having heard the strange story, questioned the gentleman in the ordinary way.

"What like is the girl?"

"Rather pretty, about nineteen years of age, dark eyes, aquiline nose, small mouth, and a mole on the left cheek."

"How was she dressed?"

A more difficult question—rather befitting the gentleman's wife. He could scarcely answer.

"This beats me," replied he; "but I have a notion she has red ribbons on a white straw bonnet. I could not say more; and if it had not been that Mrs B—— had remarked to me, on the previous day, that Nelly was a little too gaudy (and consequently she probably thought giddy) about the head, with these glaring red ribbons of hers, I would not have been able to condescend even upon this particular, so little attention do I pay to these things."

Captain Stewart noted, and several officers were sent right and left, while I sat meditating a little. "All good-enough marks these," I thought; "but the girl may have got out of the town." Going up to the gentleman, I whispered (for I wanted the answer to myself—not that I lacked faith in Captain Stewart's tact, but that sometimes I found it more convenient to take my own way, and report afterwards)—

"Is she an Edinburgh girl?"

"No," said he, in a similar under-tone, from probably mere sympathy.

"Then where does she come from?" was my next question.

"Glasgow."

"You will find me turn up, perhaps, in the morning," I said to the Captain, who had confidence in me, and did not wish to lay open my intentions, whatever they were, to those alongside.

"Very well," cried he. "I only hope you will catch the mole."

"I have caught as deep a moudiewart before," said I, as I prepared to depart.

But I wanted an answer to another question.

"Have you any reason," I inquired further, "to suppose that the girl suspects you know her friends' whereabouts in Glasgow?"

"No," replied the gentleman; "because I never knew that, neither does my wife."

"Of what bank were the notes?"

"British Linen Company."

"Enough;" and with an idea in my head—a very easy to be found one, and no other than that most animals, whether moles, or mud-larks, or men, (and far more women,) generally, when pursued, seek their old holes and lurking-places—I set out. I knew that the afternoon coach to Glasgow would leave about this very hour, and expected to be all in good time; but on arriving at the office, I found that it had left only a few minutes before. I knew that I could not make up with it on foot, and therefore hailed a cab. In the meanwhile, and while it was coming up, I made out, from a few rapid questions at the clerk,—whether there were any young girls among the passengers, what like they were, and so forth,—that there was one coming near my mark, not of the mole, or of the dark eyes, or aquiline nose, but of the red ribbons.

"I can't be wrong about the red ribbons on the bonnet," said he; "only I think there are two—one inside and one out."

"Did any of the girls change a note?"

"Yes, one of them."

"Let me see it."

"British Linen Company," said the clerk, handing it to me.

"The changer inside or out?" said I.

"Outside."

"All right," said I; and, mounting the cab—"Now, cabby, you are to overtake the Glasgow coach *at any rate*, if you should break your horse's wind, your own neck, and my collar-bone."

And the man, knowing very well who I was, set out at a gallop at once, and so furious a one, that it almost put me out of a study—no other than the examination of all the bonnets I could see in Princes Street; for I had, for the nonce, become a student of the *beau monde*, at least of the *beaux* of the world of bonnets;—in short, I was curious to know the proportion, in a hundred colours, of my new favourite one of red;—and so furious, moreover, was his driving, that the eyes of the whole street were turned upon us—those under the shadow of red ribbons being, fortunately, unconscious that I was doing all I could to reduce the renown of their favourite colour. We soon passed the Hay-weights, and were fairly on the high-road to Corstorphine. Nor was it long till I could see the red badge waving very proudly on the top of the coach, just as the clerk had told me; nay, it even appeared to me that the cabman's ambition was roused by the pennant, for he drove harder and harder, till at length the coach stopped, no doubt in obedience to the conviction of the driver that he was to get a too-late fare.

"Make haste," cried the coachman, as I got alongside and was getting out. "We have room for one, but no time for parley,"

"Room for one," said I, as I looked up into the face of the gentle Nelly, where the mole was, and where there rose upon the instant something else, first a blush as red as her ribbons, and then a pallor as white as the bonnet. "Rather think you've got one too many."

"No, the Act of Parliament says we are entitled to carry——"

"Not that girl with the red ribbons," said I, producing my baton. "You come down, Miss Helen N——." (I forgot to say I got her name from her master.) "I want to give you a ride back to town."

She wouldn't though, and seemed inclined to resist to the uttermost; but the passengers seeing she couldn't, for want of will, come of herself, took her by force, and handed her down to me, who thanked them for so pretty a charge. Having got her into the cab, I next got out her box, and, placing that alongside of her, I drove her direct up to the office. Captain Stewart, recollecting the red ribbons and the mole, and casting his eyes over her head-gear and the face, smiled in spite of his usual gravity. We soon found that the gentle Nelly wanted to prove as untrue to us as she had been to her master, for she absolutely swore that she was not only not guilty of doing anything against the laws, but that she was not even Helen N—— at all, notwithstanding of the ribbons, the mole, and the black eyes, and the really fine aquiline nose; so it did actually seem necessary that we should prove, to her own satisfaction, who she was. After searching her, we thought that the exact sum of £15, 14s. found on her—which, with the 6s. for her fare, made up the £16—would have removed her scepticism as to her identity; but even this was insufficient, and the resolute Nelly might have remained in her utter ignorance of herself till doomsday, had it not been that Mr B—— called at the office, and satisfied her that she was herself. And not only was she then convinced, but she had reason not to relapse again into her ignorance; for, during the six months she was doomed to remain in prison, she was so much by herself, with seldom another to confound her notions of who she was, that she could not have avoided herself, however willing.

The Orange Blossom

❖

HOWEVER assiduously I have plied my vocation, I have never thought that I was doing the good which our masters expect of us in stopping the sliders on the slippery scale of criminal descent. They only commence again, and when they slide off altogether others rise to run the same course. If I have taken credit for a diminution, I suspect that Dr Guthrie has had more to do with it than I. Sometimes I have had qualms from a conviction that I have been hard on many who could scarcely be said to be responsible. I have been, no doubt, often an unwelcome intruder upon merry-makings and jollifications, but then it may be said for me that these merry-makers were merry at the expense of others. Well, "you have stopped marriages where one of the parties was innocent." True, but the innocent party was attracted by the glitter of stolen gold, and why should a resetting bridegroom escape a loss any more than a resetting pawnbroker? A dowried thief in stolen orange blossom may be a pretty object to a loving snob—to me, however, she is nothing else but a thief, and if I am bound to tear her from his arms, I have just the satisfaction that I transfer her to the arms of justice, who will hug her a good deal closer.

In 1842, our office was inundated with complaints of house enterings by false keys. There had been no fewer than sixteen in six weeks, and not a trace could be discovered.

"Why, M'Levy," said the Lieutenant one day to me, "we will lose caste. Aberdeen will mock us, and Berwick hold up the finger at us. What's to be done?"

"There's a difficulty," replied I. "In the first place, I am satisfied there is only one thief; in the second place, there is only one place of deposit; in the third place, I am only one man; and, in the fourth place, I am not an angel. Yet, not withstanding, I have a hope."

"What is it founded on?"

"This little bit of swatch," replied I, showing him a paring of print not larger than two crown pieces.

"Why do you place faith in a rag like that?"

"I got it," replied I, "from Mrs ——, the proprietor of a house in Richmond Street, the last one operated on, and Mrs Thick, the broker in the Cowgate, thinks she might be able to match it."

"That promises something."

"I think I have the sex too," said I, with an intention to be jocular.

"Man or woman?"

"Woman," replied I.

"Oh, something peculiarly in the female line," said he. "I hope not an object in the *greening* way?"

"No; something preparatory to, and going before that. Can't you guess?"

"No—yes—let me see—orange blossom?"

"Yes, orange blossom," said I. "The thief wants to be married. She has laid in the dowry from the same house in Richmond Street, and finished off with the bride's badge."

Our conversation terminated with a laugh, for, after all, we were scarcely serious, and I repaired to Mrs Thick, a fine specimen of her class, who, rather than pocket a penny from stolen goods, would have surrendered her whole stock, amounting to hundreds of pounds. As I went along I continued my former ruminations on this wonderful succession of robberies. That they were all done by one hand I had, as I have said, little doubt; but, considering the short period of time, the difficulty of watching and accomplishing even one house, the multiplied chances of being seen, the obstructions of locks, the accidents so rife in pledging or disposing by sale, the many inquiries and investigations that had already been made by sharp people, I could not help being filled with admiration at a dexterity so unexampled in my experience. And then, if I was right in my whimsical conjecture as to sex, what a wonderful creature of a woman she must be!

"She is worthy of me anyhow," I said to myself; and as we illiterate people are fond of a pun, I added, just for my own ear, "I will catch her through *thick* or *thin*."

Now, don't be angry at my wit; it is better than you think; for don't you remember of one of the name of Thin, with the three balls above his door?

And not insensible to the effect of my solitary effort at being clever out of my sphere, I entered the shop of the broker.

"Now, Mrs Thick," said I, "have you got a match for my swatch?"

"Indeed I think I have," replied the good woman, although she knew she would in all likelihood be a heavy loser by her honesty. "Here's the gown," and, taking the pattern out of my hand, "see it's just the thing—aye, just a bit o' the self-same. Whaur in a' the warld got ye the swatch? Surely it's no canny to meddle wi' you, you're an awfu' man; but, do ye ken, I canna think after a' that that gown was stown."

"I never said it was, Mrs Thick."

"Aye, but it's a sign o' dead hens when the farmer rins after the fox that has loupit the yett."

"And I never said it was not," replied I, for I had reasons to be cautious.

"Weel, to be honest, Mr M'Levy, I really dinna think it was."

"And why?"

"Just because it was brought to me by that industrious creature Lizzy Gorman."

"That's the handsome hawker, as the young chaps call her?" said I.

"Just the same."

"And what makes you have so much faith in Elizabeth?"

"Just because I have kent her for years; and naebody could look into her bonny face, sae simple and sweet, without being sure she's an honest creature. Then she has hawked sae lang through Edinburgh, that had she been dishonest, she would hae been fund oot."

"Well, she does look like an honest girl," said I. "Have you had many articles from her besides the gown?"

"Just a heap," replied she. "But ken ye what, Mr M'Levy?"

"If I knew the what, I could perhaps tell," said I, keeping my friend in humour.

"This is Elizabeth's marriage-day," she whispered in my ear.

"Orange blossom!" muttered I.

"Aye, orange blossom," repeated Mrs Thick; "Lizzy's as far up as even that."

Now I had no wish that Mrs Thick should have heard my muttering, but the answer satisfied me I had muttered to some purpose.

"And who is the happy man?" inquired I; though I would not have given the sprig of orange blossom for the other sprig.

"Just a snab," replied she; "but then Elizabeth has money, and a full house, a' by her ain industry, and she says she'll set him up."

"Well, the affair looks promising," said I, adding, as I meditated a little, "unless the swine runs through it."

"Oh, it's ower near now for the sow; you're no Scotch and maybe dinna ken the auld rhyme—

> Lang to woo, and then to marry,
> That's the way to mak' things miscarry;
> But first to marry, and then to woo,
> Is the surest way to keep out the sow.

Aye, the beast seldom comes on the marriage-day to scatter the ribbons and the orange blossom."

"Not sure," said I, somewhat absent. "But letting the marriage of this most industrious girl alone, I have a favour to ask of you. Will you take care of this gown, and all the other articles Elizabeth has brought to you?"

"I will," replied she; "but the Lord kens how I'm to get them a' collected. There's a cart-load o' them; but I hae nae fear they're a' honestly come by."

"I hope so," said I, as I left the shop, with the intention of returning to the Office for a list of the property stolen from the sixteen houses, and then perhaps to call and see the bonny bride.

And as I went along, I began to gather up the fragments of my prior knowledge of my handsome hawker. She was pretty well known for several peculiarities. Her face was that of a gipsy, with the demureness of the race mixed with a simplicity which they seldom exhibit; and her dress, plain almost to Quakerism, had all that dandyism which extreme care and an excellent taste can bestow on very plain things. Quite an exception to the crowd of town-hawkers, she was far above their baskets and bundles of troggan. We see these every day. Some are enveloped in a mountain of shining articles of tin,—others are surrounded with a whole forest of wicker-work in the shape of baskets and reticules,—others rejoice in a heap of black tin shovels,—many are devoted to kitchens, where they show their white caps to the servants out of a basket neatly covered with a white towel,—the apple and orange troggars are everywhere, the red-herring female merchants being probably at the foot of the tree. Despising all these, Elizabeth was seldom burdened with more than a neat paper parcel. Even that she was often without, and indeed I had heard it often remarked that no one knew what she hawked. Yet the readiness with which she was admitted at pretty high doors was remarkable, and once in, the secret article, probably drawn from under her gown, was an easy sale—at to her, no doubt, a remunerating price—under the charm of a winning simplicity, aided by the ready tale of the interesting orphan. A little consideration of these things soon brought me to the conclusion that it was only by such an adept, thoroughly acquainted with the inside of so many houses, by means of a daring eye and a quick ear, that all these sixteen entries in six weeks could have been effected. Nor would it be too much to say that the orange blossom was not accidental, if it was an object which she had known to be in the house where a marriage was on the *tapis*, and of which she had obtained the knowledge by a prior visit.

I had now got thoroughly interested in my pretty hawker. Her movement on the scale was now upwards. It is seldom that thieves slide up to Hymen's bower; and if I had had no other motive than simply to see the young woman who could perform such miracles, I would have gone twenty miles to see her in her marriage dress, orange blossom, and all. I soon got my list completed; indeed, I was now somewhat in a hurry. The apathy with which the Lieutenant had charged me was changed into enthusiasm. Strange perversity of the human heart! I felt a jealousy of the snab. He was unworthy of such perfection. The bride must be mine at all hazards, even if I should be obliged to renounce my beauty to the superior claims of the Colonial Secretary.

Having got my list, I made again for the Cowgate, where, as I passed the stair-foot leading to the room of the intended, I saw the beginnings of the crowd which was to honour this match between the son of Crispin and the daughter surely of that famous goddess who got her skeleton keys from Vulcan for a kiss. I would pay due attention to the crowd by and by, and gratify it perhaps more than by the raree-show it was gaping to see. It was Mrs Thick I was now after; and having again found her at her old post, I went over with her as quickly as I could the long list, and became quite satisfied that her estimate of a cart-load was not much below the mark.

"Now, you are upon your honour," said I to her. "You must be careful to retain all those articles for an hour or so, for I am sorry to inform you I must take them from you."

"And can it be possible!" she exclaimed, no doubt with reference to the guilt of her industrious protégé; and then relaxing into a kind of smile, "Surely, surely you're no to act the animal we were speaking of. The bride's dressed, the bridegroom is up, the minister is waited for, and the crowd is at the door. Poor Lizzy, poor Lizzy, could ever I have thought this of you!"

"Well, I admit that I intend to be at the marriage anyhow," said I. "They have not had the grace to invite me; but I am often obliged to overlook slights from my friends."

And leaving my honest broker in the very height of her wonder—if not with uplifted hands and open mouth—I made my way to the house of rejoicing, shaded as all such are with that quiet decorum, if not solemnity, which the black coat and white cravat have such a power of casting over leaping hearts and winged hopes. The crowd had by this time increased; and among the rest was my assistant waiting for me—though ostensibly there to overawe the noisy assemblage. The Irish boys and girls were predominant, shouting their cries, among which "The snab and the hawker, hurra," would not sound as an honour up-stairs. When I say Irish boys and girls, I mean to include adults of sixty, grim and shrivelled enough in all save the heart, which is ever as young and green as an urchin's. Then who does not feel an interest in the evergreen of marriage, albeit its red berries are often full of bitterness and death? The young look forward to it, and the old back upon it—the one with a laugh, the other with a sigh; but the interest is ever the same. Nay, I'm not sure if the sigh has not a little hope in it, even to that last dripping of the sands, when even all other "pleasure has ceased to please." Excuse me, it is not often I have to sermonise on marriage, except those between the law and vice, where the yoke is not a pleasant one, and yet perhaps less unpleasant than many of those beginning with love on the one side, and affection on the other. And now I am the detective again.

"Are the constables ready?" I whispered to my assistant.

"Yes; they're in the stair-foot beyond the meal-shop on the other side."

"Then keep your post, and have an eye to the window."

"For *ha'pennies*?" said he, with a laugh.

"I'm just afraid I may reduce the *happiness*," replied I, not to be outdone in Irish wit on a marriage occasion, however bad at it.

And pushing my way among the noisy crowd, whose cry was now "M'Levy!" "He's to run awa' wi' the bride!" "The snab has stown his varnished boots!" "The bride is to sleep in a police cell!" and so forth, I mounted the stair till I came to the marriage-hall. Uninvited as I was, I made "no gobs", as they say, at entering, but, opening the door, stood there among the best of them. A more mysterious guest perhaps never appeared at a marriage before since the time of the famous visitor at Jedburgh, where the king danced; but I had no attention to bestow on expressions of wonder. The sçene was of a character to be interesting enough to any one. To me the chief object of attention was the head of the bride, where the orange blossom ought to be; and there to be sure it was, set off, as it ought to have been, with green myrtle. With this I was so much occupied, that I cannot say it was just then that I scanned Elizabeth's dress—a fine lavender glacé silk, adorned with as many knots as would have bound all the lovers in the room in silken bands; collar and sleeve of lace, of what kind goes beyond my knowledge; grey boots, necklace, and armlets; white kid gloves, with no doubt a good many rings under them. These notices came rather afterwards, my practical eye ranging meanwhile—the party being dead silent as yet—round the room, where, according to my recollection of my list, I saw a perfect heaping up of all manner of things collected from the sixteen opened houses, which the pretty bride had so industriously entered.

My survey was the result of a few rapid glances, and I recurred to the parties. The amazement was just at its height, yet strange to say the only one who stood there unmoved, and with no greater indication of internal disturbance than a cast-down eye, overshaded by its long lashes, was Elizabeth Gorman. That she understood the object of my visit, I had no doubt; nor was I surprised that a creature of her nerve, capable of what she had done, should stand before me in the midst of all her friends, and in the presence of her intended husband, as immoveable as a lump of white marble—no additional paleness, no quiver of the lip, no hairbrained glances of fear.

"And who are you?" at last cried the souter *futur*; "you are not invited."

"No; I have taken the liberty to come uninvited," replied I, as I threw my eye over the body of the young snab arrayed in absolute perfection, from the glossy cravat to the shining boots, so spruce and smart that the taste of Elizabeth must have been at the work of preparation. Nor was he without some right, if one might judge the number of houses laid under contribution for a dowry which was to be his, and by the help of which he was to become a master.

Whereupon there arose a perfect Babel of voices—"No right;" "M'Levy has no right here;" "Turn him out." To all this I paid little attention; I was more curious about a movement on the part of Elizabeth, whose right hand was apparently fumbling about her pocket. A pocket in a bride's dress!—ay, just so. Elizabeth Gorman was a bride of a peculiar kind; she had a *pocket* even as a part of her bridal apparel, and there was more there than a cambric handkerchief.

"I will help you to get out your napkin, Elizabeth," said I.

And putting my hand into the sacred deposit, I pulled out two check-keys.

With these two keys, she had opened (I speak in anticipation) the whole sixteen houses. I managed this movement in such a manner that I believe no one could know what I abstracted except Elizabeth herself, who seemed to care no more for the discovery than she had as yet done for any part of the ceremony.

"And the orange blossom," said I, "I have a fancy for this too," I said, as I, very gently I hope, took off the wreath, and, in spite of the necessary crumpling of so expressive an emblem of bliss, put it in my pocket.

The hubbub was now general, and Crispin thinking that his honour was touched, waxed magniloquent. He even put himself into a fighting attitude, and sparred away with all the valour of a gentleman called upon to protect injured innocence. Nor Dowsabell, nor Dulcinea, nor any other heroine of romance, had ever so formidable a champion; but then I did not choose to take up the snab's gage. I contented myself with stepping between one or two of the guests to the window, gave two or three knocks, and then took up my station by the side of Elizabeth. The door opened, and in came my assistant.

"I choose to claim this young woman for my bride," I said, with a little of an inward chuckle. "I will dispose of her property; meanwhile, all of you leave the room. Clear out, officer," I added, as they seemed to loiter and murmur.

And so to be sure, my assistant, to make short work of emptying the room, hurried them off, the last loiterer being the snab, whose look at Elizabeth carried as much of what is called sentiment as might have touched even her, who, however, received the appeal with the same cold indifference she had exhibited all through the strange scene. I do not say she did not feel. It is hardly possible to suppose that a young woman dressed for marriage, and in the hands of the police, with banishment before and shame behind, could be unmoved; but the mind of these creatures is so peculiarly formed that they make none of nature's signs, and are utterly beyond our knowledge. That something goes on within, deep and far away from even conjecture, we cannot doubt; but it is something that never has been known, and never will be, because they themselves have no words and no symbols to tell what it is. When thus left alone with her, it might have been expected that she would give me some token that she was *human*, but no; there she stood in all her finery, unmoved and immoveable, her gipsy face calm, if not placid, her eye steady, and without uttering a single word. "And now, Elizabeth," I said, "I daresay you know the reason of this intrusion; you are accused of having entered no fewer than sixteen dwelling-houses, and stealing therefrom many valuables, and I must apprehend you."

"Very well."

"Have you any more keys than those I have got?"

"No more."

"Were these all you used?"

"You can find that out; I confess nothing."

"Well, then, make yourself ready to go with me; get your shawl and bonnet."

And without further sign of being even touched with any feeling of remorse or shame, she proceeded calmly to put on these articles of dress.

"I am ready."

"Too serious," thought I, as I looked to a side-table and saw the wine and the cake. I wanted to give things a more cheerful look.

Was ever bride taken away without the "stirrup-cup", even a glass of her own wine?

But no, it wouldn't do. Elizabeth would neither take nor give, and so I, too, went without my glass.

"Keep the house," said I to my assistant, "till I return I will post the constables at the foot of the stairs."

And, taking Elizabeth by the arm, I sallied forth amidst a noise that roused the whole Cowgate; and no wonder, perhaps such a scene was never witnessed there before, certainly not since. Mrs Thick's hands were uplifted as we passed; nor was the wonder less among the other neighbours, who looked upon Elizabeth as a pattern of industry and strict behaviour.

After depositing my bride I got arrangements made for clearing the house of the stolen property. Every thing was removed except the table, chairs, and frame of the bed, and pages would not contain a catalogue of the fruits of this young woman's industry. But the recovery from Mrs Thick was a different process. I was up till four in the morning getting out and identifying the numerous articles of all kinds stored away in her premises.

By and by, my bride was tried before the High Court; and here I may be allowed a remark on the apparent callosity of people of her stamp. I have often noticed that these dumb, impassable victims are more ready at the end to give way than your loquacious asserters of innocence. I take this peculiarity for a proof that they bleed inwardly, and that while we are angry with them for being what we call unnatural, they are paying the forfeit in another shape. This extraordinary girl, after all her silence and apparent indifference, pled guilty to ten different cases of house-entering, and they were all effected by the two keys I took out of her pocket at the scene of the contemplated marriage. Fourteen years' transportation was her punishment, and she heard the sentence without a sigh or a tear.

I need scarcely add, that this was the only thief I ever discovered through the means of orange blossom.

The Pewter Spoon

❖

On going up to the office one day, about eighteen years ago, I was beckoned into his shop by Mr Davidson, hardware-merchant in the High Street. He seemed to have something to say to me of a very mysterious nature, for he took me ben to the back-shop, and shut the door. As for all this, and the long face, I pay generally little heed to such things, for I often find there is but small justification of the mystery inside the heads of long faces; yet I will not say whether in this case I was disappointed or not in my expectations.

"Do you know," says he, "there's a circumstance occurs in my shop, almost every day, for which I cannot account?"

"Silver disappearing from a till—a very common occurrence, according to my experience."

"No," said he; "pewter is the metal." Then, drawing closer to me—"There is a youngish woman, and rather interesting, with a mild, innocent look about her, who has come to the shop for a considerable period, always purchasing an article of the same kind."

"You don't sell picklocks?"

"No, nor is it anything in that way. To be out with it at once, it is a pewter spoon; and not being over particular in noticing either purchaser or purchases, I doubt if I would have remarked particularly even three or four returns; but she has been here almost every other day for months, gets the one solitary spoon, lays down the money——"

"Which, of course, you examine?"

"Goes away; nay, I have known her to come twice in one day for the spoon. The only construction I have been able to put upon the mysterious transaction, and even that appears to myself absurd, is, that she is abstracting, one by one, silver spoons out of some platebox, perhaps in her master's house, and replacing each silver spoon by a pewter one, to keep up the weight and apparent number."

"More ingenious than sound," said I.

"I confess that myself, and therefore am I thrown back to my wit's end."

"And not far to be thrown, in the direction of the nature of women," said I. "It is a far deeper affair than even your supposition."

"Well, I am dying to know."

"And will know before dying, but not till perhaps the day after tomorrow, that's Thursday—or Friday—it may even be Saturday; but know you will. Do you expect her to-day?"

"Scarcely, as she was here yesterday, Monday. Her double purchases are often on the Saturday."

"Not ill to account for *that*," said I. "You may look for her to-morrow, according to her routine. I am ambitious to make acquaintance with her, and shall walk opposite your shop to-morrow forenoon to wait for her. How is she dressed?"

"Always with the same shawl and bonnet."

"The ribbon is a good head-mark."

"Well, it is orange, the bonnet a chip, and the shawl a Paisley one, white, and a conch-shell border."

"A sharp colour orange," said I, curious as I am in these studies; "it even disturbs me, it is so penetrating. A woman like this could have nothing to do with green, and yet there is a verdancy about her; where, you won't guess."

"Where?"

"Why, in the absurdity of her repeating the dose upon you so often."

"Well, that very circumstance has induced me to think that she can have no improper purpose to serve."

"You don't know that vice has a weakness about it. We should always paint the devil with a limp."

"But, really," rejoined the good man, "that woman is so mild, so lamb-like, you know, so——"

"Yes, so like a fallen angel on the boards, that you can't suspect anything behind the scenes; just so. Well, you understand me—I am opposite your shop to-morrow forenoon?"

"Say twelve."

"Twelve; and you will be kind enough to come to the door yourself, just as she goes out, so that I shall know my 'nymph of the pewter spoon.'"

Leaving the shop, after thus arranging my net, which is generally not over-wide in the meshes, and as far as possible from run-holes, I proceeded to my other business of the day, scarcely ever recurring to the pewter spoon; nor do I think I would have been paying any compliment to other than very simple people if I had supposed that I saw further into the curious-enough-looking affair than ordinary observers might have done. Yet I was at my post on the subsequent day, pacing the north side of the High Street, on either side of the *Scotsman*'s stair, and noticing, without looking at, my "hopefuls;" many of whom, as they passed, gave a hitch to a side as they suddenly found themselves near me, and yet were ashamed to acknowledge their ingratitude to one who took so much care of them, when it would seem they could not take care of themselves. Among these was a *young* woman of the name of Maggy Blackwood, yet an *old* acquaintance. I saw Maggy eyeing me very keenly over about the Cross. It may be doubted whether I could detect the movements of a person's eye at that distance. I don't choose to make a question of it, yet I wouldn't advise any one, with the privilege remaining of wearing a silk neckcloth round his neck, to the exclusion of one of a coarser material and with longer ends than cambric bands, to place much confidence in my inability. I had, in short, no doubt Maggy was not only scanning me, but watching my movements. An extraordinary girl that,—her sister as well, nearly of the same age; both acute, and fitted for any business calling for my help. They had in their yet short pilgrimage tried all the games in the outlaw side of human life,—prostitution, pocket-picking, copartnership as sleeping partners with thimblers and card-sharpers, the department of "fancy girls" to blackleg lovers of the fine arts (of nature),—yet they had even till now passed through all dangers almost unscathed; at least, if burnt once or twice, they contrived not only to cure the wound, but even to conceal the scar. In the midst of all this, too, they had kept up a Siamese-twinship of affection for each other, and a sympathy of mutual resistiveness to the causes that generally so soon bring the career of vicious and dissolute women to ruin and death, of so binding and sustaining a character that, if their lives had been consecrated by goodness, one could not have resisted an admiration for them. The secret of all their success—for success it is to pass through such fires—was cunning, a quality which, like some walking-sticks, does well when green for support or guard, but when dry and old breaks and runs up into you.

No sooner had Maggy got her eye upon me, and seen me turn, than she walked quickly on, as if bent on some very commendable business, but not before I had observed the orange ribbon on the white chip, and the conch-shell border. "Ah, my nymph of the pewter spoon!" She had thought I was to come between her and her porridge, and therefore the spoon would be of no use. But was I to deprive Maggy of her spoon? Scarcely so. I stepped over to the office, to save her amiable timidity from the withering effect of my surveillance. I could calculate what time she required to go into Mr Davidson's, and get her spoon, and be out again.

And so, to be sure, it turned out; for, after waiting in the recess of the office-stair for only a few minutes, then going across the street, and placing myself a little deep in the mouth of a close, I had the satisfaction of seeing Maggy coming out of the shop, bowed out to the door by Mr Davidson, the light of whose face came over to me as a signal I didn't need. There was now little necessity for care, because Maggy was known on the streets; nor, as it appeared, did she and her sister keep her lodgings a very great secret, though they had no desire for calls or respects of dear old friends. All she feared was my observing her enter the shop; yet I saw the prudence of not throwing over her "orange" the shadow of my hemlock, and therefore kept at a distance, still following her, till she disappeared up a stair in the Grassmarket. I did not follow her into her room, because that step was not consistent with my mode of conducting such enterprises.

Bless you, that stair—with its flats looking out through their small eyes to the Grassmarket—and I were old friends; we had secrets of each other, and never thought of being perfidious in our loves and confidences. Even that afternoon, when looking about for a stray beam of evidence of any kind to assuage my thirst of light, as I went home to dinner, I felt an impulse that brought my finger softly on the shoulder of an old woman.

"Who have you living with you just now, Mrs W——?" inquired I.

"Twa lasses," was the reply.

"Their names?"

"Maggy and Bess Blackwood," she answered at once.

"Have they been long with you?"

"A gey while; maybe six months."

"And how do they live at present?" rejoined I, as I found her so very pleasant.

"Live! brawly, sir, aye plenty o' siller; very quiet, and never out till the gloaming."

"Any men going about them?"

"Seldom ane; they're quite reformed since I kenned them; they even let in a missionary at times, wi' a gey brown black coat, and a gey yellow white cravat, and after he gaes awa' the door's barred, and then I'm no sure but they pray,—only they never said sae,—but what am I to think?"

"A missionary?" said I, rather in a thinking than a speaking way,—no doubt, but *what* is his mission? I thought, as my mind began to play about the image of the pewter spoon. "And you think they bar you out that they may not be disturbed in their prayers?"

"Just sae, for Maggy especially is really very serious, sir; and then, they have a Bible; a queer book for them, ye ken."

"Well, Mrs W——," said I, seriously, "I like to see my old

pupils take to that book; and to satisfy myself, I intend to look up to-morrow or next day, between twelve and one. If you see me coming up, you'll take no notice any more than if I were the missionary himself."

"Just sae," replied she, with a kind of wink, intercepted by a look at me, whom she could not understand anyhow, for I was in the humour of gravity before dinner.

Having faith in Mrs W——, I had no reason to expect any interruption in my scheme. My pious ladies would only have more time for devotion, without any impediment to the purchase of the spoon; and it was not till the day after the next that I found myself in the wake of Maggy, with another of the same in her pocket. I allowed her to go home, to mount the stair, to get in to her holy of holies, and to bar the door if she pleased,—even half-an-hour more, just the time required for arriving at the middle of the use to which the pewter spoon would be applied, but cruelly allowing nothing for the ripening of the fruits left by the missionary with the brown-black and the yellow-white. At the end of that period, I went quietly, in my usual manner of the "taking-it-soft," up the stairs, put my finger as gently on the latch,—no bar then,—and introduced myself to the devout spinsters. I confess, I took no notice of the start and confusion into which I had so unceremoniously hurried them; but, casting my eyes round, I placed my hand upon one of a row of seven shillings laid up on the cross spar of the top of the bed—

"Tempting, Maggie, but hot," I said, as my hand recoiled from the touch of the burning coin. "Surely these come from the devil?"

The two spinsters had by far too much sense to make any protestations, or even excuses for burning my fingers; besides, they were transfixed.

"But so rude I am," I continued, as wheeling round and laying hold of a mould on the cheek of the grate, I turned out the half-impressed last coin, "I have even interrupted industrious women in 'the turning of a shilling.'"

"No use for your mocking mildness," said Maggie, as she bit

her thin lips, which she could not have bled for her biting, where there seemed no blood—so white they were. "We know it's all up, but I would rather a hundred times your sneers were damning oaths."

"And so would I," said Bess, whose words choked her.

And who should appear at that moment but he of the missionary vocation? but a most useless servant of his master; for if ever there was a time when his pupils stood in need of consolation it was now; and yet the very instant he saw me, he cried out, "M'Levy—the devil!" and bolted without leaving us a blessing! If he knew me, I also knew him. Having no assistant at the time, I could not follow him with more than my regret that he thus shied an old benefactor, for I had sent him on a mission to Botany Bay to learn good behaviour; but he returned, to take up the quadruple trade of a fancy man to my two nymphs of the pewter spoon, the utterer of the said spoon in the shape of shillings, the religious cloak of their knavery, and a most successful clerical beggar at the houses of the New Town, of small helps to widows in the Cowgate, dying amidst the cries of their famishing children. Yet I had occasion to overcome my anger some time after, by heaping burning coals on his head, in the form of a new mission to Botany Bay. I even did more, by sending out to the same place his two lovers before him, that he might not be without friends on his arrival, nor for seven years afterwards. But I am anticipating. When the shillings and the young women had cooled down so as to be fit for handling, I removed them to a safe lodging, and then went to dinner. In passing Mr Davidson's shop I gratified a whim:—

"What did Margaret Blackwood pay you for each spoon?" said I.

"Threepence."

"Cannot be, or you must be a very bad judge of the value of pewter."

"Why?"

"Because, see there are eight shillings made of one spoon, and supposing you had sold her forty, you have given for ten shillings no less than £16."

"Ah!" said he laughing, "I see I have been a little *spooney*."

Long Looked-for, Come at Last

❖

ONE of the least strange circumstances in my life is, that I seldom ever had any great desire to get hold of a worthy character without having it gratified. How that most adroit of all thieves, Adam M'Donald, did flutter my laurels! If ever there was a man who interfered with my night's rest, it was that man. For twenty-five years he had laid contributions on the good folks of Edinburgh; and yet, such was his caution, dexterity, and boldness, that he escaped trouble. Often apprehended, he was so successful in non-recognitions, alibis, and scape-goats, that he foiled every one. As my reputation increased, so increased my regret at his. At one time he was the aim and object of all my ambition. Yea, I would have given all my fame, to have it to earn again by the capture of that one man. We knew each other perfectly well, often met, and looked at each other, saying, as plainly as looks could do, "I know you love me, M'Levy, but I am coy, and will never submit to your embraces"—"Why will you not eat, Adam? the apple is sweet; and, if it should be the price of your soul, I will be a gentle master over you." It wouldn't do.

If I was a gentleman in charge, he was a gentleman at large. If I was curious in my changes of place, Adam was everywhere, and yet nowhere. If I was up to a thing, Adam was up to twenty things. If I was burning to catch Adam, as only one article, Adam was zealous to catch many articles without being caught himself. If I was vexed with disappointment, Adam was comfortable in success. Never was an Adam more envied than he was by me, and never an Adam more difficult to tempt.

It is said, that if you "wait *long enough* to become tenant of a house, you may sleep in the king's palace." I would have waited a hundred years to get possession of this man; but, probably, my good angel, Chance, thought I had waited long enough when the period came to fifteen years. Yet that was not the whole time of his triumphs, for that had extended to twenty-five—yea, he had been great when I was little, famous when I was unknown. And surely these fifteen years were enough. I certainly thought so, and some other detectives among the gods must have been of the same opinion; for in January 1835 it was reported to us that a gentleman had, on the previous evening, been robbed in the High Street of a gold watch, and it was suspected that the famous Adam was the skilful artist. To whom should this great business have been committed by Serjeant-major Ramage but to me, his natural rival in fame? Yes, that commission was the very pride of my life; and I set about its execution as if it had been a power of attorney to possess myself of a thousand a-year.

Yet the very boon was at first like a mockery. The suspicion against him was a mere gossamer web of floating surmises. No one would swear to him, and he was so defiant that I could not apprehend him without evidence to support my interference with the liberty of a British-born subject. I was pestered with advices,—a kind of contribution I never valued much, for, though they cost nothing to give, they are often dear to receive. One of the weaknesses of the regular celebrities is a kind of pride of a clever achievement, which (however unlikely it may appear to ordinary thinkers) leads them, as if by a fatality, to the scene of their triumph—ay, to the very repetition of the same act in the same place. Admitted that it is a weakness, I have often found it my strength. It will scarcely be believed, that at a quarter to seven of that evening when I got my commission, I was posted in the entry to Milne Square, in the almost certain expectation of Adam figuring again thereabout, and in the same way. There I stood, while Mulholland went with some message to Princes Street; and, before he returned, whom did I see pass, going east, but my friend Kerr, road-officer at Jock's Lodge—groggy, but not unable to take some care of himself? I knew he had a gold watch, which he guarded by a chain round his neck. No sooner had he passed, than I saw Adam, and a faithful friend, Ebenezer Chisholm, following and watching the unsteady prey from the middle of the High Street. My heart would have leapt, if I had not something else to do with its ordinary pulses,—and I could have wished even these to be calmer.

I do not say that it was a rather rebellious state of my case that made me in an instant old as ninety, and lame as palsy. With what difficulty and straining of nature I made across the street, eyeing all the while the victim and his followers. I saw them leave the middle of the street and betake themselves to the pavement, about the door of M'Intosh's snuff-shop, where they laid hold of Kerr, no doubt, as friends, each taking an arm of him, to help him on, and save him from robbers. At sight of this I got young again, my palsy left me, and I planted myself under the pend of Blackfriars Wynd. May Heaven forgive me for my adjuration, that that man, Adam M'Donald, should at that moment be put into my hands. Surely I might be forgiven the prayer when the prayer would be answered, but then it would not be till they took him to the King's Park, on his way home, where they could do their business undisturbed. Would they be fools enough to attempt a robbery of a road-officer, on the principal street of the city? Answer—I have already stated my ridiculed calculation. I saw them leave the pavement at a point opposite to the very pend below which I stood. In an instant, the feet were taken from Kerr, he was thrown flat on his back, with a sound of his head against the granite which reached my ears. Chisholm held him down; Adam, whirling the gold chain over the victim's head, rolled it up in his hand, along with the watch, and bolted,—Chisholm, at the same instant, making for the dense parts of the Canongate. But whither did Adam bolt? Into my very arms! Yes; I received him joyfully as a long lost friend. But that ingratitude, of which I have complained so often! The moment I clutched him, he commenced a struggle with me, which, if I had not been of the strength I am, would have ended in his escape. Excepting once, I never encountered so tough a job. The moment we closed in the strife, I could see his face marked with the traits of a demon, while a spluttering of words, mixed with foam, assaulted me otherwise than in the ear—"M'Levy, the devil of all devils!" responded to, without the foam, "Adam M'Donald, my love of all loves!" Nor did my grip, nor even my blandishments, calm him. He swung himself from side to side in sudden writhings, breathed more laboriously, flared upon me more luminously with his flaming eyes, which I could see in the dark; and yet he could not get away. I answered every movement by an action equal and contrary, and, as the crowd increased, his determination at length began to be less resolute. Yes, I had nearly conquered this hero of twenty-five years' triumphs, when Mulholland, having returned from Princes Street, and seeing a crowd down the High Street, made up, and laid his helping hand on my antagonist.

"Adam M'Donald," said I.

"Adam M'Donald!" echoed he, in wonder.

"Long looked-for, come at last," rejoined I.

"Yes, you have caught a man," said Adam, with a bitter sneer; "but nothing else. I defy you. I have done nothing that's wrong, and have no man's property."

"Here is the watch," said a man of the name of M'Gregor, who kept a tavern at the head of the wynd; "I was standing at my door when the robber came rushing in, and the moment you closed I heard the clink of something at my foot. On taking it up, I found it to be this watch. I give it to you, Mr M'Levy."

"I know nothing of it," cried Adam; "you cannot prove it was ever in my possession."

"I saw you throw down Mr Kerr on the street," cried a woman, looking into M'Donald's face.

"It's a lie," cried the infuriated demon.

"He's lying there yet, man," persisted the woman.

And it was true, for Kerr had been so stunned by the fall, added to his state of drunkenness, that he lay where he fell, and the rush to the wynd so confused the people that some short time elapsed before he was looked after. Just as we emerged from the wynd with our prisoner, they were assisting Kerr up. We left him in good hands, and proceeded with our prisoner to the office. I never was very fond of crowds to witness my captures, but in this case I thought I could understand a little of that feeling delighted in by mighty conquerors, crowned poets, and such celebrities in their way. We have all at times our portion of pride, and who knows, when I don't deny, but that when now taking Adam M'Donald to my stronghold I felt myself to be as great a man as any of them; for when had a conqueror watched fifteen years for his enemy? When had a poet taken as long to write his poem? The only difference between us was, that, while these think they are working for immortality, I did not just come to the conclusion that the capture of Adam M'Donald by M'Levy would be celebrated by anniversaries or jubilees. Not that I did not think that future ages, thus neglectful, would be ungrateful, if not foolish, but that I did not want to dwell upon it.

But there we are with our prisoner before Captain Stewart, after this something like ovation, as they call it, but of the meaning whereof I am doubtful; not so of my captain's reception of one who had been so long as a lion in his way; for no sooner did he cast his eyes on Adam than he exclaimed—

"Here at last! but, M'Levy," he whispered, "you have committed a grave error."

"Not at all."

"We have no evidence that it was he who robbed the gentleman last night."

"No more we have; but he has robbed another tonight, and, see, there's the evidence—no other than the watch of Mr Kerr, the road-officer."

"And where was the deed done?"

"Where, amidst all laughter, I said it would be—in the High Street."

"Most wonderful!"

I don't think so. They tell us that truth is very simple, and that lies are very knotty. I have yet a way of getting at the road where men are likely to travel, and there I meet them. I told you that robbers and thieves have a yearning for the places where their pride has been flattered, and so you see it is. Even Adam, the cunningest fox that ever went back to the same roost, with his ears along his neck, his eyes like fire, and his mouth all a-watering for the second hen, couldn't go against the common nature anyhow. But we have Chisholm to get—his henchman, a foxy-headed fellow too, who held Kerr down while Adam swept the chain over his head. I must complete my work.

But, here, as I went down the High Street again with Mulholland, I saw our difficulty in so far as Chisholm was concerned, for I doubted whether anyone saw *him* in the fray. He had learned of Adam, and knew of alibis, and scape-goats, and all the rest of the resources of men who put themselves in a position where they *must* be greater vagabonds still. So it was. We found he had gone into a publican's house in Carnegie Street, where he had collected a number of sympathisers, who were ready to swear that he was there drinking at six o'clock,—as so he might have been,—and thereafter, till long past the hour of the robbery, so that it was impossible he could have been engaged in it. Yet I was not daunted; we went to his house, and found him in bed by the side of his wife (?), who, the moment she knew our message, insisted that he had never been out of the house since six o'clock.

"That's true," he rejoined.

"An alibi everywhere," said I. "Your wife swears to your having been here; the man in the public-house in Carnegie Street, and half-a-dozen others, say you were there; and I saw you, with my blear eyes, in the High Street robbing Kerr at eight. You were thus in three places at one time!"

And my man was actually inclined to abuse my religion, because

I would not admit he was a god. I confess this roused me a little, and being, besides, impatient of his delay, I seized him perhaps more harshly than I am in the habit of treating my prodigals to get them out of the troughs of the swine, and give them bread and water in place of husks. Yet he was disobedient and struggled; then began one of those scenes which in my trade are unavoidable, and very disagreeable to a quiet man like me, who, if I had occupied the place of Simpson, would have done as he did with his children,—clapped them with the one hand, as kindly grooms do restive fillies, and put the kench over the head with the other. The wife clung to him and screamed; her fine black hair—and she was a regular beauty all over—falling over her back and shoulders, quite in the Jane Shore way, and looking, as it lay upon her white skin—where shall I get anything like it?—but what would be the use if I should try it, when I am satisfied you could detect nothing to come up to it anywhere, except in Mohammed's showroom of temptation? Then her arms were fixed round his neck, and I could see one or two rings, which should have been in my keeping, shining on fingers that were just as fine as any lady's; and why not? for she was "a fancy", and wrought none; and so she held on, crying and weeping, as the tears rolled down on a face so pure in its colour, and so delicately tipt off in the curved nose, with the nostrils wide from excitement, and the thin lips open too, and showing equally fine teeth, that my heart began to give way, though not a melter. Somehow or other, he liked the grip of this lava-Venus better than mine, and no great wonder, I suspect; and as she clung to him, and he to her, I could not separate them anyhow, until Mulholland, getting to the back of the bed, drew her to him, while I pulled him out.

"Hold her on," said I.

A request which my assistant—very modest man as he was—did not disobey, but he had no easy task, for the creature, who had got hysterical, writhed in his large hands like a beautiful serpent; till, at last exhausted, she sank in his arms, with her face turned up to him, and her beseeching eyes so fixed on his, that he afterwards declared, that if it had been possible to save Chisholm, he would at that moment have given two weeks' pay (40s.) to send him back to so faithful a creature. But I had something else to mind.

"Get on your breeches, sir."

But my prisoner was slow indeed; never before, I believe, did a man dress so slowly, with the exception, of course, of those who dress for the last home, under the impression that the clothes are to go, without a testament, to him who finishes all toilets with the hempen cravat. Yet there was excuse for him, which one might have found in his eyes, fixed as they were on the girl, as she lay still, as if dead, in the arms of Mulholland, and, it may be, not to be seen by him again, whose first step out would be in the direction of Norfolk Island.

I might notice all this, and have some qualms about my heart as I thought how strange it is that vice makes "no gobs" at good looks, but gets into very beautiful temples. Even Chisholm was himself a good specimen of the higher sort of the higher animals, and really the two should not have been what they were, nor where they were. But no help; away he must trudge. Mulholland laid the poor girl gently on the bed, and left her alone, but with little of that glory she might have been encompassed with in another quarter, if more fortunately fated.

M'Donald was easily disposed of at the trial before the High Court, but it was a tough job with Chisholm, who, with his witnesses from Carnegie Street, battled for his alibi in noble style. No use; they got a lifetime of the other hemisphere.

The Swan

❖

THE genialities of the most genial of us are not eternal; and I have found this in my own case,—not because my kindliness has been so often scorned, or received with anger if not oaths, but on another account, which the reader will scarcely suspect. We have all heard of the madman who went to the doctor at Morningside, and, with a grave face, opened his subject with—

"Sir, I am concerned about Mr ——," (the keeper.)

"Why?" answered the doctor.

"He is in a very bad way, sir."

"In what respect?"

"That's for you to find out, sir. It is for me, who hope I am a humane man, to take prompt measures for his benefit or I'll not answer for the consequences. I do enough to give you the hint. It is necessary, in the first place, that you shave his head; secondly, that you submit him to the shower-bath; thirdly, that you should bleed him freely; fourthly, that you should purge him; fifthly, that you bind him down with strong ropes to his bed; and, sixthly, that you set watchers over him of whom, for humanity's sake, I am willing to be one. I discharge my duty in making this announcement; and if my advice is not followed, you will abide by the consequences."

The keeper, though a genial man, could not have suffered all this without being angry. Neither could I resist a feeling of indignation at an act of a similar kind on the part of those under my charge.

For some time, in 1836, I was aware that many pockets were picked by two of the most cunning of their tribe I ever met, George or Charles Holmes (I forget which) and Angus M'Kay. They went always together; and if they had by their cunning resisted or baulked me,—nay, if they had even stood up to fight me,—I might still have retained my temper; but all the while the people were sending us charges, with complaints of emptied pockets, they were busy taking care of me. I believe, if they had had their will, I would have been shaved, bathed, bled, purged, bound, and watched; but their care was limited to the last. When I went home at night, I observed that they regularly followed me, saw me housed, and then went to play in their old way of lightening the pockets of the lieges. Nor were they content with seeing me home—they actually posted a companion of the name of Bryce, who went by the name of "The Watcher", to hang about my stairfoot all the evening; so that when "The Watcher" was not visible by them while plying their art on the Bridges, they could make certain that I was not in the way.

This was to my temper rather too much. I never cared for patronage, but these honours were hard to bear; and what made it worse was, that they thought I was utterly ignorant of all this care taken of me, just as if they were satisfied with the consciousness that "virtue is its own reward." I bear only to a certain extent, like the most patient, and that extent was reached. On a certain day, when I knew their pockets were absolutely filled with the results of their successes of the previous night, I observed them at their old patronising care. There they were after me, with "The Watcher" on the other side; nor did they leave me till they saw me safe in my house, at the foot of the Old Fishmarket Close, in the Canongate. For this kindness I could repay them in another way than by being excessively angry at them. They would be busy that night in adding industriously to their store, and my opportunity was apparent.

After taking my tea, I sat down and wrote a note to my assistant:—

"Send down an officer, and take up Bryce, whom you will find hanging about my stair-foot, and give him in charge at the office; then dress in plain clothes, and, with another man also plain, wait for me below the south arch of the bridge, at seven."

This note I despatched in a basket, carried by a girl who lived ben in the adjacent flat, and proceeded to effect as good a transformation in myself as would enable me to pass for a countryman come in to Hallow Fair, (then being held,) with, it was to be hoped, a hundred pounds or two upon him, received for stirks, in a pocket-book in the outer breast-pocket of his rough coat.

I was at my post by seven, and found my faithful assistant very well changed, and his companion along with him. I opened my plans to them, after being satisfied that "The Watcher" was safe. We then mounted the long stair leading to the North Bridge. We then separated, but only on the condition that we should never lose sight of each other. The streets were much crowded, in consequence of the fair. The big gudgeons, all supplied with the money derived from their sales, were stalking about; the mermaids were trying their fatal charms in every direction—not combing their own hair at so busy a time, but rather trying to tie that of their victims; and the sharks were plentiful, greedy, and shy as ever. There was that night more of concert between the two latter than we find in books of natural history, where they are represented as working on their own individual hook; but otherwise they were true to their kind: the yellow-haired sirens, when they got a victim in their arms, plunging with him to their caves—not pure coral—and there devouring him in the dark; and the blue sharks gobbling them up just where they caught them,—the one courting embraces, and the other shying them, but both equally fatal.

Of the real blue kind there were my patrons and keepers, Holmes and M'Kay—sharp, active, and hopeful—turning up their bellies every now and then, as they tried a bite. They were sure "The Watcher" was not to be seen, and therefore I could not be seen either; neither was I; and hence their confidence, and hence, too, mine. Perhaps the pleasure of that condition called *incognito*—into which, I rather suspect, all men and women, when their eyes have been glared upon by the disturbing sun of curiosity or notoriety, love to glide—was equal on both sides. Ay, where is the man and woman without their occasional mask? If you search well, you will *detect*, not only the skeleton which is behind the green curtain over the recess in every house, but also the mask which is in some spring-guarded drawer in the bureau,—often beneath the pillow,—sometimes at the back of the death-bed, when the parson (who has one often in his pocket) is praying over the expiring wretch; sometimes it is put into the coffin along with the corpse, so that no one shall ever know what deeds he or she, who looks so calm and innocent there, was doing for the sixty years of their pilgrimage in this world of masks.

Opposite Mr Craig's shop, my attention was for a little taken off my two friends—it was not my time yet to renew my acquaintance with them—by the attraction of "The Swan", a long-necked nymph, who was doing "Charlie [Holmes] is my darling", in a very good street style, to an admiring circle extending over the pavement. She was a true *Vesuvienne*, and a good devourer of the gold-fish, probably from that fine, long, white neck of hers; nor had I seen her at the minstrel trade before. Why now, when, in place of halfpennies and pennies—which I knew she despised—she might have been, like her companions of the lava streets, picking up crown-pieces, or perhaps pounds, which had been given for fat gimmers or stots in the forenoon? The question was only to be answered by me, and it was not a difficult one. I saw Holmes and M'Kay among her crowd, paying great attention to her siren strains—"The Swan" was not dying just then—that is, with their eyes; and, then, hands and fingers are not necessary to the enjoyment of good music. Nay, it was even with a little humour in his small gray eye that Holmes went and put something into her hand, very likely a small portion of the price of the foresaid gimmers and three-year-olds; and you could not have detected in "The Swan's" looks the slightest difference between the gratitude conferred on the giver and that with which she favoured some stalworth Peeblesshire feeder, who wanted to show his admiration of Charlie and "the darling" at same time, by giving her a penny.

I have said it was only I that could explain this. "The Swan" was the "fancy" of Holmes, and her singing on the street was just the *treble* of his *base* on the pavement. She collected the crowd, and he collected the money from the crowd, without the trouble of "Please, sir, help the poor girl,"—"A penny, sir, for the singer,"—or simply, "Please, sir." All that was unnecessary, when the fingers were even more subtle than the tongue. To say the truth, I was amused by the play, even to the suspending for a time my own proper part of the performance, if I did not entirely forget my anger at my patrons. Certainly, though I saw some smaller actors in the walking-gentleman line trying to do a bit of business, I had no heart for watching their pickeries, so insignificant by the contrast of the true Jeremys. I did not even notice our worthy captain, who, as he was passing to the office, stood for a moment listening to the assiduous damsel, as innocent of all this by-play that was going on, with his favourite M'Levy in the *rôle*, as if he had been one of the bumpkins from the grazing hills himself. It was not just then convenient to renew my acquaintanceship with him, so I let him enjoy himself a little, with the intention probably of reminding him next day of the figure he was cutting as a dummy, though the sharpest head in the city. At length he left, to resume his arduous duties in the High Street; and it was for me to let him go, if I was not glad of his departure, from a place where his presence could only interrupt, not only the playful tricks of my patrons, but my own.

But I must now act; to delay longer was to run a risk of being foiled, for so many good opportunities for the transference of pocket-books presented themselves, that my friends might succeed in a great effort, and be off, contented with their booty, without bestowing any attention on me. My assistant was behind me, and still kept his eye on me. I became still more entranced by the strains of "The Swan"; nor was Holmes—whom I now contrived to get near—less captivated. Though not requiring much elevation of the head, I was so intent upon catching every note of her voice, that I stood on tiptoe, looking over the heads of those before me, and with no more attention to that valuable pocket-book of mine—so proud of its contents that it poked its head out of its place—than merely sufficed to let me know that it was taken away. Could Holmes resist so ardent a gudgeon, entranced by a living, not a dying swan? Not likely, when he was, by my skill, just alongside of me, with M'Kay behind him, to get handed to him, if he could, that same pocket-book which was determined also to be in the play. I never put on a pair of handcuffs in a kindly way with more pleasure in the touch than I now permitted Holmes' hand to have its own way. My book was off in a moment, but not given to M'Kay before my assistant had Holmes in his grasp. The other policeman seized M'Kay. The strains of "The Swan" were hushed; nor did she begin again; she was too much affected to be able to sing when her tender mate was in the claws of the eagles. I was the victim, and required to keep up my character, in which I gained a kind of honour, or rather sympathy, which I had never before had an opportunity of enjoying. The crowd, many of whom were Hallow-Fair men, crowded about me, inquiring how much money was in my pocket-book; and I was in the humour.

"A hundred pounds; the price of six three-year-olds, and all I'm worth in the world."

"Might have been me," said another, "for I've as muckle in my book."

"But, Lord, how cleverly the villains have been nabbed," said a second.

"They'll no try that game again," rejoined a third.

All which I heard very pleasantly as I proceeded, still the victim along with the captors. Meanwhile my assistant retained the pocket-book, which he had caught as Holmes was on the eve of throwing it away. As yet neither of the fellows had recognised either me or my assistant, and they were indignant at being seized by unofficial personages; nor did they know in whose hands they were till they were fairly before the captain, who, as we entered, was sitting altogether oblivious of "The Swan's" strains, whatever effect they might have produced upon him while listening to them.

"Sir," said I, as I stood before him, keeping my face as much from my patrons as I could; "I have been robbed of my pocket-book, wi' the price o' a' my three-year-olds, by thae twa vagabonds there."

"Why, these are old offenders, I suspect," said the captain, not very well able to restrain himself, as he looked in my face and recollected how I had been watched and annoyed by them; "but I hope your money's safe. Let me see the pocket-book;" and getting it from Mulholland and opening it, "The price of all your stock, good sir; why, there's nothing in it but rags and paper!"

"Sold for nothing, by G—d!" said Holmes to M'Kay.

"More than your value," said I, turning round, and looking them straight in the face, in the midst of the laughter of the men; "and yet not so cheap as you think; search them."

A process not so soon accomplished, for out of every pocket there came various waifs, some of them singular enough; a net purse with two sovereigns and a penny, a small clasp leather one with some shillings, three or four handkerchiefs, two or three pound-notes crumpled up, a number of shillings and coppers, a lady's wig-frontlet carefully rolled up in a piece of paper, and other curiosities.

"We will get customers for all these to-morrow," said I; "so that it will not be necessary for the farmer to charge you for the price of the beeves."

"Who could have thought that it was the rascal himself?" muttered Holmes between his gnashing teeth.

"Ay, and he so snugly watched in the Old Fishmarket Close," said I, for a man has sometimes a pleasure to let an old friend know a grievance he (that friend) has put upon him. In short, I was for once revengeful in my humour, and what is the use of revenge unless the wrong-doer knows your triumph? "But we are not quite done yet," I continued; then, turning to my assistant, "Go to 'The Swan's' nest, and see if you can find any more of that kind of articles,—she may be a magpie in disguise."

"I only gave her a penny," said Holmes, sneeringly; "perhaps you'll find that. I've nothing to do with her."

"Beyond getting her to sing for a crowd you might work upon," added I. "You see you are scarcely masters for me; whom you took so much care of; but now I'll take care of you—lock them up."

And they were taken off, swearing and threatening in their rage and disappointment.

It was not long till my assistant brought in "The Swan", and with her a great number of valuable articles, of which she had been the resetter from Holmes. Many of them, on being compared with the books, answered the description of valuables robbed or stolen a good while before, and the charming singer was deposited in a suitable cage, where (*Charles* Holmes being her lover) she could sing, as she had done that night before,—

> Charlie is my darling,
> My young chevalier,

without adding *d'industrie*, for fear of hurting his feelings in the neighbouring cage. But by and by the tune was changed, when the Sheriff gave them their *terms* as old offenders,—not too hard terms either when it is considered how much anguish they had caused in many houses, not forgetting some anxiety in my own.

The Half-Crowns

❖

I HAVE often thought we are a little mole-eyed in social questions. How much were we to have paid the devil for our letting in mental food to the people, for the introduction of machinery, for giving up hanging poor wretches! and yet we have paid him nothing,—all movements coming to a poise. When I lay hold of a robber by the throat, we have a tussle, but it does not last long. Either he or I may be down; we don't murder each other; the forces destroy themselves, and there's peace. Where is all the expected crop of forgeries and coinings that were to spring up under the spread of the guano of education? The art of learning to write was to be the learning to forge, and electro-plating (if I can spell it) was to turn off half-crowns by the thousand. Nothing of all this. The people are better fed, the working men better employed, fewer murders, fewer forgeries, fewer coinings. I think we have rather taken from his majesty below, and I suspect he is fretful. What a fury we would put him in were we to take the young from him, of whom, in a certain class, he has had the charge since Adam coined that bad penny, Cain!

So I thought, when I told the story of the pewter spoons. I thought I had not another case of coining in my books; but I find I was wrong. Not long ago, in November 1858, I happened (I was always happening) to meet, at the foot of the stair leading to Ashley Buildings, in Nether Bow, near John Knox's Church, a clot of little boys and girls busy looking at some wonderful things, with eyes as bright and round as a new-turned-out shilling. On bending my head over the little people, and directing my eyes down through the midst of them, I found that the objects of their delight were a number (turned out to be a dozen) of beautiful glittering half-crowns and florins, all new from the mint. Was ever a nest of Raggediers shone upon with a blaze of such glory! Did ever her Majesty's face appear so beautiful to any of her loyal subjects!

On inquiry, I found that the urchins, when playing in the stair of Ashley Buildings, had found the pieces secreted in the corners of two window-soles. They were placed outside, so that any person going up the stair could reach them without entering any of the flats. I examined the places of deposit under the direction of my leaders—six of the pieces were on the window-sole of the first flat, and the other six on that of the highest. Then they had been cunningly placed in small-scooped crevices, close by the rybats. On coming down with my coins in my hand, and my troop around me, all chattering and vindicating their rights to the waifs, I was a little taken aback by the appearance of two ladies coming up the dark, dingy stair. At the first glance, and under the impression of the rustle of their heavy silk skirts, I took them for philanthropical grandees from the New Town on a visit of mercy to the hags of Ashley Land; and no wonder, for the very gayest of our crinolined nymphs, so far as regarded silk velvet and ribbons, were not qualified to tie the latchet of one of their boots. Nor was my impression changed when, standing to a side to give space to the swirl of their wide skirts, as well as honour to their progress, I looked respectfully, if not with a little awe (not much in my way) into their faces,—delicate, pretty, genteel, nor with a single indication of the flaunting lightness sometimes, in my experience, accompanying, but not adorning very gay attire.

On ascending two steps above me, one of them turned round, and, with an inquiring gaze, asked what was the matter, in a clear, bell-like voice, which was to me at the moment perhaps the more musical, because it came from such a delicate throat; but the speech was English, and we want that *spoken* music in Scotland,—at least there's not much of it among the denizens of Ashley Land.

"A little row among the boys," said I, just as a suddenly rising thought suggested something,—I won't say what.

"He's ta'en our half-croons, mem," cried a bantam, whose windpipe I could have squeezed.

Upon hearing which, my ladies turned somewhat abruptly, and proceeded down stairs. I could even fancy that the noise of their silks was increased by a flurry,—a movement altogether which I could not, even with the aid of my sudden thought, very well understand. On getting to the foot of the stair, and quit of my brawlers, I observed my two damsels walking majestically up the High Street, as if they had utterly forgotten their visit of mercy, for which their purses, and probably their Bibles, had been put in preparation. I had intercepted grace, condescension, and mercy, even when about to light, like ministering angels, on the hearts and homes of the miserable. Well, another time—mercy is long-suffering.

Just as I thus found myself a little satirical perhaps, up comes the man Richardson, who lived in Ashley Buildings.

"It's not often," said he, "that folks like me and my wife have lodgers in our small room like yon," pointing in the direction of my ladies.

"Like whom?" said I.

"Why, did you not see them coming out of our stair?"

"Yes, I saw two ladies superbly dressed; who are they?"

"Just my lodgers; your common lodging-house keepers can't touch that, I think."

"Why, no," said I; "but you haven't told me who or what they are."

"That's a hard question," replied he; "I can only say they are English, very polite, and pay their score."

"Any more?" said I; for although I had no doubt of the man's honesty, I did not wish to be forward with my half-crowns, as a "let up" in the first instance.

"Why, we are not sure of them," said he. "They are the strangest customers we ever had. They keep their door shut, and every second day there comes to them a man, as much a tailor and jeweller-made swell in his way as they are in theirs. Then the door is still more sure to be locked, and the key-hole screened."

"Did you ever hear his name?"

"Oh, yes—Mr Harvey."

"And theirs?"

"Miss Matilda Jerome and Miss Elizabeth Jackson."

"Is he English too?" inquired I.

"Yes, of the highest tone, but very condescending. He asks Mrs Richardson how she does, and she says, 'Quite well, I thank you, sir;' but this doesn't prevent her, you know, from sometimes trying a *chink*—the *keyhole* is an impossibility."

"And what has she seen?"

"Not much yet. The little is strange. The great Mr Harvey, the moment he gets in, takes off his fine suit and his rings, and puts on a fustian jacket and breeches. They work at something requiring a great deal of the fire, and then we hear *birrs*, and *clanks*, and *whizzes*—what you might expect where some small machinery is in gear."

"Producing, perhaps," said I, "something like *that*?" showing him a half-crown piece.

"Our very suspicion," replied he, as he took the piece into his hand, and seemed to wonder at the "turn out" of his little room. "But where got you it?"

"With eleven more, on two of the window-soles of your staircase."

"Hidden there by them?"

"I can't say," replied I; "but hark ye, when would be the best time for me to see the ladies and Mr Harvey together—if in the fustian, so much the better?"

"To-morrow forenoon," replied he. "They are all on the *stravaig* to-day."

"Well, in the meantime, Richardson, you are mum."

"Dumb."

And leaving my useful informant, I proceeded on my way, ruminating as usual. It didn't need a witch to tell the intention of the deposit, or the place selected for it. The false money would, of course, be dangerous in their room, and even in their pockets it would be imprudent to have more at a time than perhaps the single piece they were trying to utter. The deposit was thus a little outside bank, from which the three might severally supply themselves any number of times a-day; and though the bank stood a chance of being broken, they could lose nothing, while there would always be the difficulty of connecting them with it either as *depositors* or *drawers*. The scheme exhibited at least adroitness enough to satisfy me that the three were experienced hands. And yet, just observe the insanity of crime, whereby it renders itself a fool to itself. These clever people, no doubt, never thought that their splendid dresses, their engrossing admiration of their persons, and their exacting claims on the attention of those who would have been very willing to pass them by, only tended to the sharpening of official vision.

On making some inquiries at the Office, I learned that from what we knew as yet of the great Mr Harvey, there could be little doubt that he was a personage who for years had been driving the same trade in the south of England, where he had been often in trouble, and where not less than in London he was reputed as the best "coiner" in the kingdom. His companions were also known as adepts, whose beauty and accomplishments in another peculiar line enabled them to help the common store. Nor was Harvey limited to one department alone, being as well adapted and inclined for *taking* good money as for *coining* or uttering bad; so that viewing them as possessed of these three sources of income, we need not be astonished at their personal equipment. How little people know of the money that passes, like water over stones, through the hands of such gentry! The swell is talked of as a poor devil, with stolen finery, who lives merely in that sense from hand to mouth, which implies only freedom from want. A swell is not thus made up or maintained. It is an expensive character. The hunger and burst may haunt him as an inevitable condition; but as is the hunger, so is the burst with them—an extravagance this latter that would provoke the envy of many a fast youth, born in a mansion, and who runs through his property as fast as the horse he rides. I am speaking of England. It is seldom that we have the pleasure of seeing the true grandee here. Scotland is too poor for them. Yet I have sometimes caught them grazing on our lean turnips, when the English fields were infested with these foxes, the detectives.

So I had got on my beat no fewer than three swells, and surely a hunter of sorry thieves like me behoved to be on my honour. There is, I understand, a difficult etiquette how to *approach* the great, and how to *recede*, without showing to their circumcised eyes the back part of your person. Would I not require a lesson to save me from being dishonoured and disgraced by some offence against the code of genteel behaviour? Might they not smile at my Scotch bluntness and vulgarity, and refuse obedience to a baton of Scotch fir? One consolation at least—if the *rose* is for polite nostrils, the *thistle* is for thin skins. I scarcely think that I tried a rehearsal that night; but I was saved from all fears by my hope of being received by my great man in a fustian jacket; and as for the ladies, they might consider an Earlston gingham or a Manchester print sufficient for the trade of melting and silvering.

Next day I was on my watch, when about twelve o'clock I saw my great man enter the stair-foot of Ashley Buildings. The glance I got of him satisfied me that Richardson had not exaggerated his grandeur. Everything on him was of the best, and the jemmy cane showed the delicacy of the hand by which it was held, and by which, too, it was made to go through those exquisite twirls, so expressive of a total absence of such a thing as thought, always necessarily vulgar, when one is surrounded by vulgar people. I gave him time to be *natural*, that I might be *easy*: and then went up stairs, leaving my assistant and two constables at the foot. Mrs Richardson showed me in, but the mint was locked, on the principle of the Queen's establishment, where valuables run a risk of being taken away. I knocked and listened. Surely my grandees were in dishabille. At last my appeal, which they knew probably was not an usual one, produced uneasiness, so that the cool-bloodedness, which betokens high breeding, was reversed—low words, but quick—rapid movements—small chatterings. At length, perhaps a mere hazard, a voice inquired—

"Is that you, Missus Richardson?"

"No," replied I.

"Mister Richardson?"

"No," again.

"Who, then?"

"A friend."

And so the door gave way to the charmed word.

"Friend? why, a lie!" said the voice of a man.

"Perhaps not," said I, as I stood before them, and made my usual rapid survey.

I had been wrong in my expectation. The fustian jacket had not taken the place of the surtout, and my ladies were in the same splendid attire I had seen them in on the previous day, only the bonnets were not on their heads—adorned these with an exquisite abundance of fine hair, smooth and glossy, and done up in the first style of fashion. Yes, I defy you to have found in Moray Place more personable young women; nor if I had been there on a visit of condolence for the loss of one of their dearest friends, could I have found manners more staid and correct—I might add graceful, if I could lay claim to knowing much of the true and the false of that accomplishment. But all this I observed by one or two rapid glances diverted from my principal investigation, which latter yielded me at first but little: the indispensable bed—the table and chairs—the plate-rack, and some trunks. It was clear that they had resolved on no work that day, and no trace of their machinery was visible. My principal hope lay in an inviting press; and as I made a motion to proceed towards it, I thought I observed something like an indication that my gentleman would make free with the door; so applying my fingers to my mouth, I gave a shrill whistle, the sound of which echoed through the flat, startled my ladies out of their composure, and, what I wanted, reached the ear of my assistant, who, obeying the call, was instantly at the door.

I now proceeded to my work of search. From the lower part of the press I drew out the identical fustian coat and trousers described to me by Richardson.

"Your working-suit," said I to Harvey, who seemed to survey

the articles with extreme contempt. "A fustian coat," continued I, as I traced the blots of chemicals, and traces of quicksilver, and various scorchings, "is a thing I cannot but treat with respect, when it belongs to arms of independence. It is the fustian that makes the broad-cloth and the silks."

"They're not mine," said Harvey; "they must belong to the house."

"They ain't Mr Harvey's, I assure you, sir," said Miss Matilda Jerome.

"Perhaps not," said I, as I proceeded, "some people have a habit of possessing things that do not belong to them—*possession* just wants a point to make *property*, and perhaps this point is awanting here."

Forthwith I produced from the press several likely things—a bottle of quicksilver—some others with chemicals unknown to me—a portable vice with a screw to fix to the table, which latter had the screw mark upon it still—a hammer—files, coarse and fine—the indispensable stamp—but no galvanic battery as I was led to expect,—a circumstance which puzzled me, because I never could suppose that such adepts could be contented with the old process of salt and friction.

I had got enough for my purpose in the meantime, so, turning round—

"Please put on your bonnets and plaids, my ladies," said I, "that you, Mr Harvey, and I, may walk up the High Street to my quarters."

They obeyed with something even like alacrity, on the principle of that sensible man known to history, who, when standing at the gallows foot, said, "If it is to be done, let it be done quickly." Such are the advantages of having to do with genteel people.

I have no doubt we made an excellent appearance in our promenade up the High Street, only I doubt if any one could comprehend the possibility of such people condescending to enter a police cell. In searching the women we got, strangely enough, no bad money, but a considerable amount of good. The deposit on the window-soles had been intended for this day's work, and scared a little by its having been taken away, they had resolved on out-door adventures.

I still wanted something, as I have said, to complete the catalogue of my articles in the working department, and, above all, I required to connect Mr Harvey with that, so I applied to him for help.

"I wish to know where you live, when in town, Mr Harvey."

"In Mr Campbell's, Bell's Wynd," he replied promptly, affording still the same evidence of the advantages of having to do with high-bred people.

"Then you will please go with me and point it out."

"Certainly."

And getting again my assistant, I proceeded with him to Bell's Wynd, where, having mounted one of the worst stairs in that dark alley, we came to a wretched little dwelling of two rooms and a dark closet. How the great man could have put up in that hovel is difficult to conceive, except upon the supposition that the *swells* shrink when they get home. With the exception of a truckle-bed and a shake-down, there was scarcely a bit of furniture in the house; nor could I find a recess in any way inviting to me except the dark closet, which was adroitly barricaded by the mattress of the shake-down, upon which Mrs Campbell, a miserable invalid, lay in squalid misery. I made short work here. Laying hold of the mattress, I pulled it and its burden away from the closet door into the middle of the floor. A loud scream burst from the invalid, which, from her look I knew to be intended as a fence to the closet, and not an expression of pain. The door was not locked, the bed and its occupant having probably been deemed a sufficient bar.

"Ye've murdered me," cried the cunning wretch, so near her grave, and yet so keen in the concealment of vice. "The malison o' the Lord light on your head, and blast it! Haud awa'! my grave-claes are in that closet, and nae man will enter till that day when my soul gaes hame to glory."

"If you never die till you're *fit*, you'll live for ever," said I, when

I saw there was not a trace of grave-clothes in the dark hole,—from which, however, I brought the galvanic battery, which I had found awanting in Ashley Buildings to complete the apparatus, along with sixteen base shillings. I also got some other things of less importance.

"And now, Mrs Campbell, I will push you back again," said I, as I impelled the mattress to its old place.

"And the devil push *you* hame," she cried, "for you've murdered me."

And she groaned even in that way which aged people do when their wickedness is brought home to them; for that there was a complicity in these old people with Harvey, I had no doubt, even from the conduct of the harridan,—a conclusion confirmed by the assertion of Campbell himself that Harvey was his nephew.

I now took Mr Harvey back to the Police Office, thinking, as I went, upon the small amount of real happiness enjoyed by these adventurers among the rocks that lie in the midst of civilisation. Harvey's domestic comforts may be guessed from the account I have given. He was a man, and could bear the want of ease at night, in consideration of his privilege of walking the streets in a fine dress, and dining in the "Rainbow", with respectable people next box. But what are we to say for the women, with apparently delicate forms, and at least so much of feminine feeling as we might see shining through their really handsome faces? One might sum up all their pleasure in saying, that it consisted in promenading the streets in a silk gown. Even then they cannot be, and are not, devoid of fear. The same fear follows them home to an extinct fire, a truckle-bed with a few thin clothes, into which they huddle themselves, and try in sleep to get away from their own thoughts,—which thoughts sometimes go into the forms of dreams, wherein they take their own way, rejoicing in the tricks of a horrible nightmare. Such a being is everything but the woman she was intended to be,—her enjoyments everything but the affections and sympathies she was made to feel. Of course, I am assuming here, and I go upon appearances, that Miss Matilda Jerome and Miss Elizabeth Jackson were not originally Arabs. I might make another estimate in that case, for these are seldom touched by fear; and being against society, as society is against them, there is some inversion in them, the true nature of which, in enabling them to seek some strange kind of happiness, we cannot understand,—at least I could never understand it, and I have seen them in all humours. I suspect, however, that what we here sometimes call happiness, is only a kind of accommodation of misery. Thus they take the *sign* for the *thing*; and when they are roaring over the tankard, they think they are enjoying themselves. Perhaps they have more of the real thing in the hardness of their rebellion; for I think I have read somewhere, that man (and woman too, I suspect) is such a strange being that he can feel a pleasure in the very *spite* of pleasure. I can't say I would relish that happiness very much.

Well, I find I am at my old trade of spinning morals, without a touch of which I suspect my experiences would not be of much service to mankind; and if I had had no hope of that, I doubt if I would have been at the trouble of opening my black book of two thousand detections. I have little more to say about my grandees. They were brought to trial before the High Court, where, on the evidence of Richardson and his wife, the urchins who found the pieces, our own testimony, and the tale told by the utensils, they were found guilty. This was not, as I have said, the first, nor the second, nor the third time for the gentleman; but the ladies had never been handled so roughly before. Harvey got eight years' penal servitude, and the two belles five years each. As they sat at the bar, I could not help thinking of their appearance that day I took them for ladies of rank on a mission of charity and mercy. Surely our real LADIES, in their present rage for finery, never think how easily, and by what base copyists, they are imitated.

One word more on this subject. I am certainly not overfastidious as regards female dress. I have seen it in all its varieties, from the scanty cincture that adorned our first mother Eve, to the ingenious complications of modern taste and refinement; but I must observe, with all proper deference to the LADIES, that, in adopting the prevalent redundancy of skirt, the *imitated* have become the *imitators*, as the first of these "circumambient amplitudes" that I ever saw in Edinburgh, was sported by one of the most distinguished "Nightingales" that ever walked Princes Street. In fact, after the experience of thirty years, I find it almost impossible to distinguish the maiden from the matron,—the human vehicle for smuggled or surreptitiously acquired property from the sonsy housekeeper,—or the frail Magdalene, who knows there is a living secret to conceal, from the *robust* "habitante" just returned from an annual visit to her country cousins; nay, Paterfamilias himself, I have heard, on entering a cab or a box at the theatre, has *breathed*, if he did not *utter*, a heartfelt and pocketfelt anathema against such a superabundant and inconvenient display of hoop and crinoline.

Without attempting to quote the words of Pope as to "ribs of whale", I would simply say to all LADIES, as Hamlet said to the players, "I pray you avoid it."

The Topcoats

❖

IN the year 1845, a respectable agent in Aberdeen for one of the Steam Navigation Companies, having occasion to go down to the pier to look after some duty connected with one of the steamers, bethought himself, as he considered wisely, to put the contents of his cash-box in his pocket, so that before going home, where he kept his money during the night, he would not require to go back to the office. I have always found that people have more confidence in their pockets than even in a safe, though certainly thieves would rather reverse the faith, and I would be inclined to back them. There was a crowd on the pier, and certain parties, who love a jostle,—in which they have nothing to lose, but something to gain,—raised such a commotion about our agent as took his mind off his pocket, in place of directing it there, as all such commotions should. He accordingly lost his bag, containing about £60, part in notes and part in sovereigns. Though so far north, the young gentlemen who had "fingered" him did not show a northern adroitness in crying out, as they should have done, "Yonder's the thief making off through the crowd," whereby they might themselves have escaped notice. On the contrary, they tried to make off with their booty, whereby they brought upon them a sort of painful attention; for these gentlemen, unlike most clever people, don't like admiration or patronage, not due to their humility and love of retirement. Cries were accordingly got up, "They're off, yonder," where the fingers pointed, and two policemen, of the Aberdeen Doric order, went in pursuit.

It would appear that either the scent was too weak, or the Highland noses too strong—I mean not delicate enough for a man-chase—the most difficult of all hunts; for by the time they got to Union Street, the youths—for there were two—had hired a cab, and gone south by the coast line. This information I would have considered something valuable, and no doubt the policemen took that view as well. So getting another vehicle, with a fast-going horse, they began the pursuit; nor were they drawn off the scent, even among villages famous for Finnan haddies and red herrings, till they got to Stonehaven, where their noses became either faulty, or were not properly supplied with the scent of Laverna's ointment-box, as a learned friend once, in my hearing, called that unctuous mean whereby her children become so slippery. They, however, *caught* the driver of the young gentlemen's cab, and somehow he proved as slippery as they, having got himself anointed with the said unction, probably through the palm.

"You drove twa chields frae Aberdeen, didna you?"

"Oh, yes—perfect gentlemen——"

"We dinna want to ken whether they were gentlemen or no, ye breet," said one of the men, furious with his disappointment.

"It's not my fault if they *were* gentlemen," rejoined Jehu, who had been south; "nor am I to blame that they paid me handsomely out of a big purse. I like a man as is liberal."

"You're a tamned leear," said the other officer; "they're a pair o' big thiefs."

"Maybe we're wrang," rejoined the other; "we canna be sheer about them, for we never saw them."

"Oh, you didn't?" said the cabby, a deal sharper than the Aberdonian detectives; "then, you know they were gents—regular gents—a little out o' sorts in the garments, from roughing it, but regular gents."

"And whaur did ye set doon the fine gentlemen?" said the last sharp one.

"Why, at the inn, to be sure, where all as are gents are set down."

"And whaur did they gang?"

"I never looks after gents when they pays me handsomely."

"Then it's aw up, Saunders; we maun jeest gae back the road we cam'. Tam shame to set us on this wildguse chase."

"I'd strongly recommend your return," said the cabman, laughing within his teeth; "they're twenty miles on by this time, and you couldn't overtake them anyhow."

And these men-hunters, as reported to me, with noses so strong as to afford a good crop of red hair from each nostril, and yet so weak as to be unable to draw up a scent which, though I say it, would have made my olfactories quiver, actually did return to Aberdeen, with the opinion that they had been on the trail of gentlemen, in place of two of the most seedy blackguards that ever changed clothes with the proceeds of a robbery, and threw away the old habiliments behind a dyke. But, what was even worse, the authorities in Aberdeen did not communicate with us in Edinburgh. Meanwhile, and in perfect ignorance of the robbery, I happened to be coming up Victoria Street, with my assistant a little a-rear, when my eyes caught two faces, one of which was well known to me. Indeed, I may repeat, under the peril of a charge of egotism, that I can't forget a countenance if once its lines are well fixed in my mind; and certainly, but for this faculty, which works its way in spite of all changes and shifts of dress, or assumption of whiskers, or cutting them off, or any art of metamorphosis, I could not have recognised my old friend in his new dress, with his fine coat and overcoat, French boots, nobby hat, and so forth, all according to the highest style. Nay, there was even the air and swagger of a man of *ton*.

"Well, Jem, my lad," I said, standing right before him, "at what shop were you fitted? What an effect a change of fortune has! You were inclined to cut an old friend, and yet I have tried to put you on the way of amendment."

"What is it to you where I was fitted?" replied he, with that scowl of firmness which lies ready among the muscles to frown out at every instant.

"Nothing," replied I; "but something to you. I have a whim in my head. I want you and your gentlemanly companion up to the office."

"You have no charge against me," said he, doggedly. "Can't a fellow dress as he likes?"

"Yes," was my answer, "unless he meet the like of me, whose taste is a little put out o' sorts by inconsistency. No apology. Just come quietly along—don't want to shame a *gentleman*, you know."

And, upon my calling up my assistant, he saw that it was of no use trying a fight or a run, so gave in quietly, in that way they can all do, for they have a kind of pride sometimes in yielding handsomely.

Arrived at the office with my friends, I immediately stripped them of their fine top-coats.

"So," said I, "you choose not to say who was your tailor?"

The old answer:—"You have no business with that. What have our coats done?"

"Perhaps what the sheep's clothing did that covered a certain animal," said I. "No more argument. I detain you for inquiry."

Next day I had them before the magistrate, merely on the plea of the coats. I had no other charge; and I took this step, though I had as yet got no proof, with a view to justify my detention of them until, after a continuation of the diet, I might seek my evidences. While waiting for the case being taken up, a gentleman who was in the court came up to me.

"Why are you watching those fellows?" said he.

"Because I suspect they have been after some foul play, probably in the north."

"There's a robbery reported in the *Aberdeen Advertiser*," he continued. "I'd advise you to go to Harthill's and read it."

"Something better than the topcoats," I thought, as I nodded to my informant.

Having got the case continued, and the gentlemen again in their proper place, I set off for the Waterloo Room, where I got the paper, and read a very edifying description of my charges,—so true, that every feature corresponded to a nicety; but no mention of the top-coats. Nor did I expect it. Neither did I see then, which I did afterwards, that the Jehu at Stonehaven was perfectly right in admitting that his fine fares' clothes were only the worse for roughing it; only he might have said that nothing could be worse,—for the *Hue and Cry* described their habiliments as so very seedy, that they ran a risk of being shaken to the husk by an ordinary wind. That same afternoon I got Captain Moxey to report my capture to the Aberdeen superintendent, that he might reclaim his *protégés*,—a request that was immediately complied with. Nor did we fail to make them carry on their backs the topcoats, so that they might make as *good* an appearance as possible before the Aberdeen authorities.

But I was not destined to be done with the topcoats, for, as love or luck would have it, I was, two days afterwards, in Aberdeen at a Circuit trial,—and, as my reputation was pretty bright in the north, I was consulted by the fiscal, who thought that, as I caught the coats and what they contained, I might also catch evidence as to where they had bought them, as well as proof of where they had deposited the cast-off garments. I promised to do my best, and next morning I set off for Edinburgh, passing on my way Dundee. I was sure enough that there was no refitting at Stonehaven,—for according to Jehu's account, there was no time, whatever might be the necessity,—and bonny Dundee held out charms for my wooing,—a reluctant and shy mistress indeed, but I had conquered her before,—nay, in sober truth, a wide and dreary field, with the wind in the tail of my game. Yet the one sticking idea, to which I have already alluded, was there again in my head. The serpent burrows in the sand before casting his skin. They couldn't go to fine lodgings in that *travelling* dress of theirs; so, being acquainted so far with the town, I went to the Overgate, where the waifs are thrown up, among the rotten wood, dulse and tangle, and dead star-fish. Got a clue to a likely lodging-house, where tramps find rest to their limbs,—but, alas! not often to their minds,—up a very close close, then up a stair, at last confronted by a door. Knocked with a detective's hand, softly and gently; and why not?—crime angers us no more, however we may lament it, than does the dead subject the anatomist, who is to lay open the mysteries in that forsaken tenement where once was the warmth of God's breath. An old woman opened the door,—always old these door-openers, poor souls, for there is no joy outside to them, and they can, at least, let others more hopeful and happy out and in.

"You keep rooms for letting, my good woman?" said I.

"Ay; do you want lodgings?"

"No," said I, as I stepped in, and sat down; "but I want a lodger, or rather two."

"You look vexed, guidman," said she, gazing into my face, which somehow got full of sorrow on the instant.

"You are a mother, no doubt?" said I, lugubriously enough, and yet not all a feint; "but I hope you don't know what it is to have lost a ne'er-do-weel."

"Atweel do I," replied she, "and mair; but whaur are ye frae?"

"Edinburgh."

"And maybe ye'll ken Mr M'Levy, the thief-catcher?" she continued. "He grippit my laddie, Geordie, in Leith, and put him in jail; but they tell me he's no a hard man; and oh! if I could just get somebody to see him, and maybe he would deal gently wi' him. Ken ye the man?"

"I'm rather intimate with him," said I; "and if you will tell me your son's name, I will try what I can do."

"Geordie Robertson."

Bad case, I recollected; housebreaking in Leith.

"I will try," I again said. "And now one good turn deserves another. My two sons, I fear, are no better than yours—perfect vagabonds. They ran away last week, and I'm just seeking for them to get them home again to their disconsolate mother."

"Weel, there were twa callants slept ben the house last Thursday," said she. "What-like laddies are they? But, eh, fule that I am, ye wad maybe ken their claes?"

"Too well, my good woman; worn and ragged, I fear, and"—it would be out—"no topcoats."

"Topcoats!—the deil a topcoat had they, puir callants; but, Lord bless you, you maun hae gien them siller, or they maun hae stown it frae ye, for they came in next forenoon wi' new suits—topcoats an' a'—rowed up in muckle parcels, and then they despised the auld rags just as if they had been ashamed of them. They tirred to the skin, and awa they gaed like gentlemen, leaving the auld skins, as I may say, just whaur they tuik up the new. I'll show ye them."

And trotting away, she returned in a few minutes with the precious wardrobe,—a little the worse for roughing it, but gents' notwithstanding.

"The very identical clothes," said I; "and good *evidence*—of my misfortunes. Now, I'll just pin some bits of paper to the coats and breeches. Can you write?"

"I can sign my name—no muckle mair; but what for?" she added, suspiciously.

"Just in case they should deny that they have brought such a disgrace on their father and mother by wearing such beggarly clothes."

"To shame them, like?" said she, with a faint smile.

"Precisely."

"Just as they do in the foundlings I hae heard o' some-gate abroad, whaur they keep the duds, to mind the unfortunate creatures o' what they aince were?"

"The very thing."

"And a maist sensible thing, sir," continued the woman; "but there's nae care o' that kind taen wi' my Geordie."

"I will see about him when I get to Edinburgh," said I, as I cut the pieces of paper from the back of an old letter I had; and having got all the articles labelled, I got Mrs Robertson to mark them with her name. And now—

"I will pack them off to Mrs Justice," said I. "You will let them remain till I send for them."

"Nae doot, and thank ye, Mr Justice," said she. "But oh! will you mind that fearfu' man, M'Levy, and saften him wi' kindly words; and tell him I'm a lone woman, who looked aye forward to Geordie helping me in my auld age. Ay, just mak your ain case to him, and say that maybe his ain bairns may live to need the help o' a kindly hand, even like yours, Mr Justice, and maybe ye may saften his heart, and get him to deal mercifully wi' Geordie Robertson."

"I will do the best that Justice can do for him," said I, smiling inwardly at so strange a scene,—almost oppressive to me, however, for my playing, as it were, with God's favours, and repaying the use of His leading hand by a falsehood; which yet, for good ends, so far was justifiable, at least as His own world goes, and we go by necessity along with it.

And bidding Mrs Robertson good-bye, I hastened and got a man to carry the bundles, which I had addressed to the fiscal at Aberdeen, to the coach-office,—thereafter intimating my gift to the good Lady Justice, at the same granite city, by a letter, which I wrote in Mrs Hendry's inn, near the Fishmarket.

So far I had succeeded according to what I have always thought my luck, but which a friend has often told me is something he calls instinctive logic,—words I can't well detect the meaning of. Whatever it may be called, it must again serve my purpose in respect to those top-coats, the source of which had become a *crave*. I beat about till I came to "The Globe," where I entered with that question in my mouth I have put so often, and to so many different kinds of people. Finding a likely face—

"Did you, about Thursday last, fit out a couple of young men with clothes?"

"I think I know what you mean, Mr M'Levy," said he, smiling in my face,—an Edinburgh shopkeeper come over here, but quite unknown to me there. "Yes, we did; and what is more, I knew one of the fellows in Edinburgh; but we had no right to refuse their custom, you know."

"What did they buy of you?" asked I.

"Why, whole suits. They were quite flush of money, and I'm rather astonished they did not fear exposure, from the contrast between the shabby outside and the rich pockets within."

"Any sovereigns?" said I.

"Plenty."

"Such gentlemen couldn't do without topcoats."

"Not likely, in this cold weather,—and with delicate constitutions, you know," smiling.

"And tender training," I added.

"Ay."

"Read that," handing him the Aberdeen newspaper, "and tell me if that description applies."

The young man glanced over the "Literary Portraits"—"The very men to a hair."

"You served them yourself, and can speak to their identity?"

"Yes, we don't forget these customers."

"Not likely," said I, as my mind recurred to what I knew of their habits. "No customer, I suspect, like a newly-enriched thief,—never hucksters, nor haggles, nor chaffers about shillings?"

"No, nor pounds. Then, they get so fanciful. They buy whatever is most fashionable, cost what it may."

"I see you know my children," said I, inclined to be more communicative to this intelligent lad than I generally am. "Yes; they put on a red hackle to catch a gudgeon like me."

"Or a golden pheasant's feather," said he; "no doubt fond of the *Dighty*."

"Or make themselves phantom-minnows, to tempt me to rise more effectually."

"Yes, or even a 'terrible devil,' to make sure work," added this knowing dealer in soft goods.

"Well, but to business," said I. "There can be no doubt they got the topcoats from you?"

"The match of that hanging there," replied he, pointing to a coat.

"The very twin-brother," said I, as my eye glanced on the 'charming' garment. "Ah, ironed by the very same goose?"

"The same goose."

"Your name?"

"James B——."

"Some more gifts to Justice," I muttered to myself, as I left him, to make a study of any indications I should meet of St Crispin's qualities emblazoned over doorheads. I tried only one before I entered a likely shop, into which I was tempted by seeing in the window some showy French goods,—the pheasant's feathers.

"You deal in French boots, Mr G——?" said I, bowing as I entered.

"Yes, sir," replied the man, "but I would recommend our good Scotch make, such as these;" and the garrulous dealer went rattling away in the old there's-nothing-like-leather way; "why, sir, these Frenchmen beat us hollow in fine work, but—would you believe it?—they are perfect cobblers at a coarse, useful, crush-clod article. They seem to lose not only their genius but sense in it, just as if they thought they threw away their work on it. No, sir, they can't comprehend a neat-rough, or a rough-neat, anyhow, and so make a bungle."

"Let me see those boots in the window," said I, after allowing his wind fair swing.

"Jacques Moinét, Rue de St Hilaire," I read out, and compared within, as I remembered the name on those slight and genteel feet-coverings I had helped to draw off from two gentlemen in the office in the High Street of Edinburgh so shortly before.

"Did you sell two pairs of these to a couple of youths on Thursday last?"

"Yes; they said they had been roughing it in the north, and had got out at elbows a bit; but plenty of money."

"Sovereigns?"

"I saw they had them, but they paid me with a couple of notes."

"How did you come to get notes and yet see the sovereigns?" said I.

"Why, no doubt a little weakness, to show they were gentlemen; when the one drew out his notes, the other brought forth a handful of the gold bits, and so generous were they to each other, they seemed to strive for the honour of paying."

"Then you thought them gentlemen?"

"Only from the excuse of roughing it, and the money," replied he, with a smile; "otherwise, I would have thought them Q.C.'s; not exactly Queen's Counsel," he added drily, "but queer customers."

"Something in that way," said I, handing him the "Literary Portraits," and then watching to study the face of this also rather Q.C.; and truly, if it had been one of the children's mock phizes, made out of India-rubber, it could not have gone through its twitches of transformation more ludicrously.

"The very men;" he cried, as he burst out into a laugh, with the identical India-rubber wide mouth; "the very men, sir. You have got the foot-mark in the soft mud."

"Your name on the door?" I rejoined.

"Yes."

"And you can speak to the gentlemen, if you saw them?"

"Perfectly. I could have no hesitation."

"And perfectly willing, I presume?"

"Yes, if called upon by the authorities."

And so, I finished my labours in Dundee, which were something to amuse me on my journey south. I immediately despatched the names, with a short jotting of precognition, as a companion to the bundles; but, oh, the vanity of human wishes! The reader will scarcely credit me when I tell him, more pathetically than lies in my way, that these children of mine were insensible to, nay, ungrateful for, all this trouble of their father, Mr Justice. They actually refused my gifts; for when tried at the next Aberdeen Circuit, they pled guilty, without intending amendment; and thus all my trouble was comparatively vain, except that they got "twelve months" to think over their ingratitude to their loving, but disconsolate father.

The Belfast Key

❖

I HAVE never been able to ascertain where all those images of people go to in my mind. I am sure they are not packed up, each with its little film of card away back, the last got being always nearest the eye, like a barrel of herring on its side; for in that case I could not get out some fifteen-year-old one, as I do so easily, to confront it with some of my children, who have been away round the world and come back again. Nay, the older they are the brighter they are, and then they don't trouble me any more than if they were dead,—like the flies in Dr Franklin's bottle of Madeira, I have read of somewhere,—and are always brought alive again just when they're wanted. Neither do they trouble me, as they certainly do others, who have what they call a fancy, where the little things are eternally getting restive, rising up and flapping their wings, and flying hither and thither in confusion, bothering the soul, so that it becomes terrified at midnight with ghosts and phantoms, and producing hysterics, and Heaven knows what more. I have no fancy. If I had had, I would have been dead long ago; for how could I have borne such a host of thievish and murdering-looking likenesses of banished or hanged men, rising up on me in myriads, and haunting me everywhere, as if I had banished or hanged them in spite of the innocence they all protest, and sometimes look so much like? No! thank Heaven, I sleep, and have always slept, not like a top with its unobserved whirl, but like a log. And if I should be wakened, to catch some Bill Brash who has taken it into his head to come back from Norfolk Island, whither I had sent him, I find the image of Bill as ready at my call as if it had been fluttering and tormenting me all these seven years.

It is now a pretty old story, that of the lifting of two piles of valuable tweeds—worth a hundred guineas—from the door of Mr Young's shop in the High Street. I got notice almost on the instant, and hastening down, saw how the affair had been managed. The glass door inside had been shut, and the piles had lain on either side of the space between the outer door and the inner. The affair looked curious. The piles were four feet high, and every web rolled on a pretty heavy piece of wood, so that it would have been a considerably tough job to have *snatched* even one and made off with it in the very heart of a passing multitude. The shopmen had, of course, their theory, as all people in such circumstances have. There must have been, they thought, at least half-a-dozen about it, each taking a piece and running off with it, just as ants do their bags when they want to get them out of the sun. I knew better; such a scene would have been noticed outside, because the very *succession* of the liftings would have taken greatly more time than the pauses of passengers could have permitted. In short, I saw that one person could do it better than a dozen, taking quietly, after a survey, first one web and then another, depositing in succession, and coming and going. Then there was the inevitable conclusion that the webs were not far off,—a great point; but the webs *were* deposited, and would be where they were; so my case was not one of chase, and Time to be taken by the forelock.

Nor was I long in getting my theory confirmed. Just as I was inquiring up and down for a hint, I met a woman who said she had seen a young man turning the corner of Borthwick's Close, with a piece of cloth under his arm.

"One piece?" said I.

"Ay, ane," replied she, a little groggy; "and plenty, for, my faith, he was staggering wi' the weight."

"Do you know where he got it?"

"No; but he looked as if he had come up the street, and what was I to think but just that he was a snip? and then they aye walk quick, the snips, they're so glad to get on their feet."

"They don't stagger, though," said I.

"Sometimes on 'little Sunday,'—that's Monday,—for they're aye a day or twa ahint the other workmen in their weekly jubilees."

I listened patiently, for I never repress witty witnesses; their conceit makes them say more than your grave informants, who have no tickling inside their clay heads.

"Did you see enough of him to enable you to speak to his appearance?" I inquired again.

"Only the hinder-end," said she, with a groggy smirk, "which is aye big in them. I could swear to the hinder-end o' a snip, but no to a particular ane, for they're a' alike; the swivel, too, that maks them rock sae when they're in a hurry, is a' o' a piece; and then, they aye snuff with the right nostril, which they haud to a side, to save what they're sewing."

And so on she would have gone,—for, as I have said, she had had a dram,—but I had got all she could tell, and, inquiring her name, I got on with my thoughts. Could it, after all, be possible that this bold fellow had returned and returned to the treasury, and picked off twenty bales of goods all one by one? The man that achieved this was worthy of my acquaintanceship, and even this consideration alone would have inspired me to a capture; but then, such an artist could scarcely have been unknown to me, unless he were a new importation, and that was unlikely, for he must have arranged his resetting-place, and have known the closes.

On what I had got, my theory was formed. Going down to Hunter's Square, I went south by Blair Street, till I came to the Cowgate, and then along to the foot of Borthwick's Close; I then stepped into a grocer's shop,—always the historical register-office of the neighbours, who can't do without their penny candle, red herring, and ounce of tea.

"Any strangers about the close, Mr Heron?" said I.

"I believe the turner's son has come home," he replied.

"You mean by the turner, the old man whose shop is there, but who lives elsewhere?"

"Just so."

"But Brash can't live in the shop?" I rejoined.

"Not sure, the father is weakly, and has not been working for some time."

"And perhaps the son may sleep among the sawdust?"

"Not unlikely. I'm sure, at least, he hangs about here, for I saw him lig-laggering wi' the women opposite my window yesterday."

"But he has never bought any cheese, or herring, or bread, or a candle, and taken it away as if to use them somewhere here about?"

"Yes; he bought bread and herring yesterday,—no candle,—and he went up the close with them."

"If he had been living with his father, he wouldn't have come here."

"No; the family were never customers of mine."

So far well enough. There was some one in that close, who, if *my* memory served me, was very well able, from *experience*, to do the bold and clever thing that had been done; but it was no business of mine to be seen thereabout just at the time when I wanted somebody, and when some other body might say to another body, that M'Levy was there, for the people had got into their heads that I could be nowhere but where I should be. I would rather, at that juncture—it was now getting late—be among the light-o'-loves. Really, in these very squeamish days I know not how to get rid of my old vocabulary; we used to have good sturdy names for a certain class,—not those of Mohammed's paradise, with the black eyes they have at their heavenly birth, but those who have black eyes of another kind, generally given by one to another, and not just so productive of love. So I have been careful in avoiding slang,—a kind of language rather beneath me,—but then, certain names are useful, if not necessary. Were I a scholar, I might coin an appellation for them—not a reproachful one, perhaps; for vicious and immoral as they are, alas, who can tell the insidious temptations that were employed to render them the fallen guilty beings they have now become,—outcasts possibly from a comfortable home, to become the criminal creatures you now behold? Under whatever name you like, I was accordingly soon there, with a notion, not at all unjustified, that my tweed-lifter—like other people who have done a great feat and made a fortune—would, in place of going home and snoring out his triumph, go where "pleasure waits him," were it for no other purpose than just to give his relieved heart some play, or get some recompense for his trouble. And who that by his own hands had made £100 in half-an-hour, upon a capital of a bad shilling, would not feel happy, and inclined to be among merry people, like these black or blue-eyed damsels, always jovial, even in the very midst of their wretchedness and tears,—not tears of joy, pure and unmixed, as they were wont to be in their days of innocence, and before this moral blight had fallen upon them.

I was thus naturally led to Hyndford's Close,—a very good specimen of a rut in a dried stream of lava, which, I fancy, is just a kind of cinders. I went through several *establishments*; and last came to the great one, with nine or ten beds, if you can call by that name the four fir-posts, with the lath bottoms, and the pieces of yellow cotton sheets, and scarcely less yellow blankets, and strips of old carpets or horse-cloths spread over them, and the pillows,—little bags, sometimes filled with teased oakum, among which I have often found jewels and gold watches. In that house I once discovered as sharp a trick as ever I played, if it was not sharper than the discovery. I had traced a £20 watch to the pocket of "The Crow," and there lost it just as she was supping her sheep's-head broth out of a capacious bowl, with what they call a horn cutty. I searched about everywhere and could not find the watch, yet I was certain it was in that room. I had almost given up, when I noticed her very slow with her kail. I knew it wasn't fear prevented her satisfying her appetite, for "The Crow" feared me no more than she did her mother, whom she was in the habit of thrashing, because, as she said, the old woman had taught her her trade. There must be some secret under this sudden want of appetite. The kail would not go down in the bowl, because she would not put them down into her stomach. I suddenly caught a thought. "Let me taste your kail, Bess;" and my first sup was of the watch, which she had slipped into the bowl when she saw me enter. When she took flight to the South Sea, I would have taken a year from her banishment for her magpie trick, Crow as she was.

I need not say how vain it is to question these queens of Rougedom—another modern name—as to any gentlemen of the light-fingered tribe being among their subjects,—unless you are to go direct contrary to their contraries,—nor with what confidence they lie in your face as they hold up their queenly countenances. They are all of a piece, these queens, and a strange piece indeed. You may know every section by mark,—the purple face, always with a rotten-like tumefaction about it, set on the thick bull neck, which again is placed on the untidy bosom—beneath which a heart throbs, rankling with bitter feelings against society, whose laws have excommunicated them from its pale,—all surmounted with the sleazy mutch, set off with a crop of faded French flowers, collected from her subjects. And there is pride in this corporation, as she looks big, talking of "*my* house," sometimes, at least once in my experience, "*my* establishment," "*my* young ladies;" sometimes these one day without a shoe, and the next (a pawn redemption-day) decked out with articles every one of which has its eventful history; how it belonged to some fine lady in Moray Place,—how it came down to the lady's maid,—how it ran the gauntlet of passing turn about among the household, with a dogging envy of its possessor for the hour,—how it had charmed a "colley" from George Square to Hyndford's Close, where he lost his watch,—how it has been pawned a hundred times, and yet retained its power of drawing.

Even with so proud a dame I seldom did more than give her a nod, as I opened the door and took my walk, as I did now among the beds and cells. I searched everywhere,—all the working bees out among "the flowers of Edinburgh" to bring home the *honey* in the shape of *money*,—but there was, far ben, with a window looking into a ruinous area to the east, a room I remember very well, and the door of which I had passed. I returned to enter, but found it shut, and locked inside. These crazy hindrances I have often made short work of, by putting my back to them, in obedience to which they generally fly open, with the advantage of anticipating the preparation the inmates honour me with. I applied that force-key now, for I knew that any suspected denizen of that inside heaven would rather jump the window for the opposite place than welcome me to his bower of bliss. A gas-burner was flaring away right in the faces of three persons, two women and a man. I saw nothing, of course, but the three faces, with the six eyes looking clear, but in nowise bewildered with anything like consternation, only the man did not seem easy in a position which, judging from the apparent cosyness, he might have thought enviable by *some* whose tastes lie in that heavenward direction.

"You seem to be very comfortable, my friend," said I; "I am sorry to flutter your wings in that paradise."

A growl repaid a handsome compliment; but such is the way of the angels in these paradises.

"I will thank you to get up," said I.

"Don't, Jim; he has no right," said the guardian angel on the left.

"Ay," said the other on the right, "what right have you to disturb *decent* people in their own apartments?"

"Come, I say, get up; don't you see I'm waiting?"

"Shan't," growled the man; "you've no charge against me. I came to Edinburgh only yesterday."

"Where from?"

"Belfast."

"What street?"

"Huntly Street."

"No such street there, I suspect," said I. "Come, get up, and dress, and the ladies can cover their faces with their hands."

"Won't do, Bill," whispered the left one; "it's M'Levy; if anything's wrong, it's all up."

"So you won't rise?" I persisted.

"What for?" roared the swain, getting at once into a rage, as he probably contrasted our cells with his present angel-guarded position.

"Just to don your clothes," said I; "I want to know if, by searching, you can find anything in the pockets which I may think curious in the arts; but I have some delicacy in rifling pockets. There may be money in them, and you might charge me with a deficit. Come."

"I never rifled pockets anyhow," said he, as he fixed his eyes on me, with a look that did not change my conviction that I had had his image for a good many years in my mind, associated with the honours offered to him by a judge, and a jury, and a full court, before he sailed for Norfolk Island.

Yes, even though thus translated, with the light of his sister angels shining on him, I knew him the moment I threw my eyes over him.

"Well," he cried at length, as he started, and stood before me, yet, I thought, under the belief that I did not recognise him.

"Quick and cover; here's your breeches. I will be your footman; here's the vest, and next the coat, stockings, neckcloth, boots,"—all in succession, with proper intervals. "All right; now you are in a position to appear before the ladies."

"What next?" said he, sneeringly.

"Ripe, and tell me what is in your pockets."

"There's a handkerchief," said he, pulling out, "a penknife, a quid of tobacco, a pipe, a bit cheese, an empty phial,—that's all. Does any one of them belong to *you?*"

"Nothing more?" said I. "Try again. I thought I heard the phial strike against a bit of steel, perhaps a key. Come, out with it; I am curious in keys."

But he wouldn't.

"I'll help you, my good fellow," said I; "you know I'm your flunkey."

And plunging my hand into the right outside-pocket of his coat, I brought out a good-sized outer-door key.

"Where's the door that key opens?" asked I.

"In Belfast."

"Belfast again, and in Huntly Street! No doubt the house will have a number too—10,060?"

"No. 11."

"Well, we shall go there to-night," said I. "Are you ready?"

And not waiting for a reply I took him gently by the arm, and moved him out. The inevitable all-up was now in the ascendancy, and he went like a lamb till we got to the High Street, where I gave him in charge to my assistant, there waiting. I had the key in my hand; and, coming to Borthwick's Close,

"This way," said I; "I have a call to make before setting out for Belfast."

Nor did I take any notice of the change that, like a flash, came over his countenance. He was a ruddy healthy fellow, new from a voyage, and had not yet taken on the close-colour, but he was in an instant pale enough to satisfy even Despair herself. Proceeding down the close, my man and assistant before me, we came to the turner's shop.

"I want to go in here," said I.

"I have nothing to do with that place," said he; "this is not Huntly Street, Belfast."

"No, nor No. 11; but just you open the door," (handing him the key,) "and let me in."

Though the key seemed to burn his fingers, he was yet so satisfied of the all-up necessity, that he seemed to grasp it nervously, and proceeded with his own hand to open the door.

It was much too dark to see into the hole, but there was light in an opposite window; and getting, upon a rap, the end of a halfpenny candle, I came over.

"I want to see," said I, "whether this turning-lathe turns out any tweeds."

And straightway our eyes beheld all the webs of Mr Young's two piles of cloth, built neatly up against the wall. I counted them carefully, for I had a pride in the exact number—thirty pieces, all there, not one wanting.

"You can identify these, Mr William Brash," said I, looking my prisoner directly in the face, "as the webs of cloth you stole from Mr Young's shop-door some four hours a go?"

"Brash, not my name."

"Not now, but it was before you went on your travels; for which jaunt you were indebted to me, I rather think."

His courage couldn't stand my last appeal, and he seemed as well satisfied that I could do no more for him as any one with a cancer could be with the doctor who administered a hemlock poultice, which could nip, but never heal.

Having taken him to the office, and provided for him carefully, as a valuable addition to our stock of moral curiosities, I got the thirty bales up, which were all safely delivered to Mr Young; but that gentleman, I rather think, had no less difficulty in accounting for the seizure, so near his premises, than in understanding how these thirty heavy pieces could have been carried away, in so short a time, by one man. That there were no assistants, was admitted by Brash himself who was sent abroad a second time for ten years.

The Padlock

❖

IF we are required to be sharp, why not? Is it not that there is sharpness brought against us? If we had honest people only to deal with, we would not be needed; if only the committees of mistakes and blunders, we would require only common acuteness; if only honest rogues to expose, we would do with merely ordinary powers; but when we have to encounter ingenuity, sharpened to a razor-edge by rapacity, dishonesty, and fear of punishment, we must be even more than razor-edged. It is impossible to form any idea of the wonderful devices of practised thieves without being acquainted with them. Just look at animals with instincts of preservation, and see how wonderfully they work them; and then consider that men and women have not only these instincts, but reason to help them, and you may come to have a notion of what such as I have to encounter in bringing offenders to justice. I offer a case that may help you.

Sometime in 1856, two stots were stolen from a park in Linlithgowshire. Information was sent to us, with a view to discover whether the beasts were disposed of here. Stephen Cook, an Edinburgh man, was suspected; but the Linlithgow officers, taking the charge very much upon themselves, chiefly conducted the investigation. I did not interfere, having something else to do. The Linlithgow officers failed. They were not even sure that Cook had stolen the beasts; and as little were they successful in getting hold of Cook, who was a very mysterious kind of being. Some of the butchers seemed to know such a man as a kind of middle salesman, occasionally selling them a beast, which, as they thought, he purchased from some grazier; but where he lived, or how far he engaged in this trade, they could not tell. Having paid him the money, they were done with him; and no suspicion ever entered their heads that he belonged to the Rob Roy order.

Though not undertaking the search in 1856, I was impressed with some kind of romantic idea, which had taken hold of the Linlithgow officers, that Stephen Cook was a mystery. His mother's house, in Allan's Close, was known; yet this gave no clue, for the mother knew far less about her son than any one else. He went about the country; he was neither of this profession nor that; he was seldom or ever with her; in short, she knew less about her son than even the Linlithgow officers, who thought they knew he was a cattle-lifter, as well as a cattle-seller. These notions stuck to me, and often I thought of Stephen Cook, for whom, indeed, I retained a kind of affection, merely because, like other people, I am not proof against mysteries. There is only this difference, that, while the other people only dream over them, I have generally a desire to unravel them, and make them no mysteries at all. In short, Stephen Cook passed into the back of my box of memories, and there his image stuck, ready for any light to bring it out.

It happened that, two years afterwards, on 15th December 1858, another stot was stolen from a park on the Dalkeith Road; and information having been sent, Stephen Cook became all at once one of my desires. On inquiry, I ascertained from a Mr Purves, a butcher in Edinburgh, that a beast answering the description—for a stot has marks as well as a man—had been sold to him—by whom? no other than Stephen Cook. The mention of the name made me start. Stephen Cook again, thought I; even the mysterious Stephen Cook, who is unknown to his mother,—lives nowhere,—only turns up to Mr Purves to sell him a beast,—and then disappears, no man knows where. It is clear that Stephen Cook and I are destined to be acquainted. The matter is settled by the powers above, and there's an end on't.

I had not forgotten Allan's Close, but in the meantime, in case of disappointment there, I asked about among the butchers. Still the same answer,—"Know nothing about him,—appears occasionally and disappears,—never drinks the luck-penny,—never chaffers long,—gets his money and off, till the next time; but when that time may come round no one knows,—that's all." I don't despise the ingenuity of other men; I knew that the Linlithgow officers had searched the mother's house,—and, no doubt, they did it thoroughly,—but the "idea" I have spoken of so often is with me, somehow or other, my guide, in spite of all arguments,—ay, sometimes a little mirth now and then, as if the humorous gentlemen were certain that I was wrong for this once, anyhow.

It was under this guidance, accordingly, that next morning—for I wanted no time to be lost, in case Stephen Cook should take a fancy to a stot somewhere else, perhaps in Angus, where they are so fat—I got up about six, before the men leave their beats, and, having dressed in my ordinary way, I took the road to Allan's Close. I saw there the man on watch, and told him to remain at the foot of the stair, while I would take his lantern and try to find an honest man in the dark.

I then went up three stairs, and came to a door. I rapped more than once, when, at last, a voice came from behind,—

"Wha's there?"

"Are you Mrs Cook?" asks I.

"Yes; what want you at this early hour?"

"Just to speak a few words to you; open the door."

"Can ye no tell me what it is? you may be a robber for aught I ken."

"No, no, my good woman; I would be sorry to harm you, but you *must* open the door; or, just to tell you the truth, I will force it; I am on the Queen's service."

I could detect the effect of this announcement in a flutter behind the door. I even heard the quick-coming breath, and the nervous movement of the hand as it began to finger the key, but I did not consider this an evidence of the woman's guilt; anyone would have been startled by such an announcement. The door was opened, and I entered, showing myself my way by the lantern.

"Have you any one in the house with you?"

"No, sir," she answered, in a poor way; "I am a lone woman; there is no one lives with me."

"But haven't you a son?" I asked.

"Ay, sir; but he is never wi' me."

"How is this? has he any house of his own, that takes him away from his mother?"

"No; yet he seldom or ever comes here."

"Then where does he live? he must live somewhere."

"Dinna ken; he never comes here."

"When did you see him?" I then asked, more and more impressed with the strange character of my hero.

"I havena seen him for twa or three months, sir."

"Did you see him two months ago, then?"

"Ay; I think I did."

"You only think you did; could you be sure if I were to make it three months?"

"Weel, perhaps."

"If you know so little of him," I continued, "do any of the people below-stairs know him?"

"Oh, no, they ken naething about him; we hae nae-thing to do with the folks on the stair."

"Did any of them ever see him?"

"I'm no just sure if they ever did; but I dinna ken; maybe they may, and maybe they mayna."

"Well," said I at last, "I must search your house."

"Oh, ye're welcome to do that; but, besides my cat and myself, there's nae leeving creature here."

"And the mice," said I, as I began to peer about.

"And the mice," said she.

The woman went and put on some dress, and I went through the two rooms, opened the presses, looked below the two beds, and saw no sign. I then got her to open any drawers she had, to see whether there was any men's apparel—coats, or shirts, or shoes,—but no, not a trace that any male creature had anything to do with that house. Like the former officers, I was at my wit's end, and my "idea" was getting to be a fiction.

I forgot to say, that the house was at the top of the stair. Outside the door of the dwelling there was a kind of coal cellar, a dark hole with a door. I opened that, and threw the light of the bull's-eye upward; but nothing was to be seen, but a bucket or so, and cobwebs. After throwing the door to, my eye was next arrested by another cellar-like door, which was securely guarded by a padlock. Why is the one door open, and the other padlocked? I thought. A cellar is not usually padlocked.

"What kind of a place is this," said I.

"It leads to the roof, I fancy," she replied. "I dinna ken the use o't; maybe it belongs to the landlord."

"Then, who has the key?"

"Dinna ken, sir, and canna tell."

"But I must get in, Mrs Cook; and if you haven't the key, I will go to the landlord; and before that, I'll try the people below. Yes, I will knock every soul of them up."

"Oh, it will make a noise in the stair, sir; and I hope you'll no do that."

"Well, I can knock off the padlock with an axe," said I, and proceeded into the house again for such an instrument.

"Lord bless me," she cried, as she trotted after me, "have I no tauld ye the door just leads to the roof? and what in the name o' that's gude can you want there?"

"And why should you want to prevent me?" said I, laying hold of her axe. "If I choose to take a walk on the roof, that surely can do you no harm."

"There's nae use for breaking doors ony way," she cried, as she became more excited. "'Twill rouse a' the neighbours."

"Indeed it will, and it would please me better to get the key."

"Aweel then, but you'll no seek up when you see it's just a trap-stair leading to the roof."

"We'll speak about that after the door's open; come away with the key, for I know you have it."

And then, what appeared to me very strange, she seemed to grope in a box of ashes.

"Surely the key cannot be there?" said I.

"I dinna ken, I am just looking, for ye ken it's o' nae use to onybody, except maybe the sweeps; and really I take little care o't; and—losh, there it is—but you'll sune be satisfied that it just leads to the roof."

A long parley this, but far from being useless,—the key, with its position among the cinders, was just as mysterious as my old haunting gentleman, Stephen Cook the cattle-lifter.

I then went and undid the padlock, with the old woman beside me, watching every motion. I opened the door, and looked in.

"Now, you see, sir, that I was right; just a trapstair for the sweeps,"

And a trap sufficient to catch a rat of my size it seemed to be, for the passage was so narrow that the effort would be to crawl and even force your way up, by squeezing the sides.

"Are ye no satisfied now?" said the indefatigable woman.

"Not until I go up and come down again," said I, as, going to the top of the common stair, I called for the policeman.

He came up directly, and taking his station at the bottom of this strange passage, I put in my head and shoulders, having previously given the man his lantern to hold for a little, and hand up to me when I ascended. I found it a tough job for a man of my dimensions, but I forced my way; and having got to the top, there I was in a garret, with the bare cupples running along, and the roof joists overhead. I now told the man to hand me the lantern, which having got, I began to glance about the bull's-eye light here and there, till I fixed it upon a man lying on a mattress in the corner. He must have thought me a strange visitor at that hour in the dark. Indeed, he could scarcely have seen my person—only the round disc of the bull's-eye glaring upon him. There was my mystery,—Stephen Cook. I took him up, he was tried at the High Court, and got twelve months. It will at once be seen, that the padlock was resorted to as a cunning mode of impressing one with the idea that the opening was to an outside lumber-room, where it could not be supposed that any one could sleep; but it was the very padlock itself—resorted to by cunning to divert suspicion—that roused my suspicion.

The Boots

ONE morning, in the year 183–, information was sent to the office that a shoemaker's shop in the West Port had been broken open, and a quantity of new boots carried off. I got the intelligence, and having been always impressed, as I have said, with the conviction that in all such cases an hour at the beginning is worth a whole day afterwards, I hurried down to examine the shop, and have a few words with the man. On looking about, I ascertained that the robber or robbers had been wonderfully moderate in their depredations, after having been at so much trouble. Only a few pairs had been taken away, and, as it were, picked out pretty deliberately. Then, why at so much trouble with so humble a shop, when so many larger ones, containing valuables, might have been entered, with perhaps less manipulation, and with a hundred times more booty? I at once fell on the suspicion that some one acquainted with the shop was the depredator; and, moreover, that he was single-handed—altogether upon his own hook, as we say. On this supposition, I questioned the shoemaker back and fore, and he soon began to see that some one of his own people must have done the deed. Nor was it much longer till he singled out a discharged workman, who had come to him as a kind of tramp from Glasgow.

"His name?" asked I.

"John G——."

"Is he presently employed?"

"No, he is going about idle."

"Did he ever hint of any intention of going back to Glasgow?"

"No, he told me in the shop here that he was going to Inverness."

"What brought him to the shop? Had he any other thing to say than that he was going to Inverness?"

"Now, when you set me a-thinking," replied the shoe-maker, "he had *nothing* else to say."

"And therefore he came just to say that," I muttered, giving expression rather to my own thoughts than wishing to enlighten the shoemaker.

I did not see that I could get any more, nor was I dissatisfied with the mere fact that the peripatetic snab had been at the trouble, before supplying himself with more boots than he could wear the soles of in his journey, to make this kind communication to his old master. Thieves and robbers are great speakers by contraries, so that were you to *follow* them round the world, you would meet them mid-way about the Cape of Good Hope at that moment when you had no hope. They use an easy cipher, which we have only to turn upside down; but it is not that you must seek them south when they have sworn they are on the tramp for the north,—you must often expect them at "Loch Drunkie," in Perthshire, when they have been bent on drinking the sober waters of the crystal "Ninewells" of Berwickshire,—one well not being enough for the demands of what Dr Miller calls—so obscurely to simple people like me—their *nephalism*, which I have *detected* means no more than just temperance or sobriety. I must get my snab with the boots anyhow; and it was clear I could get no further help from the master.

On leaving the shop, I went direct to Princes Street,—of course with an idea in my mind, and somehow I have always been contented with one idea when I could not get another; and the advantage of sticking by one is, that the other don't jostle it and turn you about in a circle when you should go in a straight line. My line was accordingly straight enough, but not to *Inverness*. I went west, intending to question some people at the Hay-weights as to what kind of folks had passed about that early hour in the morning when even the most passable-looking gentry on the stravaig are kenspeckled. I suspected he would have a bag; and a man with a bag on his back at gray dawn does not usually carry it as an offering of faggots to the rising sun; and then a bag has a mystery about it even to those who never saw Burke with his. On going forward I met a man who had clearly come along the Glasgow road—even a better customer than those at the Hay-weights: at least I never yet encountered a traveller on a solitary road who was not able to tell me something about the wayfarers he has met on his way,—nay, though they belong to the inferior tribes, he will notice whether it is a Brownie or a Hawkie, so curious are people about common objects when they have nothing uncommon to occupy their minds.

"How far have you come?" said I.

"About ten miles," replied my man; "and the deil clip them short, for I'm tired, and my boots are clean worn through."

"And what is that you are carrying?" said I, with that unavoidable curiosity that belongs to us.

"Just a pair o' thae same things," replied he; "I got them cheap for five shillings frae a pedlar, about twa miles on."

"Let me see them," said I.

"Weel, I didna steal them ony way, and ye're welcome," he said, as he undid the paper, and showed me a pair of boots, with my West Port customer's name stamped upon them. A cab at this moment came up.

"Ho, there!" I cried to the cabman, who drew up; and, turning to my friend, "You'll just step in, and ride a bit with me. I want to speak to you a little about the boots."

"The boots!" said the man, as he obeyed me almost mechanically, perhaps as much through fear as a kind of notion he had that I was to drive him into town; but when he heard me tell the driver to go on at a gallop along the Glasgow road, and found himself carried along at so hard a pace, he cried out, "Lor', man, this is my road hame again, and it's to Edinburgh I am bound!"

"Well, well," replied I, "you'll be in Edinburgh by and by; but I am curious about the boots. They are so good and so cheap that I would like to get a pair from the same pedlar, and I'll just take you with me to help me to bargain for as cheap a pair to myself."

"The deil's in you for a queer chield," he replied, in amazement; "but this is ae way and a half to buy a pair of boots. I canna gang—stop there!"

"Be quiet, sir," said I, showing him my baton, the sight of which calmed him in a moment. "Drive on."

Nor did my astonished friend speak a word more for several minutes, confounded as he was with his new position. The driver, who knew me, kept his whip in a whirl, and our speed rather increased than diminished, till we got beyond Corstorphine, when my companion shooting out a long neck,—

"Yonder he is," cried he.

"Stop," said I to the driver, "when you get up to a man with a bag."

Nor were we very many minutes when the cab stopped, and my snab—for it was the very man—stopped also to see what was to turn up. A moment satisfied him that he and his bag were the cause of all this trouble, though I am not sure if he knew me, only the sight of his customer probably told him that he had been informed on by the ungrateful wretch he had favoured with so good a bargain. In a moment, the bag was thrown off his back, and he was off at only a cobbler's pace.

"No use, my friend," I cried, making after him; "I want a pair of boots of you."

And seizing him, I brought him back to where the bag lay.

"Open it," said I, "and let me see your stock. You sold this man a pair at five shillings, and why not favour me?"

Even through his suspicion and doggedness there gleamed a small light of hope in his eye, and having opened the bag and shown the boots,—

"Oh, I'll take them altogether," said I, "and this man's pair to the bargain."

And throwing the bag—into which I placed also the countryman's pair—into the cab, I put him up too, by which time he knew that he was fairly caught, and became very quiet.

"To Edinburgh, again."

On arriving at the place where I took up the countryman, I set him down.

"And now, sir," said I to my prisoner, "you pay this poor man his five shillings, and I'll *pay you* for the whole stock when I get to the High Street."

The five shillings were reluctantly tolled out. The countryman was overjoyed beyond measure, and I took Mr Snab to the office. The shoemaker got back his boots, and my friend six months in a place where a pair would have lasted him, if they had been *lasted* by so cunning a hand as his own, for six years.

The Ingenuity of Thieves

❖

It would not be a hopeful sign of the further triumph of the good principle over the evil if the devil's agents could show us many examples where they have beaten us, and been enabled to slide clean off the scale. Since my first volume was published, I have been twitted with cases where we have been at fault. I don't deny that there are some, and I will give one or two, of which I have something to say. In the meantime, I have consolation, not that I have contributed much to the gratifying result in being able to point to the fact, that, since the year 1849, the Reports of the General Board of Prisons have shown a gradual and steady decrease of the population of our jails. I am free to confess that this result is only, to a small extent, due to us, and the reason is plain enough. The old rebel has had the advantage of us. We have, until very recently, been acting against him on the principle of those masters and mistresses, who, with a chuckle in their hearts, lay pieces of money in the way of suspected servants to catch them,—something in the Twelvetrees way, only they don't wish their unwary victims "to die on the spot;" nay, having caught them, they only turn them off to rob and steal elsewhere. Yes, in place of our philanthropists meeting the arch-enemy at the beginning, when he is busy with the young hearts, detecting the first throb of good and turning it to a pulse of evil, we have been obliged to wait until the young sinner was ripe and ready for our hardening mould of punishment. There was no Dr Guthrie there—a good way cleverer than the enemy, I suspect, and capable of checkmating him by nipping the canker in the early bud; and then we have been hampered by our legal governors, who have been, and still are, always telling us we must keep a sharp look out for what they call, in their law jargon, an "overt act," the meaning of which, I am informed, is, that we must wait until the rogues are able to do some *clever* thing, sufficient to show us they have arrived at the age of *discretion*, and become *meritorious* subjects for punishment.

With this advantage over us, it is no great wonder we are sometimes outwitted; nay, the wonder rather is, that we succeed so often as we do, and I think it might be a great consolation to our philanthropists working among the Raggedier ranks, when I tell them, as I have already done, that I don't hold the enemy at so much count as many do. His terrible reputation is due to our own laxity. We let him into the camp, hoof and horns, and then complain that we can't drive or pull him out, whereas we have the power, if we would only exercise it, of *keeping* him out. To my instinctive way of looking at things in those days of improved tactics in war, it seems something like folly to trust to the strength of the wild boar's tail in dragging him out when we can so easily barricade the hole.

Viewing crime even in its diminished extent, there is another consideration which has often opened my eyes pretty wide. We are always a-being told that the human heart has really some good soil in it—(I don't go with those who think that people inherit evil as they do sometimes six toes)—and that, though the devil has always a large granary of tares, we have an abundance of good seed from Jerusalem. I would just ask what use we have been making of that good seed? Have we not been keeping it *in* the bushel just as we keep the light *under* the bushel? In my beat I see a routh of the tares; then I get a sickle put into my hands, and I cut away just as the gardeners do when they prune in order to make the old branches shoot out with more vigour, and, behold, the twisted saplings, how stiff and rigid they become!

But I suspect I am here getting out of my beat. I set out with stating that I had got thrown in my teeth cases where, by the ingenuity of thieves, we have been defeated. They are not cases of mine, any how. I may take one or two that relate to one of the most successful artists of the tender sex that ever appeared in Edinburgh, viz., the well-known Jean Brash. I knew her very well, but, strange as it may appear, her ladyship always contrived to keep out of my hands; not that she came always scaithless out of the hands of others, any more than that her victims came without damage out of hers, but that she usually, by her adroitness, achieved a miserable success, sufficient to form the foundation of a romantic story. At an early period, she could boast of some attractions, but she could boast more of making these run along with her power of *extraction;* yea, she had three wonderful powers, viz., those of captivating her cullies, retaining them if she chose, and of losing them by capturing their means. Of the last of these she was more proud than of the others, and if she could, in addition, enjoy the triumph of deceiving an astute constable, she got to the top of her pride—a creature or *fiend,* otherwise strangely formed, for if she seduced and robbed by instinct, she strengthened and justified the inborn propensity by a kind of devil's logic, to the effect that, as she had ruined her immortal soul for the sake of man, she was not only entitled to receive from him the common wages of sin, but also to take from him whatever her subtle fingers could enable her to lay hold of by way of compensation. On one occasion, when, as I think, she resided in the Salt Backet, and when I had occasionally my eye upon her with a look of official love, which she could return with a leer of rather a different kind from that wherewith she wrought her stratagems, she had sallied out, after night-fall, to try her skill on hearts, gold watches, or little bits of bank paper. Doubtless, no more now than on any other occasion, did she imitate the old sirens of whom I have read somewhere. She did not sing them into her toils, that is, her art was not thrown out any more than when a cat purrs at a mousehole. Her power could be in reserve, and yet be available, so that a man in place of being a *dupe,* might flatter himself that he was a *duper* seeking for her charms in the shape of shrinking modesty. So probably thought the happy Mr C——, a mercantile traveller in the hard goods line from Birmingham, but not himself a Brummagem article of false glitter,—a sterling man, if one might judge from the value of the money he carried. In her demureness, Jean appears a real jewel, and he would secure the prize, yet not in the way of an "*un*commercial traveller," for he could and would purchase, and surely in so modest-looking a creature he would make an excellent bargain. Look you, here is a little consolation for us, as we wander about seeking for the vicious to catch them and punish them into virtue. We see occasionally the vicious prowling, in the shades of night, seeking the vicious to deceive them into further vice, and yet sure to be deceived in turn and brought to ruin, while they are trying to make a capital of pleasure out of a poor wretch's necessity. So it has always been: voluptuousness gets hysterical over modesty (Jean Brash's modesty!) and how can we be sorry when we see it choked with the wind-ball of its desire? Then, look ye, is it not a little curious to see vice so conservative of virtue as to become a detective?

Well, Jean is caught by the commercial traveller, how unwittingly the reader may pretty safely guess, and not only caught, but led as a kind of triumph to the Salt Backet, where resides one of those "decent women" who take pity on errant lovers; probably if Jean had said that the house was her own, he might have doubted of a modesty which could belie itself at home among friends. Then, as they say love has quick wings where there is a shady grove in prospect—not always of sweet myrtle—not seldom of common pine firs, with a good many nettles and thistles growing about the temple—so they were speedily under the auspices of the decent priestess. How long it was before the heart of this lover, which had only been for a little absent from his commercial interests, returned to these so as to make him alive to the conviction that he had been robbed of a hundred-pound Bank of England note, I cannot say, for I was not in this case; but certain it is, that rather quiet part of the town soon echoed to a cry of horror, to the effect that he had been relieved from the anxiety of carrying about with him a bit of paper of that value.

Of all this I have no doubt, because I was perfectly aware that Jean was a woman who could confer the boon of such a relief from anxiety as easily as she could transfer that anxiety to herself; nor could any one who knew her doubt that she could contrive to make the care a very light one. Even the more romantic part of the story which "illustrates" the memory of this remarkable woman, I have no proper right to gainsay—how the commercial traveller rushed down stairs and bawled out at the top of his English voice for a constable—how the constable made his appearance while the traveller kept watch at the door—how they hurried upstairs to seize when they should discover the money—how they found Jean quite in an easy state of conscious innocence—how she adjured the constable to search the house and her own body, and satisfy himself that the unfortunate man was in error—how, for that purpose, she quietly handed to him a lighted candle placed in a brass candlestick, and well fixed there by a round of paper not to oscillate in the way of unsteady lights—how the constable searched for the missing note with this candle, so fixed by the paper roll at the end thereof, all the while that Jean was muttering to herself, "The fool has taken the wrong end"—how he failed in his search, and how the traveller gave up all hope, if he did not suspect that he had lost his note elsewhere, and therefore resolved to avoid the fearful exposure of committing the woman—and how Jean was at length left quietly in her state of innocence. The reader may guess that Jean at her own time undid the piece of paper from the end of the candle, thus rescuing the "Governor and Company of the Bank of England" from their temporary degradation, and enjoying a quiet chuckle at her successful ingenuity.

Now, I confess I never liked very well to hear this romantic bit of Jean's history, and simply for this reason, that I was not there to hold the candle.

On another occasion—though I am bound to say I have heard the credit of the adventure ascribed to a young unfortunate of the name of Catherine Brown, who lived in Richmond Street—our Jean was pursuing her *nomade* vocation in Princes Street. The night was dark enough, and the hour late enough, to inspire adventurers with sufficient confidence to flirt a little with the coy damsel, without being detected by curious friends. There are always numbers of these shy and frolicsome fish who are fond of poking their noses into the dangerous meshes, without any intention of entering the seine, where they would be pretty sure to be caught. The regular tramps, such as our heroine, are quite up to these amateurs, hate them heartily, and sometimes make them pay, and very deservedly too, golden guineas for silvern words. I can't say I have much sympathy for them when they fall into misfortune, and ask our help to get money restored to their pockets, which pockets they voluntarily placed within the range of curious fingers. Why, if these fingers are delicate enough to be fondled and kissed without recompense, the men show a bad grace in complaining that the same fingers fondled in their turn a bit of gold or paper supposed to be beyond their reach. Of course we do our duty, but always with a feeling in such cases that the victims did not do theirs, and impose upon us the trouble of rectifying the results of their folly, if not vice. Such fire-ships show enough of light to enable these gay yachtmen to steer sufficiently aloof. (Were I able to be fanciful myself, I would not need to borrow the words of one of our well-read Lieutenants.) These young men play round the rancid candle-light of impurity, which at once enables them to see reflected in their self-conceit their immunity from danger, and imparts a little heat to their imagination. Rather fine language for me, but I see the sense of it.

With one of these gaudy night-moths our famous heroine had forgathered; and thinking probably that if he did not choose to consider her soft hand sacred from his squeeze, she was not bound to esteem his pocket tabooed against the prying curiosity of her fingers, she made free with the contents thereof. At least the youth thought so; for on the instant he bawled out to the passing bull's-eye that he had been robbed. The constable, who knew Jean—as who didn't—immediately laid hold of her, and as there were no passers-by to complicate the affair, the money would of course be got upon the instant. It was no less than a five-pound note, at least so said the young man; but Jean, whose coolness never forsook her, simply denied the charge.

It was a matter of short work for the constable to search her so far as he could,—an act in which he was helped by the young man. Her pockets were turned out, but with the exception of a scent-bottle, a white handkerchief, and some brown pawn-tickets, nothing was found there. All round the pavement the light of the lantern showed nothing in the shape of the valuable bit of paper, and there was no sympathiser to whom she could have handed it.

"You must be under a delusion," said the policeman.

"Impossible!" cried the youth. "There are as many folds in a woman's dress as there are loops and lies in her mind. March her up."

To all which Jean replied with her ordinary laugh of consummate self-possession, if not impudence. Nor was she at all unwilling to march—rather the contrary. She knew what she was about.

"Come away," she said, "and we shall see who is right and who is wrong."

And so away they went. Nor was it long before Jean was examined by one of the female searchers of the Office. No five-pound note was found upon her; and though the young man raved incessantly about the absolute certainty of the theft, the policeman, and not less the lieutenant on duty, was satisfied that there must have been a mistake,—a conclusion which the redoubted Jean confirmed by a cool declaration, in all likelihood false, that she had seen the young gentleman in the company of not less scrupulous women a very short time before. There was only one thing to be done—to set Jean free.

"And who is to pay me for all this time?" said she, as she turned to the lieutenant a face in which was displayed a mock seriousness, contrasting vividly with the wild, anxious countenance of the youth. "I could have made five pounds in the time in an honest way, so that I am the real loser; and who, I ask again, is to pay me?"

A question to which she no more expected a reply than she did the payment of her lost gains in an honest way. And with head erect, if not indeed with an air of injured innocence, she marched out of the Office. Yet nothing would satisfy the young man that he had not been robbed; and he too, when he saw that he had no hope, left with the conviction that he was a greatly injured innocent.

The matter died away, leaving only the impression of some unaccountable mistake or indetectible priggery, though probably the presumption was against the woman, whose genius in this peculiar line of art was known to be able to find her advantage in a mystery through which the most practised eye of official vision could see nothing.

A day or two passed. No more was heard of the young man, who no doubt had made up his mind to the loss of the five pounds; nor did the constable, who was again upon his beat about the same hour, think any more of the mystery, unless perhaps the place brought up a passing thought of wonder how the bit of paper could have disappeared in so very short a time. A woman came running up to him. It was Jean, and she was all of a bustle. Laying hold of the man by the left hand—

"What now," said the constable, who knew well that something not altogether useless to Jean was coming.

"In one of your high jinks?"

"No; I have a secret for you, man."

"What is it?"

"Oh, you're such peaching fellows, one can hardly speak with you. Would you like the young sprig's five-pound note? He can't afford to lose it, and my conscience is queezy."

"Ah, ha!" cried the constable, "Jean Brash's conscience!"

"Aye, man, even Jean Brash's conscience," replied she, a little grandly. "A queer thing maybe, but still a thing. Aye, man, I would tell you where the five-pound note is if you would keep me out of the gleg's claws."

"Well, I will," replied he, getting into official cunning. "Tell me where the note is, and I will do my best for you."

"Ah, I know you won't, and so I can't trust you with an admission which you would use against me; but suppose I were to make a sign, eh? A nod is as good, you know, as ——"

"Well, well, give me the nod to lead me to the note."

"And you will say nothing? Well, who's your tailor?" she cried, laughing.

"What has that to do with the note?" responded the man.

"Something that may astonish you," said she, as she still held his arm, and fumbled about the cuff of his coat. "He gives you a deep cuff. Very convenient as a kind of wee pawn."

"Nonsense. Get off. You are trifling."

"Not just," she replied, again laughing and thrusting her nimble fingers, so like instruments of legerdemain, deep into the cuff—"not just. Suppose you were to find the note in here after I am gone, would you just say you got it there, and nothing of me?"

"Perhaps I would."

"Then search your cuff," she cried, swinging his arm to a side, "and you will find it."

And running away, she threw behind her the words: "But be sure and act honourably, and give it to the prig."

The constable was a little confused, but he did not fail to begin to search the cuff, from which Jean, while pretending she had deposited the £5 in the receptacle, had absolutely extracted the spoil,—the identical note which she had placed there at the instant of her seizure on the night it was stolen, and which he had carried about with him for two days, altogether unconscious of the valuable deposit.

The man could swear, as in a rage he searched and found nothing, but he couldn't detect, and I don't think he ever knew the trick played off upon him; for it came out long afterwards when Jean was safe, and in one of her fits of bragging, how she did the authorities.

These are not *my* experiences, and I can give no guarantee of their truth; but, as I have said, I should have liked to be the man who held the candle, supported in the socket by such a valuable bit of paper; and I must add, that I should have liked also to be the man who wore the coat with the deep cuff.

So much for such talk as goes on amongst us. But I have had enough of experience of Jean to enable me to say that she was the most "organic thief" of my time. So much was her *make* that of a thief, that I doubt whether training in a ragged school would have had much effect upon her. The house she occupied in James' Square was a "bank of exchange," regularly fitted up for business. In the corner of a door-panel of every bedroom, there was a small hole neatly closed up with a wooden button, so as to escape all observation. Then the lower panels were made to slide, so that while through the peep she could see when the light was extinguished, she could by the opened panel creep noiselessly in on all fours and take the watch off the side-table, or rifle the pockets of the luckless wight's dress. She made occasionally great catches, having once "done" £400; but she was at length "done" by the paltry sum of 7s. 6d. I have heard that she is still alive in Australia, and married, perhaps driving, like a pastoral Arcadian, "the yowes to the knowes."

The Urchin

❖

MY reminiscences, I find, contain so many of those turns which are called coincidences, that it may be asked, why so, when such occurrences in ordinary lives are so very few and far between? Yet it is to be remembered, that I was always on the trail of crime, and that when these startling incidents occurred, I was at the place, and among the persons, where some such discoveries might transpire. In short, as I have said, if Chance so often favoured me, I was as often poking at her.

In that close or pend leading to Tweeddale Court, so famous as the scene of Begbie's murder, by Coulson or Moffat, a robbery took place in July 1848. It seems that a small manufacturer of Galashiels had come into town with some bales of rather valuable goods,—tweeds, shawls, &c.,—and that during his sojourn here, he had taken up his residence in a flat led to by a door on the right-hand side of the pend. While the man had been out, probably disposing of some of his goods, some persons had entered the house with false checklock keys, and made a clean sweep of his bales. One person could not have done the deed, because the weight was at least equal to the strength of two stout men or full-grown youths. We got notice instantly, and I set out on the adventure of trying to recover the poor man's stock-in-trade.

The greater part of stolen things find their way generally to the bad houses, for it is among these the male thieves—and here I suspected that sex—almost always lurk, with this advantage that they can get the women to help in the disposal of them. In this instance, the probability of the housebreakers being among these haunts was, to my mind, increased by considering the nature of the articles stolen, particularly shawls. I accordingly commenced a search among the brothels, expecting chiefly to find some pair of shoulders adorned with so envied an article as a fine new plaid, in justification of which expectation—the short time taken into account—I may just state, what is well enough known, that the desire to put on new fancy articles overcomes all prudence, and defies the danger of the mere recentness of the theft. Yet my calculations in this instance failed, though I believe I visited twenty of the most probable dens in the Old Town, neither finding the said adorned shoulders, nor the bales from which the adornments might be taken. Discomfiture generally, I may admit, or rather boast, nettled me, and I was on this occasion very loath to give up, however harassing my labours. I wandered and wandered everywhere, as curious an observer of plaids as a Galashiels weaver or Paisley manufacturer. This may be said to have been very vain, for I did not know the patterns; and then hasn't almost every woman a shawl? Very true, but then I knew so many of the likely ones, as well as their tawdry dresses, that I might have found it somewhat fortunate if I had met such as Jane or Kate Smith, or Lucky Maitland, swaggering away under the pride of a Galashiels plaid, span new, and all her own too.

But I did not meet these celebrated personages in any such condition, so tempting to culleys. Completely worn out, and as yet without hope, but still stiff enough in my determination, I was dragging my legs up Blackfriars' Wynd, intending to give a look in upon the paradises there, to cheer me in my terrestrial troubles. Perhaps I would have continued my searches into that hopeful sphere, Halkerston's Wynd, where Lucky Maitland and her nymphs spent their happy days; for when I began these hunts I was, like the red-coated hunters,—who can never tell when they are to be home to dinner, because Reynard does not condescend to tell them where he will be caught,—entirely uncertain when I should give up. A sniff might inspire me, and blow my soul up into a flame, at the very moment I was among the cinders of, I won't say despair,—for I don't know what it is,—but of considerable pulverisation. Indeed, I couldn't tell the humour I was in, but it was not a good one; just in that state when a little whisper would revive me and bring me up again. I believe I was so far gone that I had my hands behind my back, not the best sign of a detective on duty, when a little urchin of a girl—with just as much upon her as would entitle one to say she was an improvement upon Eve after the catastrophe of the apple—peered up into my face, and with a leer, which might either have been fun or devilry, cried—

"Man, do you want a shawl for your wife?"

"Shawl, eh! ay," said I.

"Because thae twa women there," pointing to Jane and Kate Smith, whom I had the honour of knowing, "hae bonny anes to sell."

"Ho there, lasses!" I cried on the instant, and going slap up to them in an intercepting way; "I want to buy a shawl from you."

"We have nae shawls," said Kate.

"Wish we had," said Jane.

"Then what bundles are these you have under your arms?"

"Nae business of yours," said the one, and then the other.

"If it is no business of mine to buy a shawl, having no wife, neither is it yours to sell. Come, let me see them."

The women knew me, and probably thought there was little use in battling the watch with me. At least I got easily from them their respective bundles, which I undid upon the spot, and found, to my great surprise, a fine Galashiels plaid in each.

"You would not sell them," said I, "and now I will take them for nothing; and what's more, I will pay no price for you; so come along with me to the Police-office, to answer for the manner in which you got this stolen property."

After some of the ordinary cursing, they went along with me, and I took them to the office, where they were retained. I was aware I could get nothing out of them, and therefore lost no time in going away to Halkerston's Wynd, where I knew they lived, with a famous mother of harpies,—no other than the said Lucky Maitland.

On entering the den, I met the old mother at my first approach, stationed with the determination to keep me out,—the best reception I could have got. She was growling like a she-bear whose cubs are in danger.

"Ye hae nae business here,"—the old address I have heard so

often,—"there's naebody here but decent folk—awa' wi' ye!"

"It's not indecent folk I want, Mrs Maitland," said I; "it's dishonest folk; and if you have none of these about you, you need not be afraid."

"Ou ay, the auld gibes. Man, can ye no just say, 'I'll be d—d but I will be in?' Faith, I would like the ane better than the other."

"But I came here to please myself, mother," said I, "not you;" and so I pushed her to a side, and went forward, followed by the hag, muttering her sworn wrath.

On getting further in, I found sitting, or rather lying, in a dark small room, two "halfins," as we call them,—neither men nor boys,—whom I knew to be Glasgow thieves—James Wilson and John Morison. They were living there among half-a-dozen probably of young women, among whom, though so young, they could keep their places, if not command them, by the charm of money got by thievery. I may mention that people are often under the mistake of estimating such youths by the common standard, not being aware that they have lived twice their years, and have more cunning, trickery, boldness, and "worldly wisdom" of their kind, than probably their fathers. The women were all out, but what is the day to these owls? When night comes, they revive like torpid snakes, and revel in all the sins of Gomorrah, amidst ribald songs, oaths, dancings, jolly bouts, and prostitution. I would stop the next night's revelries anyhow. Without saying a word, I called in my assistant to take care of the young tigers, as well as the old tigress, while I should search for the Galashiels bales. Search! why there they were, piled up between two truckle beds, almost entire, if the plaids carried by the Smiths were not all that had been taken out of them.

"Whence came these?" I said to old mother.

"They're a hawker's, what left them here this morning; and a d—d ill-pleased man he'll be when he kens they've been stowen frae him by riff-raff o' police."

"Step up to the office," whispered I into the ear of the constable, "and bring down two men to carry up the bales, and I'll remain here in the meantime."

"An' ye'll be blaming the twa puir callants," she continued, "wha are as innocent as the baby born yesterday."

"I never said they were guilty, Mrs Maitland," said I.

"Na, na! ye canna say that, God be thanked; I ken their parents,—decent, honest folk, as mine were, an' a' my kith. And wha says no? I wad like to see him, and maybe thae nieves an' his nose would be as sib as lovers' mou's."

I sat down on a crazy easy-chair, and allowed her to go on; for I knew the woman, and that to try to stop her was to excite her.

"An' wha turned your nose this way? Was there nae scents in Blackfriars' Wynd, or ony ither wynd, that ye cam' here, whaur the deil a thief or limmer is ever seen frae January to December? But touch thae laddies if ye daur. They're brither's sons o' mine."

"The name of the one is Morison and the other Wilson," said I, more for amusement than anything else.

"It's a lee, sir; but the police are a' leears, every mother's son o' them. Were I a man, and a' men were like me, we would rise upon ye and hang ye like Porteous; but no on a barber's pole—it's owre guid for ye," and then she laughed hideously.

Nor would she have stopped for an hour, if my assistant, who had met two constables at the close head, had not come in, and put an end to her oration. I proceeded to put the bales on the men's backs, amidst the terrible cursings of the hag; and having despatched them, my assistant took one of the youths by the arm, and I the other.

"Good day, Mrs Maitland," said I.

"And an ill day to you, ye scoondrels," she yelped, as she followed us. "But a waur's waiting ye, when ye'll roast in hell-fire, for banishing and hanging honest men's bairns, when it's yoursel's should be in the rape; but indeed a rape's owre gude for sae cut-throat ruffians."

The remainder—if remainder it could have been called, which would have gone on till next morning—was cut short by the shutting of the door as we left her, but not without being honoured by a scream of vengeance, which made all the old tenement ring. Even when up near the top of the close, we heard her, as she had sallied out, yelling at the top of her husky voice, and calling down upon our heads all kinds of punishment.

But luckily there are two sides to a question. If Mother Maitland cursed us, the Galashiels manufacturer saw the case in another light, and showered upon us his blessings, and probably he would even have gone the length of reversing the deserts, by hanging the good mother at her own door. Nor did I forget her either, for when I brought away the thieves, I merely left the resetter for a little, till her rage cooled. In a short time, I sent for her to join the four already in custody, as fine a company as ever met together to enjoy the pleasure of a pannel-box.

On examining the bales, I believe they had just been taken in time,—a day would certainly have reduced both their bulk and their value; as it was, they were entire with the exception of the two plaids. And I believe further, if the manufacturer had been able to find out the funny urchin, she would have been clad, very much to her wonderment, from top to toe, in real genuine tweed; but if goodness in this case went unrewarded, not so evil, for the whole four were duly punished. The Smiths got twelve months, Wilson eighteen months, Morison fifteen months, and the good Dame Maitland, six months.

This case suggests a remark. The judges, when they pronounce such sentences, no doubt think they are inflicting punishment, and philanthropic people will even pity the victims. Yet I have often doubted if our prison punishments are really punishments to them. The thraldom, no doubt, keeps them from the objects of their wishes; but their lives, in spite of their assumed jollity and wild mirth, are really in such opposition to human nature, that they never can be called happy: so that if their punishment is an evil, it is only one evil in place of another; and so we find them treating their sentences with a levity which is just a symptom of a kind of despair influenced by drink and debauchery.

The Pirates

❖

ALMOST every case which has come into my hands, and in which there was difficulty in tracing, has had something to mark it as demanding a treatment suited to its peculiarity. In following that treatment, I have had occasion, in conformity to the latitude intrusted to me, to differ from my colleagues, but seldom with much cause to repent of my pertinacity. In the case I am now to narrate, this occurred to a greater extent than in some others; and, perhaps, it is on that account—for the transaction itself is of frequent occurrence, the robbery of a tar—that I recur to it.

In 1845, we were called upon by a sailor of the name of Geddes, a Newhaven man. He was in that state in which these good-natured fellows often are, after having passed a night in some of the low houses, in the midst of half-a-dozen of depraved women, collected around him by the attraction of a bunch of notes. He came in very unsteady, and withal jolly, with the indispensable quid in his mouth, and the hitching up the breeches as usual. I asked him his errand.

"Why, you see," said he, "I was boarded and robbed by a nest of pirates over in that creek there," pointing towards the other side of the High Street.

"When?" said I.

"Last night, second watch."

"A very loose watch, I fear," said I. "Why didn't you keep a better look-out?"

"Right, sir; but then you see we had too much grog, and got hazy about the eyes, so that we couldn't see the enemy nohow, until fairly boarded, and now it's all up with my cargo."

"What had you on you? have you been at sea?"

"Why, yes, your honour, I had been cruising in the South Sea, and came to Leith yesterday, where I laid in a cargo of notes, twenty-eight of 'em, and wanted to have a scour among the fire-ships up in this dangerous sea, and so got robbed you see; everything gone, sir,—not a penny—nothing left, but this piece of seal-skin, with an inch or two of pig tail."

"You have paid for your fun," said I; "but where did this happen?"

"I think the name of the creek," he went on, "is Galloway's Close. The captain in charge of the pirates, Hill, or something of that shape. Then there was Nell, Grace, Moll, and Agnes; but I couldn't tell one from t'other now."

"But why didn't you take care of your hard-won money, man?"

"And so I did,—lockers bolted and barred; but they silenced me with their charges of gin and whisky, and when I went to sleep, scrambled up the sides of my craft, and robbed me of every penny. So if you can't make sail and catch 'em, I must off again to sea; but catch me next time,—I'll give that creek a wide berth, or my name's not Jack Geddes."

"Can you tell me what like the women were?"

"All of a piece to my eyes—just women, every one of them, that's all; all the same you know when a man's groggy; but I wouldn't mind it so much if they hadn't sheered off, and left me a disabled hulk, without a biscuit in the locker, and nothing to comfort me, but a sore head and two quids or so."

"You have mentioned four names; do you remember any more?" said I.

"No, can't say,—half-a-dozen anyhow."

"Why had you so many sweethearts?"

"Oh, we like a choice you know," said he, laughing; "at first there were only Nell and Molly, then one told t'other as how I had a rich cargo, and so the fleet collected."

"Well, I'll try what can be done for you," said I.

"I hope you'll give 'em a taste of the grating and cat anyhow."

"Wouldn't it be of more importance if I could get the money?"

"Oh yes; wouldn't require to go to sea again; and then mother would get something, you know, and old father."

"If you had given it to them to keep," said I, "you wouldn't have been here to-day."

"Yes," he replied, with a comic kind of seriousness stealing over his face, if there was not something like a drop gathering in his eye, of which I was the more certain that he brought the sleeve of his jacket over his forehead. "Yes; the old ones will get nothing till next time, and I'd rather not see 'em till I've gone to sea again, and come home and make 'em happy. I'll keep out of Galloway's Creek next bout, I warrant."

"Would you know them if you saw them?"

"Wouldn't I know the cut of the enemy?" said he, getting into his old humour. "They came too close quarters for my not knowing 'em."

"But you cannot tell which of them took the money?"

"No; I just remember a low room, stoups and glasses, and a fleet of women. I was singing 'Tom Bowling', and Nell was helping me,—others singing something else, and one or two dancing,—all merry and jolly,—when I must have fallen asleep, for the next thing I remember was that they were all off, the gas out, and nothing to be seen but darkness—and all my money gone; nothing but the seal-skin pouch and the quid to go to sea with again."

"It's a hard case, my lad," said I; "but you have brought it upon yourself by your folly. I'm sure you all know well enough of these tricks, and yet they are always coming fresh upon us. I will set about trying to get hold of the pirates, as well as your money. Call back in the afternoon, and in the meantime keep a look-out about the streets, and endeavour to lay hold of them."

So away he went, hitching in the old style. I had no great hopes of his case. The women he had mentioned were known to me very well, as residing in, or frequenters of, a Mrs Hill's establishment, in the close he had mentioned; but they were experienced hands, and so well up to "planking" such an easily disposed of article as money in the shape of bank-notes, that to get hold of the thieves was making scarcely any progress. But the difference I have alluded to was as regards the first step. Going direct to the den is often held to be the best method of getting hold of a beast who is glutted with prey; but women, even of their depraved kind, are not exactly beasts, though in many respects worse. They are not altogether deprived of the glimmer of reason sufficient to tell them that their lair will be the first searched. To go there is simply to give them warning, and put them on their guard. Yet this is the common way of many detectives; and I was only taking my old way when I insisted, against a contrary opinion, that we must in the first place avoid the house.

But there is another consideration, derived from the inevitable nature of women. The moment they get hold of more money than will serve them for their always crying immediate wants, including the eternal whisky, their very first thought is dress. They will go a-shopping at all hazards. Their trade is to attract, and it often enough happens that the very shawl, or bonnet, or gown which helps to ensnare the victim, is the produce of a robbery similar to that they will practise upon him; so that, I believe, it has occurred that, as the money is distributed from one to another, a man has been caught and robbed by means of the cash he had in his pocket a night or two before. There is a pretty bit of redistribution here, very instructive; but I believe it's all one whether understood and felt or not. If sin were to be cured by the scab of its own cautery, it would have been off the face of the earth some thousands of years ago, down to the pit, never to be allowed to come up again to taint this fair world.

Proceeding upon my theory of avoiding the house, I, accompanied by one or two constables, betook myself to the Bridges, where are the shops most frequented by women of this stamp. I just wanted to know if the thieves were true to their old nature. They had had time enough to sleep off the effects of the whisky, and to awake to little else than the madness of their conviction that they had each a bundle of notes in their pockets, which it was necessary they should scatter, by purchasing new things, to enable them to get quit of the old rags. I accordingly kept pacing the Bridges, as if in no hurry consequent upon the sailor's story; and I believe if they had seen me, they would have been satisfied either that Jack was still in Mrs Hill's, or that he had never been to the office. On the other hand, if I had seen *them*, I could have read money in their eyes. Yes, as I have hinted before, if you know the general cast of the features of people who live from hand to mouth,—and a very artful hand sometimes, in the case of that class over whom I exercise a fatherly care,—you can almost with certainty tell whether any windfall has come in their way, for you may be assured that nothing but money can make them look happy; and then the happiness has a kind of hysterical excitement about it that carries a mark to a good observer. Nay, when a good haul is got of £20 to £100, there is often observed a commotion in the whole sisterhood, even among those who don't participate in the plunder, for doesn't it show that there are prizes in their lottery?—their fortunate turn will come next; the victims are getting rich and unwary;—and, above all, there is the inevitable envy of the lucky sister or sisters who have been so unspeakably fortunate, without taking into account that there will be drink going in the "happy lands" for a week to come, until the money is all spent and gone.

After keeping up my watch for more than an hour, I observed Helen Mossman and Grace Edwards coming out of a respectable shop, each with a neatly tied up draper's bundle. I kept my eye upon them. They had the happiness of shopping in their hearts, and were babbling, as money-holders do; nor did they seem to have any fear of being laid hold of, though, of course, they did not see me. In the midst of their talk, they met Agnes Pringle and Mary Cameron bouncing out of another shop, where they also had been getting their neat paper parcels, and then they commenced a quadruple conversation apparently extremely interesting to them, for they laughed heartily, and even, you would have thought, turned their eyes contemptuously on the passengers on either side of them as if they said to themselves, "We have been shopping as well as the best of you;" for to what woman is the pride let alone the pleasure, of shopping not dear? But as I stood and watched them, another thought occurred to me. There stood four women, who had taken from a poor seaman the wages of a year's voyage to the other side of the world, and left him not so much as would get him a day's tobacco, while he had an old father and an old mother looking to him for help, and only to be met with the miserable intelligence that their hopes were blasted. What did this poor fellow do to them that they should render him penniless, even make his stout heart swell with pity for these parents, and bring the tear to his eye, to be brushed off in shame of what he thought his weakness? No, they cared nothing for these things,—Jack was not even mentioned, only collars, and ribbons, and handkerchiefs, to deck them out for some other seduction.

I was in no hurry. Here I had Jack's Nell, and Moll, and Grace, and Agnes, all in a neat clump, while, if I had taken the advice given to me, I might not have had one of them; for a visit to Galloway Creek would have sent Sarah Hill, the daughter of the keeper of the house, out upon a hunt after them, to tell them to keep out of the way; and this they might have done till every penny of the £28 was gone. My men were now behind me, for they had also seen the birds getting into the net; so, stepping up to them, —

"You are blocking up the way, my ladies; walk on."

"Walk to the devil!" said Nell Mossman. "The street is not yours."

"We will walk any way we please," said another.

"Which way do you want us to walk?" said a third.

"This way," said I, pointing north; "this way, come along."

And so they did; for in spite of their bravery they began to get alarmed.

I walked along with them to the Tron.

"Oh, not that way," stopping them as they moved for the Canongate; "this way, past the Tron."

"And why that way?"

"Never mind, come along, and here is a friend who will go with us and bear us company;" and who's this but Jack, all sober and tidy, with a clean light at his poop and a fine breeze in his main-sheet?

"All right," he cried, as he came up; "direct for port, four passengers and a valuable cargo."

And Jack came to my side, as the cowed and heartless creatures still kept mechanically trudging by our side.

"Old mother and father have a chance yet," said I, in a low tone to the tar.

"Oh, God bless you, sir," rejoined he; "were it not for them I wouldn't have cared a d—n, but since ever I saw you this morning my heart has been thumping against my ribs, like a moored lugger against the wooden fenders of a pier, all for the thought of the old ones."

And there the drop came again.

"D'ye know, sir," he continued, "I had made up my mind——"

"For what?"

"Not to see 'em after eighteen months' absence, but just away to the West Indies again to-day."

"This way, ladies," said I, as we came to our haven.

And as they turned and stood for a moment in hesitation, though they had seen plainly enough for several minutes whither they were bound, Jack stood and surveyed his jolly friends of the preceding night's revelry and madness. There was a good-natured triumph in his clear eye.

"Why," cried he, with an oath, "this is so jolly good a thing, I'd have the same fight again to have these land-pirates at my stern."

"Step in."

And thus I had the entire company within my harbour; and then we began to unload the outlaws, an officer being sent to the house to search it. A part was found there, and the rest had been pretty fairly distributed, so that, making allowance for the purchases and a few drams, we got, one way and another, almost the whole of Jack's £28. Thus old father and mother would have a chance, after all, of getting a few comforts through the mean of their good-hearted son. Yet, I believe, the most curious and lamentable feature of this case is that to which I have partially alluded,—the utter want in these women of anything like a sense that they had done anything that was wrong in reducing *a poor man* to beggary. It is nothing to see them hardened in cases where the victims are rich,—the "serve-'em-well" doctrine applies there with perhaps a touch of retribution, for such women are in that predicament from the selfish licentiousness and hollow-hearted deceit of rich seducers.

Nor, do I believe, did they feel more when, tried by the Sheriff and a jury, they got their rewards: Helen Mossman twelve months, Grace Edwards six, Agnes Pringle and Mary Cameron nine, and Sarah Hill, the bawd's daughter, as resetter, seven. "The pirates' doom."

Decision

❖

I need hardly say how very much is due to decision in the business of detection. A single minute will often peril the object of your inquiry, and then, it does not often happen—at least I have not found it—that the patience that is required in ferreting is joined to the power of dashing at an emergency. A very singular case, where I had an opportunity of testing myself in this way, comes to my recollection.

On the 4th of January 1858, as a man, whose name has by mischance been omitted from my book, was going along the head of the Cowgate, he was instantaneously set upon by three young men, thrown down, and robbed of his watch. A man of the name of W. Duncan who came up at the moment to lift up the stunned victim, met the robbers as they made off. It was dark, and he had a difficulty in catching marks so as to be able to identify them. All that he could say when he came to the office was only general, so that it would have been impossible to proceed with any certainty on his description. In addition to this disadvantage, it happened that any information that I could get from him was got at the door of the office, where I met him as he hurried in. I was just on the eve of setting out on a hunting expedition, accompanied by my assistant Reilly, with a draper who had got taken from his shop a quantity of goods, and whose case was urgent. However, I got so much from Duncan,—enough to point my mind towards three young men—David Dunnet, Robert Brodie, and Archibald Miller, the last of whom I knew to be a returned convict.

Of course, it was impossible that the man could give me any general marks of all the three, nor did he, but it was going far to point out the gang that I got something indicative of one; for when once a gang is formed they fall into a fatal regularity of almost always acting together, so that if you get a clue to one you may consider it a clue to them all. So general have I known this habit among thieves, that I have not found it happen often that while the copartnership lasts they betake themselves to individual adventures. The reason of this is perhaps evident enough. Thieves and robbers have their lines of acting, much like players, and when they determine to go in partnership they agree as to the kind of speculations they will engage in. The particular line of the three I have mentioned was robbery of the person; and, knowing this, I was the more easily led to the conclusion that they were the parties implicated in this affair. Yet, withal, I must confess that I possessed nothing like a conviction; and, indeed, so much was I taken up with the draper's business that I sent Duncan into the office to report regularly, when the lieutenant on duty would, of course, set the proper detective on the scent.

In the circumstances, the affair was soon out of my mind, occupied as I was with the poor draper, who sighed for his goods, and no doubt thought that I was the man to repair his loss. A reputation thus gets a man into toils, but I hope I never regretted this consequence, so long as I could give my poor services to anxious, and often miserable victims. How often have I walked through Edinburgh in the middle of the night, and far on in the morning,—when all were asleep but those who turn night into day,—accompanied by some silent man or woman, groaning inwardly over a loss sufficient to break their fortunes and affect them for life—threading dark, noisome wynds, entering dens where nothing was heard but cursing, and nothing seen but deeds without shame, endeavouring in the midst of all this sea to find the sighed-for property, or detect the cruel robber. Wearied to the uttermost, I have often despaired, at the very moment when I was to pounce upon what I sought, redeem my spirits, and render happy my fellows.

In the present case I had a task of the same kind. We went through a great part of the Old Town, up-stairs and down-stairs; through long dark lobbies, and into all kinds of habitations, but the draper was not that night, at least, to be made happy. We had entirely failed, and were all knocked up by disappointment and fatigue. If the robbery in the Cowgate had scarcely taken hold of me when we set out, all interest in it had passed away, if not all recollection. Some hope had taken us over to the far end of the Pleasance, and we were returning by that street. It was now between twelve and one,—a dark morning, as it had been a dark night,—every sound hushed, and all thought, it may be said, stilled within us. In short, we were fit only for our beds, to which we were hastening as fast as our weary limbs would carry us. I think we had got as far as the foot of Adam Street, when up came three young fellows so rapidly that they were within a yard of us before they saw us or we them.

"Seize them," I cried.

And instantly we sprang upon them. I seized Miller and Dunnet each with a hand, while Reilly engaged Brodie. Straightway a fierce struggle ensued, during which I cried, "Search Brodie."

And no sooner was the cry uttered than Brodie threw something away from him to a considerable distance. The sound of the article charmed the ear of the draper, and instantly running to the spot, he picked up a silver watch—the very watch that had been taken from the man in the Cowgate three hours before. In the meantime the struggle continued, and no man can form an idea of the energy of robbers when caught suddenly after an exploit. Their blood is up before, and the terror of apprehension gives them a power which is just that of self-preservation.

At length, and receiving some aid from our valiant draper, who lost the sense of his loss in a kind of revenge against the class from which he had suffered, we succeeded in quelling them, whereto we were probably aided, too, by passengers who stopped to witness the *mêlée*. We landed them all safely, and they got their reward. Brodie, who had the watch, was sentenced to seven years' transportation; Miller, the returned convict, got two years' imprisonment; against Dunnet, not proven, for there was no proper identification. I have said that Miller was a returned convict. I am not sure but that the old notion that punishment tends to reformation hangs yet about many minds. For God's sake, let us get quit of that. I have had through my hands so many convicted persons, that the moment I have known they were loose, I have watched them almost instinctively for a new offence. The simple truth is, that punishment hardens. It is forgotten by the hopeful people that it is clay they have to work upon, not gold, and, therefore, while they are passing the material through the fire, they are making bricks, not golden crowns of righteousness. Enough, too, has been made of the evident enough fact that they must continue their old *courses* because there is no asylum for them. You may build as many asylums as you please, but the law of these strange nurslings of society's own maternity cannot be changed in this way. I say nothing of God's grace,—that is above my comprehension,—but, except for that, we need entertain no hope of the repentance and amendment of regular thieves and robbers. They have perhaps their use. They can be made examples of to others, but seldom or ever good examples to themselves. That they will always exist is, I fear, fated; but modern experience tells us that they may be diminished by simply drawing them, when very young, within the circle of civilisation, in place of the old way of keeping them out of it.

Nievie, Nievie, Nick-Nack

❖

I need hardly say that the mere value of a stolen article has little to do with the amount of the guilt. The rapacity that strains after a big booty will condescend to a very small one. And, certainly, in so far as regards the discovery, while a valuable thing creates more interest, and therefore multiplies the means of detection, there may be as much of a curious peculiarity in the *trace* of the small robbery as in the large one.

In April 1845, we got intelligence that a uniform coat, belonging to a porter in a Life Assurance Company in Edinburgh, had been stolen from the lobby by one of the "prowlers," or thieves that go about studying doors and windows, ready to enter on the instant and take advantage of any laxity of care that presents itself. The boldness and sharpness of these worshippers of Chance are extraordinary. I have known instances where members of a family have met them on the inside stairs, and even in rooms, and they have generally an answer that serves them for the moment, till they get off. Then there is the well-known trick, to send the servant in with a message, and when she comes tripping along with the answer she finds the lobby cleaned out. No open door is safe in Edinburgh for a moment; and even intermediate doors that are shut are often opened by the prowler. In the present case, a glass-door formed no impediment. The coat was snatched off the pin, and the red-necked official was deprived of his dress badge.

The article with its red neck was what we call kenspeckle, and it was further distinguished by having upon it buttons, cast on purpose, with the name of the Assurance Company upon them; so that it was not one of those things I could look for in a pawn-shop or a broker's. It would get first into the hands of a tailor, to be shorn of its peculiarities, and transformed into a shape that would enable the thief to get it disposed of; but then no ordinary tailor would have anything to do with it; and, therefore, it appeared to me that it would cast up in the hands of some low snip, who devotes himself to such transformations. There is a difficulty about all such things, but here it was increased by the exclusion of the ordinary places of deposit.

This small affair of the red-necked coat tickled me a little. I took a fancy to finding it, for we have our pet subjects, and I believe I would rather have discovered this coat than have been the means of finding a hundred stolen pounds. After all, however, my anxiety owed something to a conviction at that time of being "done" by the prowlers. They were as thick as wasps about other than paper-hives, and every day was bringing in charges of lobby thefts which defied us. Now here was an opportunity that might not present itself again,—a kind of regimental dress, which spoke its character everywhere, and was so likely to leave recollections on those who might have seen it. Nay, I got dreamy about it. It was doubtless in the hands of a tailor, father of a prowler; and if I should thread through every close in the Old Town, dive into every den, interrogate every snip connected with thieves, I would have it. Then, how fanciful I turned; I dreamt as I walked about I would see the buttons adorning the jacket of some one, whether honest or dishonest, most probably a thief; and I believe I did examine buttons whenever I saw them on a suspected coat. But for a time these fancies were not made facts. I don't know how many snipperies I visited, how many pieces of *red cabbage* I took up and examined, how many *bachelor's buttons* I inspected, all in vain. I had just one hope left, and that pointed to North Gray's Close, where one Alison lived, who had a son one of the prowlers. The recollection of him came last; and if this effort failed I might bid adieu to my coat.

I think I was on the Mound when the thought of Alison came

into my head, and I lost no time in directing my steps towards North Gray's Close. I had got to about the Bank of Scotland, and looking up Bank Street, whom do I see but my young friend Alison himself, standing speaking with one of his brethren? They were engaged, too, in some magical-like movement of the hands, Alison turning his closed fists about each other as the children do in the game—

Nievie, nievie, nick-nack,
Which hand will ye tak'?
The right or the wrang?
I'll beguile you if I can.

"You'll not beguile me," I said, as the old rhyme came into my head.

And slipping forward, I came upon the two without being noticed, and just as they were nick-nacking in great glee.

"There is the 'nieve,'" said I, seizing Alison's hand; "and there is the 'nick,'" snatching a button from it; "and there is the 'nack,'" as I took him by the shoulder. "Where got you this, my lad?"

"Oh," replied he, sneeringly, "a button frae an auld sodger's coat."

"What regiment?" I inquired, scarcely able to restrain a laugh in the exultation of having got my button.

"Life Guards Blue," replied my confident lad, who was quite jolly in the conviction that I could make nothing of a button.

"The Life Assurance Company?" said I, carrying on the joke; "not far wrong,—and blue with red facings, eh?"

His laugh went away down about the nether lip, and there hung; and so stunned was he that he could not speak; but they're all subject to revivals.

"Won't do, you see," said I.

"Done by a button, by G—," swore the graceless young fellow. "I got it frae Williams, and he got it frae——"

"No one," said I. "You got it off the coat you stole from a lobby in George Street; and if you forget about it, I may bring it to your recollection by informing you it had a red neck."

And now this clever young artist attempted to play me off with a dodge. Putting his hand into his pocket,

"There's twa dizzen o' buttons for you," said he, with a leer; "maybe I hae stown a' the haill twenty-four coats they belanged to?"

A bold and dangerous trick. But he thought he had a chance by thus putting me off my scent of the one coat; whereas in the other view he had none.

"Well, we shall see about these buttons, too," said I, "when we get to the office."

"Do ye no ken we play at buttons, man?" said he, again on a new turn, as I was walking him up.

"Yes, and at coats too," said I; "but the right hand's nicked this turn, anyhow."

Having got him safely lodged, I hurried away to another quarter, where I was afraid I would be anticipated by Williams, the other button-player, who had run off when I laid hold of Alison. Proceeding to North Gray's Close, I went straight in upon the father, old Alison, who was sitting *à la* snip on his board, very busy, no doubt, as I thought, making "stolen coats look amaist as weel as new." He looked up as I entered. I knew him, but he didn't know me, though doubtless he had heard of me.

"I want some red clippings," said I, "for a purpose. Have you any?"

"I'm no sure but I hae," replied he. "Are they for catching mackerel?" he added, with an attempt at humour, for the Alisons were apparently a funny family, if I could judge from the button-player.

"No," said I, laying hold of a red neck lying in a bundle of *cabbage*; "they're for catching sharks; and by this," holding up the bright article, "I intend to take two."

"Ay!" said he, as he sent his eye through me like a Whitechapel sharp-blunt, and no doubt made a wrong stitch, which he tried to undo as he caught my eye.

"This is the red neck of an official coat," said I; "and I'm anxious to get the body of it."

"It's a cursed lee!" cried Mrs Alison, who was sitting by the fire; "it's a piece o' my mither's auld red plaid."

"Why," said I, "I thought these old red plaids were made of a kind of cloth they call camlet; but this is of fine West of England broadcloth."

"Braidclaith here, or braidclaith there," replied she, "that's a piece o' my mither's auld plaid."

At that moment a sharp voice, which I knew to be that of Williams, sounded from the door—

"Jack and the buttons are up the spout!"

And I heard the step as he made off, having, no doubt, made this announcement in ignorance of my being within, and with a wish to put the father and mother upon their guard.

"What can the daft laddie mean?" said the mother, looking stupid, but alarmed.

"He means," said I, "that your son John has been apprehended for having in his possession the buttons belonging to the coat of which this is the neck. Now, you see, the buttons are of no use without the coat, and the coat and the neck should go together; and therefore I will thank you to tell me where the coat is."

"And wha the devil ever heard o' a man catching a coat by the colour o' the buttons?" replied the wife. "A coat may hae ae kind o' buttons the day, and anither the morn. Ye may as weel try to catch a dog by the colour o' a single hair. Ay, man, though ye were M'Levy himsel', you couldna do that."

"But M'Levy tells you, just here at this moment," said I, "that he will do that. Bring me the coat, and I will match it with the buttons, as well as with the red neck."

"Weel, if you're M'Levy," replied she, "we're in the gleg's claws. But gleg or no gleg, ye'll no do that, for the coat's no here, and never was here, and Johnny has just got the buttons someway we ken naething about."

"Just as you've got the neck," said I, "in a way you know nothing about. Come, I have no time for this palavering. Out with the coat, or *the ticket.*"

“The ticket! what ticket?” cried the wife.

“What ticket?” echoed John from the board.

“The pawn-ticket for the coat.”

“What coat?” again rejoined the pertinacious dame.

“Ay, ye may weel say, What coat?” added John, looking up from his work, which he had still kept at all the time.

And so they went on bamboozling me till my patience became exhausted; besides, I felt so much pride in the strange discovery of the button that I could not bear to be nicked in return by a cunning snip and his wife. I must have the body of this coat, whatever might be the fortune of the many others which had figured with the other buttons got from Jack. So I began my search without saying a word to my two sharp ones; but not-withstanding all my diligence, I could not find anything like a fragment of it among the many pieces and clippings that were there, as the last traces, no doubt, of the twenty-four so wittily alluded to by the son. I was nearly at my wit’s end; although I had alluded to the pawn-ticket, it was rather as a chance-thrust; for, after all, the made-up coat with its new buttons might have been sold to some of the old-clothes-men, and I had no mark on it whereby I could discover it. But I was not yet done.

“I must ask a favour of you, Mrs Alison,” said I.

“I houp,” replied the wife, “it will be to get leave and liberty to make an apology to decent industrious people for suspecting them o’ theft, and searching their house.”

“Why,” said I, “it is just that you will search your pocket,”—the uniform depository of these little bits of paper,—“and try to find for me the pawn-ticket.”

“The pawn-ticket?” again cried she.

“What pawn-ticket?” rejoined the snip.

“I have told you already,” said I; “and if you don’t comply on the instant I will search you myself.”

“Weel,” cried she, as she began to see how the affair was going, “suppose I had a pawn-ticket in my pocket, what about it? Isn’t the pawn-shop the poor body’s bank? and am I to be ca’ed a thief be-cause I pledge something to keep me and my bairns frae starving?

Here," said she, drawing out a ticket; "and what can ye mak o' that? It's just for a coat; and there's plenty o' coats in the warld."

"Have you any more?" said I, putting my hand into her pocket, and pulling out an old hussey, more like a tobacco-pouch than anything else.

And there, to be sure, was a number of these same little enigmas, which I had no doubt had some secret connexion not only with my much beloved coat, but also those of the twenty-four kinds of buttons.

"Ah," said I, as I examined them, "the pawn-shop is indeed the poor man's bank, and your family must have been often starving, and as often bursting, by these pledges and reliefs."

I thought I had brought them to reason, but no.

"Just tell me," said I, "which of all these little bits of paper is the token of my coat."

"What coat?" again from the wife.

"What coat?" again from the snip.

"Why," said I, "to satisfy your curiosity about this wonderful coat with the red neck, and the buttons with the Assurance Company's name on them, of which you know nothing, and about which you are so curious, I will accompany you to the Police-office. You can wait there till I bring the coat to you, and you will have plenty of time to examine it."

"Were you the muckle black deil himself," skirled the woman, "I'll no move an inch. This is my castle, puir as it is."

"And this board is my throne," cried Snip, grandly, "and nae man will make me budge an eighth."

"Do you see this?" said I, dangling my handcuffs. "Would you like me to lead your majesty and your queen, as a public show, along the High Street of Edinburgh?"

I have often had occasion to notice the wonderful effect of the dangling of these hand-binders. It is quite magical, especially where the hands are *not clean.* They are a terror to that instinctive love of liberty which seems in man to have its temple in the arms—by which man defends himself from enemies, embraces his friends, and makes the bread of his life. You may gag his mouth—even a woman's mouth—or bind the legs, with comparative indifference on the part of the victim; but the moment you threaten the hands, the spirit is kindled, and all possible resistance may be expected to be offered, and would be, but for another charm, that of authority. There is the love of freedom and the instinct of obedience to the powers that be, so that the human creature is at once a king and a slave. My monarch of the board and his queen were now to act the slave. They were as quiet as the Brentford dignitary after his fall; and, having got themselves dressed, without ever having cried out, "What coat?" they were taken up as resetters, and lodged where there was no throne to sit upon.

My charmed button had done much; but it did more. In a very short time I got from the pawn-shop my coat, which had been very nicely remodelled by old Alison, but not so changed as to be beyond identification; and were I to say what the twenty-four buttons produced, I might be accused of exaggeration. I can at least say that that button of the Assurance Company insured many a lobby against the risk of prowlers for a long time, and that, too, without the company getting a penny of premium; but what was more, that same button was the means of procuring for old Alison, and his wife, as resetters, and young Jack, as the prowler and thief, sixty days of Bridewell, without the luxury of playing "nievie nick-nack" with his brother prowlers.

I may remark that the public are often under the belief that when a system of depredation has been carried on for a time, there are many hands employed at the work. It more often happens that they have all a centre in one or perhaps two individuals. I stopped the shutter-punching mania, as well as that of the bag-snatching, by one capture in each case.

The Hay-Seeds

❖

I HAVE heard it said that the clue of a man's destiny lies at the foot of his cradle. I don't pretend to understand this saying very well, but I know there is a clue that leads somewhere; and that although there may appear to be a break in it now and then, I have noticed the junction, where there seemed, to common eyes, to be no connexion whatever. I have already given a good many cases where the peculiar traces that bind a lawbreaker to his crime were so minute, that it seemed impossible to discover them; and if they had not been discovered, the destiny of the man could not have been said to be connected with the act, so that God's ways could not have been justified to man. But they were discovered, and hence our faith was confirmed. Of this kind of cases, no one ever struck me as being more curious than that I am about to narrate, though the thing stolen was not, any more than in some other cases, of very great pecuniary value.

Some years ago, two or three young thieves were seen lurking about a house in Brandon Street, on a Saturday night. Their attention was directed to a front-door, which no doubt they wished to be open. One was seen to go up and examine the checklock, and then come away and commune with his friends. Then there was a jingling of keys, as if they had been turning out their stock of skeletons to know which would fit. At length they succeeded: the old customer tried his hand again, the door was opened, and by and by the two who were on the watch outside got handed to them three topcoats, with which they made off, while the chief thief quietly shut the door and walked off. All this play was noticed by one who could neither run after them nor identify them; and when notice came to the office, we had absolutely nothing to go upon.

Next morning (Sunday) Mr Wilson called the officers and gave them their commission. "It is not the value of the coats," he said, "that makes me anxious about this case, but the certainty I feel that if we don't get hold of the thieves, our books will be filled with cases of the same kind. Now let us see who shall be the first to bring in the gentlemen and the coats. I need not say," looking to me, "who I expect to be the man." I had confidence enough, and although there was no clue, I believe I smiled at the compliment, just as if I had said, "Well, Lieutenant, they shall be with you in a very short time." The truth is, that the theft was no sooner intimated, than my mind went away about Stockbridge, where I knew a covey of these wild-birds had alighted, and were picking up their food in the streets near by; and my mind took this direction as a consequence of my experience that thefts by combination are generally traceable to a partnership which is as active while it lasts as it is shortlived. Nor are there many of these partnerships existing at a time,—sometimes only one, doing an amount of business, generally in the same line, which induces the good people to think the town is filled with robbers.

I and my coadjutors went together, going, by my leading, along Fettes Row, and intending to make some forenoon calls at Stockbridge. We had emerged by the side of St Stephen's Church, and just as we were on the eve of turning down by the front of it, I happened to cast my eye up Pitt Street, when my attention was arrested by two young men standing speaking to each other at the entry to the house and shop of a tailor in that street. One of the lads had his coat off, and I believe it was the white shirt-sleeves that first caught my eye.

"A little in the wildgoose-chase way," thought I, as I neared them,—"going to catch feathers from a plucked bird."

Notwithstanding, I proceeded, and just as I got within their eye-shot,—my own was discharged farther down,—one of the two made off up Pitt Street, but not before I discovered he was no other than one of my suspected at Stockbridge. The coatless one slunk in, and, leaving him safe enough, I made off after the fugitive. I traced him to the turn of Heriot Row, and saw him running west at full speed. It was Sabbath morning, and it was not for a decent person like me to be pursuing thieves on the Lord's day, though I was sure they were not running to church. So I turned my steps back to the tailor's shop, where my white-sleeved gentleman was now likely completing his toilet, to appear as gay as possible in presence of his Sunday-out housemaid, who would be ready for him as usual, about the time when her mistress would be thinking her devout Jenny would be walking churchward, to the sound of the Sabbath-bells.

On getting down-stairs, I knocked at a door, and straightway there appeared before me my coatless customer, still uncoated and holding in his hand a big knife. The apparition startled me a little, but did not drive away my wits. I must get the knife out of his hand. He looked fierce, but that was no reason why I should not look the very opposite.

"Put on your coat," said I, "and come out and speak to me,"—a process he could not very well have gone through with the gully in his hand.

Obedience to a soft request is natural, and my man, laying down the knife, with which, after all, he had perhaps been cutting his breakfast loaf, donned his coat, and came out to me, leaving the knife behind.

"Who was the lad you were speaking to a little ago at the door?" inquired I.

"I was speaking to nobody," replied he, with a very determined air,—a denial which resolved me at once. How much more I have often drawn out of a denial where the denied fact was clear, than I ever did out of an affirmation, though clenched with an oath!

"Now," said I, in pursuance of a resolution which may appear unauthorised, if not foolhardy, but which I took my risk of,—for with me it has always been "no risk, no reward,"—"you take your hat, while I keep hold of you," remembering the knife, "and then I will take you where you may get some help to your memory."

And having kept hold of him till he was covered, I took him up the outside stair and committed him to one of my brethren, who quietly led him up to the office.

Having despatched this worthy, I kept watch at the door until the officer returned, then betook myself to examine the nest from which I had taken my bird. At the foot of the stair I met an old man, the master of the youth, and, as I afterwards learned, his uncle. Though he had not formerly appeared, he had heard enough to satisfy him of what had been doing, and was clearly prepared for me.

"Though you have not often customers on Sunday morning," said I, "I have a commission for three topcoats, and want them upon the instant."

"I sell nothing on the Lord's day," replied my devout gentleman; "neither do I work on that day."

"But you are not forbidden to answer a plain question on that day," I rejoined; "and I ask you if you have about you three topcoats; and as you don't traffic today, I shall take them from you for nothing, to relieve your conscience."

"I have nothing of the kind," sulkily; "do you take me for a thief?"

"Not just yet," said I; "but wait there a little, and perhaps I may do you that favour when I come upstairs."

And without waiting for an answer, I shot down a very tempting inner stair, leading to an underground kitchen at the bottom, and below the back of which, where there was a recess, I found the very things I was in search of. In all which proceedings, though there was a dash of haphazard, there were not wanting probabilities, which were at least sufficient to move me, and in the following of which I was thus rewarded.

"I will take you for a thief now," said I, as I came up the stair with the three coats over my arm. "Though you could not sell clothes on the Lord's day to a man, you could see yourself to the devil by telling me a lie. These are the coats."

"Oh, they will be my nephew's, John Anderson," he cried.

"No matter, they have been found in your house, and you go with me."

And the devout little old man was so far cured of his devotion, that he neither preached nor prayed, probably because he had not a willing audience, and hypocrisy lose its cant before justice. He went quietly to where his nephew was; and now it was necessary to catch the other birds, who I suspected were those who brought the prey home. There was no difficulty about them; William Ferguson I had seen in the morning talking to Anderson; we got him on the same night at the house of his father. But there was another spoken to by John Anderson, as having been actively engaged in the robbery,—the brother of William Ferguson, called John. I had always such a desire to see my friends together, that it vexed me when any one was absent from a meeting, where the sympathy was generally so complete, that no one contradicted another, but all were bound together in the bonds of friendship, rendered tighter by a cause of common interest. If I had got none of the others, I would probably have been less solicitous about John; but John I must get, or my peace was not of that kind which consists in duty done. There was a difficulty about this John. I had never seen him, neither had any of my detective brethren; and that he had made a desperate bolt, there could be no doubt, having in all likelihood heard of the capture of Anderson in the fore-part of the day. Another officer considered he had got a string in the direction of Leith, because he had heard at the house of the father that they had friends in that quarter. I did not try to turn his nose, seeing he was holding it out so snuffingly in that direction, and accordingly allowed him to run on, with the only fear that the organ would stick in the earth, before he got to the burrow, so keen was he in testing the ground traces; so away he went.

As for myself, I had another notion. I have often found that Edinburgh thieves, when disturbed in their sweet security, make, like the deer, for the water,—not to swim, and distribute their peculiar odour in the fluid, but as a means to get away. And Fife is often the destination. Somehow they think policemen don't cross waters,—loving rather to search on dry land, after the manners of the bloodhounds, which are always at fault in lochs and streams. At any rate on this occasion, it came into my head that my friend John would make for Newhaven early in the following morning, to catch the steamer that then plied from that pier to Burntisland. So on Monday I got up before daybreak, or rather in the perfect darkness of the prior night not yet modified, and having dressed myself, I took my dreary way to the old fishing village. The day was beginning to break when I arrived at the pier, where I took my seat on the edge of one of the hauled-up boats. The fishermen had been down to the Isle of May, and having arrived with five or six cargoes of fish during the night, were all ready, in their thick pea-jackets, long boots, and red night-caps, for the fish-fair which is held on the pier almost every morning during the fishing season. The regular fishwomen were beginning to come down from the village, with their peculiar dress,—the loads of petticoats, of their favourite colours, yellow or red-striped, with the indispensable pea-coat, and close mutch enclosed in a napkin. Then there came the crowds of the Edinburgh fish-hawkers, almost all young Irish hizzies, resonant of oaths, and each with the hurly, without which she could do nothing in her wandering trade.

By and by, the crowd, and noise, and hubbub increased to those of a regular fair; nor, amidst all the picturesqueness of the scene, was the indispensable fun wanting,—of such a piebald kind, too, with no similitude in the traits of the Irish jokes and the regular fishwives' Scotch humour,—yet with gradations of caste pervading the masses, the stately Newhaven dames appearing like grandees among the tattered callets of the High Street, and the demure and mute fishermen over topping all, and only condescending to smile at times as some witty exclamation burst upon their ears. And there was I, sitting in the midst of this at six o'clock in the morning looking for a young man I had never seen, and had only got described to me by an accomplice, who might have given me a lying portrait. What hope could I have of his being there, or of recognising him if he came? Not much; and yet enough, for the crowd being almost all women, I could devote my attention easily to a newcomer. The boat to Fife could be seen coming over the Firth on her way to Granton

Pier, whence she would come to Newhaven, thence to start on her passage across. I was meanwhile busy enjoying the scene before me, not a little amused by the remarks of some of my High Street children, who knew me well enough, if more than one had not been through my hands. It was now their turn for revenge—

"Och, woman, the thieves are so scarce in Edinburgh, he'll be to catch haddies this morning!"

"Ay, he'll to be handcuff the John Dories with a string."

"And maybe tak' them up to Haddie's (Haddo's) Hole, woman."

All which, and much more, I bore with good temper, the more by token I saw a young man coming sauntering down through the crowd, whose appearance claimed my special attention. He was very like the description given me by Anderson; yet my marks were so dubious, I could draw no very satisfactory conclusion. He paid no attention to the scene about him, and was clearly bent for the other side of the Firth, but he had no bundle, and had all the appearance of being on the "tramp",—not, however, as a tradesman on the search for work, but rather carrying to me the well-known aspect of one of our Edinburgh scamps, seedy, haggard enough, and clearly out-o'-sorts. He passed me as he went down, but the light of the morning was yet so hazy, that I required a nearer view. I rose from my seat, and followed him down the pier, getting as close to him as I could, with a view to a better comparison of his face with the image I had formed of him from Anderson's account. While thus examining him, I observed on his coat some hay-seeds. "That lad," thought I, "has had hay for his sheets;" and I then recollected that, in the gray dawn, I had observed a large hay-stack on the right side of the road coming down from Edinburgh. Slight as the suggestion was I felt myself certain that he had been sleeping in that hay-stack all night; and no one will betake himself to a bed of that kind without some motive of concealment or refuge. At least if he was not my John, he ought to have been; and every look, after the view of the seeds, seemed to send a back energy down through my arm, imparting something like a crave in the fingers to lay hold of him; but then I was among a crew of fish-women, who would have proved troublesome to me, from recollections of kindness received from me, either by themselves or some of their friends; and I required to have recourse to tact. So, going up to him carelessly,—

"Raw morning, my man."

"Ay," with some confidence, almost enough to shake the hayseeds out of my mind.

"You'll be for Fife, I fancy?"

"Right," replied he; "when will the boat be here?"

"You'll see her near Granton, yonder; she'll be here in a quarter of an hour. We have time for a dram to keep the sea-air out of our empty stomachs."

And what eye that has been closed on a bed of hay in a raw night would not leap at the cheerful word "dram?" And so did his. Cold and breakfastless, he jumped at the offer.

"Come up to Wilson's," said I, "and I'll stand your glass besides my own."

And thus I managed him, for he had no notion but that I was an intended fellow-passenger. In two minutes after I had him seated in Wilson's, with the gill of whisky before us.

"Come, my lad," said I,—for truly I had some pity for him, so cold and heartless he looked,—"you will be the better for this."

And giving him his dram, and taking my own, of which I stood in some need as well—

"Are you from Edinburgh?"

But here he faltered for the first time, even with the reviving whisky scarcely down his throat.

"No; Cramond," said he, irresolutely.

And yet, if I was not mistaken, he came down the pier by the Fishermen's Square. I was now getting confidence, and he was not losing it. So I beat up my advantage, for I had no authority yet to take out my leather strap.

"It is strange how friends meet," said I, cheerfully. "I did not think that Jack Ferguson would have forgot an old fellow-workman."

"Well, I don't remember you," said he, without a protest against my soft impeachment.

It is said that omission is not commission; a proverb not altogether true, I suspect, for here was just as good an admission that his name was John Ferguson as I could have wished in the very ardour of a search.

"And how is Bill, your brother?" said I, without telling him that I had lodged the said Bill in safe quarters on the previous night.

"Oh, well enough," he replied; and yet just with a trace of repentance that he had said it.

"Yes," said I, now perfectly sure of my man; "he is well enough, for he's in prison waiting for you, as his accomplice in a robbery of three coats, in Brandon Street, on Saturday night."

The words were not out when he started up, as if a cannon had been fired close by his ear, and made for the door.

"Come," said I, laying hold of him; "you can make nothing by flight in this thoroughfare; you may as well be easy. Here's a drop of whisky in the stoup yet. Take it kindly, and then I will fit you with these," taking out my cuffs.

And such is the accommodating spirit of these fellows,—so intimate with reverses, and mixing sin and sorrow with indulgence and indifference,—that Jack sat quietly down, and taking up the stoup, poured out the remaining half-glass, took it off, and then took on his curb.

"Well now, Jack," said I, for I was curious on a point, "didn't you sleep all night in the haystack up yonder, on this side of Bellfield?"

"Yes, I did," he replied; "how do you know that?"

"Why, by these hay-seeds on your jacket," said I. "Don't you see that if you had had these upon you last night before going to bed, and had taken off and put on your coat, as honest men do, these seeds would have been shaken off? and then, don't you further see, it was very unlikely you could have got these seeds upon you this morning, when newly out of bed? So, Jack," I continued, "it was really by seeing these very small particles upon you that I was led to the thought—for I was not sure about you—that you were skulking for some cause, and, therefore, very likely, one of my friends."

"Good God! is it possible?" he cried; as if he had been on the instant made aware of something he had not thought of before.

"Yes," said I, "it is possible and real. It is not I who am The Thief-catcher;" and as I pronounced the words I pointed my finger to the roof, and looked in the same direction, with a solemnity I really at the moment felt.

Nor was the effect less apparent upon the face of the struck youth. A tremor seemed to shake his heart, and I thought I observed a moisture in his eye, which had so often and so long no doubt been red and dry with the effects of his outlawed and dissipated life.

"Yes," he said, "there is another thief-catcher higher than you, and I feel His hand upon me with a firmer grip than that of these cuffs. I will, if God spare me, be a different man. I will confess the robbery. Yes, I will convict myself and Anderson, ay and my brother, if they and my father should murder me for it; and if you don't find me changed, my name is not Jack Ferguson."

"We may get you made a witness, and free you," said I.

"I don't want," he replied, resolutely; "I would rather be punished along with them, and, if I can get into their cells, I will try to get them to change their course of life."

This was almost the only case of penitence in a confirmed thief I ever witnessed. In the same mood, I took him up to the office. It was afterwards arranged somehow that the devout little old man, the resetter, should be accepted as a witness, probably for the reason that he was less guilty than the others, though, in my opinion, he was the worst of the whole gang, let alone his hypocrisy, which only aggravated his resettership—a far greater crime than theft or robbery. They were tried by the Sheriff, and got, respectively, eight, six, and four months. Whether Jack wrought out his penitential fit, I never ascertained. He got out of my beat, and I sincerely hope into another, traversed by a better angel than a detective.

The Ash-Backet

❖

IN the case I am now to give, I have no reason to make fault with my horn-and-hoof friend. I could find none of his ordinary weakness, for he certainly did not only his best, but in a style so adroit, that if he had been the only person in the world he would have had reason to gratify himself with his own blessing—always, of course, framed so as to suit the wish that formed it; but, fortunately, he is not the only person in the world, for he was foiled in even his very best laid scheme, so that Burns might have put him in company with the unfortunate "mice and men", only he had no name to give him beginning with the lip-letter; and then the rhythm would have suffered, as a friend of mine said, knowing I could not discover such learned niceties myself.

A watch was amissing one morning from a house in Picardy Place, in 1834. The story was mysterious. A man called Gardner, a sleazy connexion of the servant's, had been in the kitchen; and when the girl's back was turned he had slipped into the drawing-room, where he had been seen by the lady, who he probably thought was out. She missed a gold watch and running into the kitchen charged the man. He denied. A policeman was got, who searched him, but the article was not found on him. When he was brought up to the lieutenant he was discharged, though an old offender, for the good reason that no man saw him take the watch, nor was the same found on his person. Then the servant was suspected by us, but the lady had such faith in her that she could not join us in our suspicions; and the whole affair was rendered doubtful by the fact, that the door had been open during the forenoon while the girl was down to the cellar for coals.

It was altogether, in short, a mess, in which no detective "idea" could be discovered by Genius herself. There were suspicions as evident as millstones looked at through a microscope,—collusion between Gardner and the servant, the hiding of the watch by the latter, and so forth,—but these were rebutted by other considerations. The servant had been there for years with nothing amissing, and people don't fall into the devil's hands all at once with a fling as lovers do; and then the open door was enough itself to let in wind sufficient for the dispelling of these thin clouds of gas smoke.

When in the evening I walked down to Picardy Place, I did not take credit to myself, nor do I do so now, for supposing I could, merely by walking the street and looking at the door, clear up the mystery. I went only because the place had for me the usual charm of places where secret things have been done. It was dark, and about nine o'clock. I was passing from York Place to Picardy Place, north side, expecting to see nothing thereabouts but those spectres of cinder-women, who, once in the lava streets, have a liking for charred things. After all, they are not very troublesome to us. If they get a silver spoon now and then, and don't give it up, we can't say much: the thing is thrown out, and they are so poor. Strange beings though, with characters never studied, for what interest can there be in a poor creature going about grubbing among ashes, and picking up things you would wonder at? For it must be confessed, that cinders, to give them a gleam of heat at night in the holes they live in, are not the main object. Hopeful souls even in ashes, they expect something to "turn up" out of what others cast away. Yes, I say, they have characters,—they won't steal unless the thing comes half in their way, for they have no courage to enable them to be regular thieves. Then they have almost always been *Vesuviennes*, as they are to the end shrivelled toys of man's heartlessness, and all their anger burned out of them by misery. To ask how they live would be vain, for they don't live,—they only breathe and sigh, on food that is enough for their appetite, which is gone.

I saw them at their work, shadows of creatures going from backet to backet. They never look at you; they don't think they have any right to look at a human being, having renounced the thoughts and feelings of our kind. And few look at them; fewer still give them anything, while sturdier petitioners get shillings and sixpences. But as I was thinking something in this way, I saw a male cinder-wife—excuse the expression; a man went up stealthily to a backet, and bent down, and then left it again. I could not comprehend this any-how. Why had he not the bag? and without the bag, what could he do with cinders? I suspected he had seen me, for he stood in the middle of the street for a time till I had passed. My curiosity was excited; yet, after all, what more easy than to suppose he intended transporting the backet after turning out the ashes? a bit of humble larceny often enough practised by the lowest class of thieves. I stood at the turn of Broughton Street, and saw him approach the pavement again. This time he was bolder for his great enterprise, for I saw him lift the backet and carry it off towards Leith Walk.

"And not turned out the cinders," muttered I, as I came up to the spot where the utensil had lain.

Small things strike more sharply at times than big. I must see. He will empty it on the middle of the street. No, he doesn't; he carries it on and on. He didn't intend to empty it, and I might be left in rather a curious mystery.

"Well, my lad," I said on getting up to him, opposite the end of the north side of Picardy Place, "what are you to do with the backet?"

The old answer—

"What's that to you?"

An answer which, if he had recognised me, as he didn't, he would not have ventured, though I knew him. He had been six times through my hands, but I shied his looks, and kept my hat well down.

"I want to know what you intend doing with the backet?"

"The backet?"

"Ay, the backet."

"It's my own."

"No, I saw you lift it."

"I'm going to empty it."

"Why?"

No answer.

"Then, Gardner," said I, looking at him, "why *don't* you empty it?"

"And so I do," he said, as he heard his name; and suiting the action, not only to the word, but the fear, he threw it down, and was for off.

"No, my old friend," said I, as I seized him; "not so fast, or there will be a greater *dust*."

As I held him, I cast my eye, not without an "idea", upon the ashes. There was something else there than charred coal. I stooped, still holding on by my man, and picked up a gold watch.

"How was I to know that was there?" said he, with an air of triumph.

"Because you put it there in the morning, when you were in Miss ——'s house, under the fear of a search."

"It's a lie, and a foolish one; how could I know that it would be allowed to remain?"

"Easily answered," said I; "but it is not my intention at present to satisfy your curiosity. Take up the backet and come with me."

In the meantime, up comes the servant, crying out if any one had seen a man with a backet.

"Yes," said I, "here is the man and the backet too."

"You, Gardner!" said the girl, "what, in the name of wonder, do you want with my backet?"

"It was not the backet he wanted," said I, "but this watch which your mistress missed in the morning."

The girl's head ran round as she looked at the man and me, and the backet and the dust.

"Good heavens!" she cried, "I will be blamed and ruined. It will be said I put it there that he, who is my cousin—oh that I ever knew him!—might find it when I put out my ashes at night."

"Never you fear," said I, for I saw by the girl's unfeigned surprise that she was innocent. "The whole story is clear enough."

"Ay, to you and to me," said she; "but how will I get my mistress to see it? Yes, the backet was in the kitchen, and when the policeman came it must have been put there by Gardner."

"All too clear to need so much talk," said I.

"Oh!" cried the terrified girl, "but will you come with me now, and satisfy her?"

"No; I must take this precious cousin of yours to the office, backet and watch and all, and you will be called upon in the morning; meanwhile, go home and tell your mistress that M'Levy requested you to say that he thinks you innocent. If the lady has a spark of sense, she will see it all herself."

But still she wept pitifully.

"Ah, sir, our family have been ruined by this blackguard; my father fed him and cled him, and he has been a disgrace to us all through life; and now, at last, he would be the means of making me suspected of robbing the best of mistresses."

All the while, the hardened scoundrel looked as unmoved as the piece of wood which he used as the means of his villainy.

"Dry up your tears, my good girl," said I; "we'll never trouble you again, take my word for it."

And still blubbering, so that the passers-by began to stand and inquire, she hung by me, imploring me to go with her and satisfy her mistress. It was with some difficulty I shook her off, but at length I succeeded; and as I proceeded upwards, I still heard her sobbing among the crowd. Gardner was silent—perfectly unaffected at the misery into which he had brought his relation. He was safely provided for.

In the morning I went to Picardy Place. The girl opened the door, with a look so thankful, as if she considered me her preserver.

"Have you told your mistress?"

"Oh, sir, I couldn't. I have not slept a wink all night."

"Not told her, foolish girl!" said I.

"No; but you will, and then she will believe."

"Of course she will, and she will be better satisfied when she hears, as I hope she will by and by, that Gardner gets a passage over the seas."

The girl ran quicker than she ever did along that lobby before, opened the door, then shut it behind me,—to watch and listen, no doubt; and who could blame her?

In a few words I explained the whole story to Miss——, a sharp and benevolent woman; she saw through the trick in a moment.

"But your poor servant is in a terrible state about it, lest you should suspect she had any hand in it."

Without saying a word, she went to the door,—

"Mary," she called, with a loud voice.

No answer; Mary was caught; she was standing up by the wall, so that her mistress could not see her.

"Mary," louder still.

"Yes, mem," said a voice at her very side.

"Stupid girl, come in here;" and she took the timid creature by the hand, and dragged her in.

"What are you afraid of?"

Whimpering and sobbing.

"Give up; I have no fault to find with you."

"Oh, but you have been so kind a mistress," she said, in a choking kind of way, "that I could not bear—no—I could not bear—bear the very thought that you should suspect me."

And then came another burst.

"Girl, have I not told you that I am satisfied with Mr M'Levy's explanation, and that you are no more guilty of taking my watch than Mr M'Levy himself?"

"God bless you, mem, and God bless you, sir, and now I'm happy."

And happy she ran away, relieved of a night-mare which had been upon her throbbing bosom all night, and, not contented with its night work, had clung to her all the morning.

"Ah, this accounts," said her mistress, "for the miserable look she has borne since ever she rose; but that girl will be dearer to me than ever."

That same day Miss——and Mary came up and were examined. There was no doubt of Gardner's guilt, yet it was viewed as a strange case, altogether without precedent. The magistrate said that "there really was no substantial evidence against the man upon which he could be charged for stealing the watch. It was altogether circumstantial; no doubt he did it, but no one saw him put the watch in the receptacle where it was found, nor was the watch actually, in a proper sense, found upon him. He might say that if he wanted to find the article, he could have rummaged the backet,—a far more likely act than running away with a load of dust. Indeed, it is not easy to see why he should have followed a course which was so likely to bring upon him the very people on the pavement. It is clear, however, that he may be charged with stealing the backet itself, and, if you please, the cinders; and, as I am told he has been convicted before, the issue will be the same. It is proper for me to add, for the sake of the girl, that, in my opinion, she is perfectly innocent. It is impossible to bring home to her even a suspicion; for even, on the supposition of concert, how could she know that the ashes and the watch would not be tossed into the cart before her cousin came to take it away? Then she was not on the stair watching the result of a scheme; she came down only after the article was taken away, and finding it gone, ran after the thief, not even knowing it was Gardner that took it."

Good news for poor Mary, and, perhaps, better afterwards, when her never-do-well relative was transported for seven years, just for stealing a backet. He was obliged to swallow the shell and throw out the kernel.

In this case, vice did not show her usual weakness. Everything was adroitly played, with the single exception, perhaps, of his running away with what he might have searched; but then he did search, and it was only when he heard the cart that he gave way to what appeared to him to be a necessity. Is not all vice a necessity? If it weren't, I fear I would have skeely for breakfast.

The Look-Out

❖

PEOPLE who boast of a little courage are generally very averse from the cunning that skulks and gets behind screen and defences; they can't submit to such degradation; and therefore it is that when a man is found at this kind of deceit he is set down as being a coward. I fear, however, that my courage would be pretty doubtful if it were measured in this way, for I have often enough been *perdu* in holes that would scarcely hold me, peering out for curiosities in my way, with much zest, and not at all ashamed when, bouncing out, I could catch a robber by the throat and bring him to justice.

Some sixteen years ago, Mr Tibbetts, hat-maker on the South Bridge, was greatly annoyed by that kind of disappearance of property over the counter which has no *per contra* of the appearance of cash. It is a common thing, and speaks ill for the honesty of our people as well outside as inside the counter. In this instance, the affair was a puzzle; for while Mr Tibbetts suspected his lad, there were disappearances that could not be accounted for by his dishonesty. Articles went amissing while the lad was there, but the same thing occurred when he was not there. He had tried many ways to get at the real truth, but as yet had failed, when he applied to me.

I went and examined the shop, and got all the information I could get; very unsatisfactory it was. In some views the lad seemed to be the thief, in others not; so that I saw nothing for it but a secret watch. I looked about me for a hiding-place. Mr Tibbetts recommended beneath the counter, where I might hear something but see nothing. I must have a lookout, but the difficulty was where to find it in an open shop, every corner of which was known to the lad, and where any screen or artificial covering would have been suspected in a moment. At length I fixed upon the recess behind the fan-light on the top of the door, where I could see all that took place in the shop, as well as take a look out on the street, if I chose to have a variety. Of course, I behoved to be as careful in the one direction as the other, for verily it would have been a strange thing for M'Levy to have been seen doubled up behind a fanlight in a hatter's shop, waiting for a victim. To render my look-out complete, I proposed that he should surround me with bandboxes, as the milliners' apprentices are sometimes seen on the street. The notion pleased Mr Tibbetts, and was the more acceptable, as it had often been the custom to place hat-boxes there when there was no room for them elsewhere.

Mr Tibbetts was in the practice of opening the shop in the morning himself about eight o'clock, going home to breakfast at nine, when he was relieved by the lad. To make sure work of both suppositions,—as well that implicating the lad as that applicable to outsiders, whoever they might be,—I proposed to mount into my look-out, with my bandboxes about me, as soon as the shop was opened. Next morning at eight I was accordingly at the shop. I got up to my place by means of a ladder, and Mr Tibbetts began his part by piling up before me the bandboxes, which, as he placed them, I arranged in such a way as that I could see over the entire shop and yet not be seen by any one who had no suspicion of my being there. All things being thus prepared, we took to our respective offices; occasionally, when no customer appeared, speaking of things in general, without my feeling much of that discomfort I had awarded to so many, viz., that of a prison; myself for once being a prisoner. It is said that if every room of a house were seen into by a secret watcher, it would be a show-box even more wonderful than a travelling exhibition; and I rather think, from my experience, the remark is true. About half-past eight, a respectable-looking man, whose appearance was familiar to me, as going up and down the High Street, but whose name I did not know, came in.

"I want some hat-trimmings," said he, giving the trade description, which I did not well understand.

Mr Tibbetts showed him some specimens of hat-trimmings but the customer appeared to me to be very ill to please, so that the suspicion got into my mind that the man had some other object in view than to get the article wanted; nor was I wrong.

"I must go up-stairs for it," said Mr Tibbetts.

"Just so," said I to myself; "and while you are upstairs. I will see what the very particular customer does."

And I did see it. No sooner was Mr Tibbetts mounted to the other storey, than the very particular customer swung himself over the counter, filled his outside pockets with trimmings—he was not now particular by any means—from a drawer; and then, vaulting over again, resumed his position.

"Ah," thinks I again, "if you just knew that M'Levy is here, up in the fanlight recess, looking down upon you with these eyes!"

But he did not know it, and that was his comfort; and then lo! all his particularity had vanished.

"Oh, just the thing."

And, after all, the quantity he bought—no doubt of an old fashion he didn't need—was so small in comparison with what he had in his big pockets, that the one, the smaller might very well represent the amount of his real honesty; the other, the larger, standing for his assumed honesty or hypocrisy, whereby he cheated the public more effectually than he had done Mr Tibbetts.

After he had gone, I shot my head over the bandboxes.

"What is that gentleman's name, Mr Tibbetts?"

"Taylor, a small manufacturer in the Canongate, and an honest man, I believe."

"Very honest. Bring the ladder as quick as possible, and let me down."

"What do you mean? That man surely did not steal anything?"

"I'll tell you when I'm down. I never shoot secrets at people as if they were partridges."

So he got the ladder, and let me down.

"That man," said I, "is off with trimmings of at least ten times the value of what he bought of you."

"An old customer, ill to please," said he. "Ah, I see now where my goods have gone; but why did you not tell me to stop him?"

"Just because I didn't wish," said I. "He will lead us himself to the store; and, besides, it's close upon nine, and I don't wish your shopman to see me, which he might have done if there had been a protracted bustle here."

"Ah, I see," replied he.

"I wait for you on the opposite side: join me when the lad relieves you."

I took my new station, and by and by I saw the lad enter and relieve his master; who, coming out, walked on his own side towards the north. I then joined him.

"Taylor," said I, "the moment you went up-stairs, sprang the counter, filled his pockets, and again took the outside, and met you as like an honest man as the most other very honest men are like themselves."

"You perfectly astonish me; though any man had sworn—"

"Yes, yes," said I.

Just the old thing, which I hear rung in my ears every day, and which I have no need to repeat; because, really, I must proceed upon the cruel and very selfish principle of taking the greater part of people for rogues until they are proved by some test honest,—not that I think honest people are fewer than others say, but just that I have somehow a difficulty in taking their own word for it.

"And where are you going?" said Mr Tibbetts.

"To Taylor's house, to which you will please take me."

"Why, I am almost ashamed to face the man," said he.

"That is a feeling I never felt," said I.

"I mean for the man," said he.

"Ah, that is another question; that feeling I have often felt, and a very painful one it is."

And so, under our necessity, we went to the house of our honest man, which we were not long in finding; neither were we long in discovering the goods. Laying my hand upon them, as they were yet warm as it were from the fevered hand of guilt—

"These were taken from Mr Tibbett's shop within this half hour," said I.

The man, while betraying astonishment, did not quite lose his confidence.

"No man can say that," he replied; "these are the goods I bought from Mr Tibbetts. He went up-stairs for them, and there being no one in the shop but myself, who could take it upon him to say that I stole them?"

"You don't deny it," said I; "you only assert that no one could see you."

"Yes, I deny I stole them," said he; "and, therefore, I conclude that, as there was not a single soul in the shop, you must have got your information second-hand, and that second-hand is a liar."

"How can you be certain," said I, "that no one saw you?"

"Because I have eyes," said he. "I repeat, there was no one who could by any possibility see my movements, all honest as they were, in that shop. Did you, Mr Tibbetts?"

"No, I was up-stairs."

"Then I repeat, and will stand to it for ever, that no one upon this earth saw me steal these trimmings."

"Upon *this earth*," said I, looking him in the face in than kind of way in which those eyes of mine, of which I am little proud, have often enabled me to see things under the skin, and which, I am free to say, were never turned by another pair; "but there might have been one *above* who saw you."

The statement struck him, but he recovered quickly.

"Are these your goods, Mr Tibbetts?"

"Yes," said he; "I looked in my drawer," (a circumstance I have forgotten to mention,) "and found as much as these amissing."

"And, therefore," rejoined Taylor, "you fix on me, though no one saw me steal them?"

"The one *above* excepted," said I; "and by this authority I ask you to step up with me to the Police-office."

The evidence was too much for guilt, and he came away, I taking the trimmings along with me. He was duly lodged in safe quarters, to think on the value of what he had stolen, and compare it with the worth to him of a character.

"Now, Mr Tibbetts, will this account for your losses?"

"Not at all, unless the boy has been done in the same way.

"Then I will test him, but not from above again. In the first place I can't get up, he being there; and in the second place I suspect some outside sympathisers; so I will take another position. But I will better reserve this till to-morrow morning."

"Yes," said Mr Tibbetts; "your only chance is when I am out, between nine and ten. It is now nearly ten, and he will be expecting me."

Next morning, accordingly, I was at my post at nine opposite the shop; nor did I require to wait long. I soon observed a sleazy, hawking-looking dog walking backwards and forwards, and occasionally looking in at the window.

That is a resetter, said I to myself; for I have a knowledge of the tribe, always cowardly and side-looking, never with the firm defiant eye of a confirmed thief.

Thus watching my man, I saw him slip suddenly into the passage of the common stair to the south of the shop. What next? Almost what I expected,—the lad came to the door, looked north and south, and round and round, then, going to the common stair, peered in. Ah, everywhere, thought I, but right opposite, where I am. So it is always, when people wish to do something wrong; they look about for danger, which they don't wish to find, and therefore they never look in the proper direction. If they did, they would seldom do the evil thing, for, though the danger is not *patent*, it may always be seen, if the wish were away and the eye left to the guidance of honesty and wisdom. Although I was not known to him, he might have looked into the drawer whence he was to abstract what he abstracted, and then consider that his master could not but miss his goods. That was his proper direction, but he looked out in place of within. In a minute after, he came to the door again, with a bundle behind him, looked about again,—what trouble vice puts itself to under the aspect of prudence!—and darted into the entry. A clever-enough trick, as he thought, but then I had a motive for dashing in as strong as his, and I obeyed it. Hastening over the street, I was in upon them just as the lad had handed the bundle to the resetter.

"What is this?" said I, laying hold of it.

"Some clothes of the boy," said the man, "which I have got for my wife to wash for him."

"And your wife washes span new hat-trimmings?" said I, pulling out an end.

The usual dashed and blank looks of those who are catched red-handed.

I took them both direct to the office, where Taylor was before them, though the parties were in no way connected. As for the man, I felt nothing. I had sympathy for the boy, who in all likelihood was led into this breach of trust by the older culprit. The law makes allowance for the authority exercised by a husband over a wife, whereby she is often freed, while the real truth is that the authority is often reversed; but there is no allowance for that cunning persuasion exercised by full-grown men over mere striplings—a very deadly thing, and I am satisfied very common. The father and mother of a thief, who have trained him from youth upwards to the habit, get clear because they didn't do the deed, and the wretched pupil is made the scape-goat of their sins. I have seen hundreds of boys and girls convicted and sentenced who had, considering their years and education, no more moral guilt on their heads than the unfortunate cat bore while under the hand of the monkey. So in this case the lad and the man got sixty days each; but it was just a wonder that the latter was punished at all, for if he had not been caught in the act, he might not have been discovered without a difficulty not applicable to the thief himself. The time apportioned to Taylor scarcely repaid his crime. But Mr Tibbetts' evils were all cured in twenty-four hours. I never heard more of his being exposed to robberies of trimmings or anything else.